The Triumph of Campaign-Centered Politics

by

David Menefee-Libey
Pomona College

CHATHAM HOUSE PUBLISHERS
SEVEN BRIDGES PRESS, LLC
NEW YORK • LONDON

Seven Bridges Press, llc
135 Fifth Avenue, New York, New York 10010

Publisher: Robert J. Gormley
Managing Editor: Katharine Miller
Project Editor: Melissa A. Martin
Production Services: *TIPS* Technical Publishing.
Project Manager: Robert Kern
Composition: Lorraine B. Elder and Kay Ethier
Cover Design: Inari Information Services, Inc.
Printing and Binding: Versa Press, Inc.

Library of Congress Cataloging-in-Publication Data

Menefee-Libey, David John, 1958–
        The triumph of campaign-centered politics / by David J. Menefee-Libey.
        p. cm.
    Includes bibliographical references and index.
    ISBN 1-889119-19-9 (pbk.)
    1. Politics, Practical — United States — History — 20th century. 2. Political parties — United States — History — 20th century. 3. Electioneering — United States — History — 20th century. 4. Democratic Party (U.S.) — History — 20th century. I. Title.
    JK1717 .M46 1999
    324'.0973 — dc21
                                                                    99-6066
                                                                        CIP

Manufactured in the United States of America
10   9   8   7   6   5   4   3   2   1

For Wendy, Sam, Ike, and Nell

Contents

Preface

Eugene McCarthy, speaking from experience as a member of Congress and presidential candidate, was fond of saying that "Being a politician is like being a football coach. You have to be smart enough to understand the game, but dumb enough to think it matters." Growing up as one of McCarthy's constituents, I always saw politics as a bewilderingly complex game, much harder to understand than the touchdowns and field goals my beloved Vikings fought for. Yet, watching as Lyndon Johnson tried to explain the Vietnam War and later as the Watergate Committee did its work, I had no doubt that the game mattered.

The game was also changing. My first direct exposure to politics was meeting Minnesota Governor Karl Rolvaag at the Littlefork County Fair, and several times I listened to Vice-President Hubert Humphrey regale gatherings of the faithful in northern Minnesota towns. I quickly learned, however, that much of the real game of politics had moved out of the party gatherings and union halls and into less personal settings: the evening news, television commercials, direct mailings, and so on. This left me with a vague unease because I liked to have my politicians where I could see them for myself and decide first hand what I thought of them. Still, the United States is a big country, and the human business of representative democracy is bound to be imperfect.

I have spent much of my adult life studying and teaching politics, trying to figure out how campaigns and elections work. In many ways, this book is an attempt to explain what I have learned, to explain the game of electoral politics and how it has changed since Eugene McCarthy and Hubert Humphrey first ran for Congress in the 1940s. In short, it is a book about how campaigns and elections work, focusing especially on the practical business of representation, deliberation, and choice. I argue that campaigns and elections in contemporary America are best understood as campaign centered in each of these dimensions, and I do my best to explain the development, practices, and implications of campaign-centered politics.

This is also a book about political parties. Parties have been central to most of the important developments of American history, just as they were central to the Senate impeachment trial of President Clinton. Parties are important in and of themselves, but they also offer an excellent lens for seeing and understanding the emergence of "the new politics" since World War II. I try to show in this book how the triumph of campaign-centered politics has transformed parties and how the parties in turn have shaped common political practices and institutions.

This is a personal book. I'm not sure that anyone fully shares my point of view or fully agrees with my analysis of contemporary American parties, campaigns, and elections. Nevertheless, I couldn't have written this book without tremendous help.

Ira Katznelson, David Greenstone, Garth Taylor, Jack Knight, Margaret Weir, Gary Orfield, Gerry Rosenberg, and Mark Hansen helped guide my research in its early stages. The Brookings Institution's Governmental Studies Program generously provided me with the Robert Hartley Research Fellowship, which enabled me to go to Washington, D.C., and begin the field research and interviewing that provides much of the empirical core of the book. I thank Paul Peterson and his colleagues at Brookings, who created a tremendously rich intellectual and political setting for my research. I owe a special debt to former Brookings research fellows Tom Weko, Joe White, Mark Rom, Ken Mayer, James Lindsay, and Bob Copeland, as well as to Paul Herrnson, who co-authored an article with me in the early stages of this project. I thank them and hope that I contributed as much to their work as they did to mine.

Pomona College proved to be a rich environment for continuing my research and writing the manuscript. The ideas here reflect countless conversations with my colleagues at the Claremont colleges. I am particularly indebted to the late Fred Krinsky, who had a remarkably rich understanding of American politics and society as well as an unflagging commitment to the democratic values I hope this book embodies. I am also indebted to the Pomona students who heard many of the ideas expressed here in rough form in the classroom and whose curiosity, criticism, and optimism and have led me to sharpen and clarify every aspect of the book.

This project has developed more slowly than I would like to admit, and I have accumulated more debts than I can possibly repay (or perhaps even remember). It would take pages to list the generous colleagues who have read and commented on individual chapters or arguments over the years. Several colleagues have read the full manuscript in various stages of its development and provided helpful criticism and guidance: Dan Mazmanian, Larry Dodd, Barbara Salmore, Sandy Maisel, Steve

Schier, Vicki Shabo, and Walter Dean Burnham. I owe a special debt to Charles Hadley, who had the generosity and patience to read and provide essential help with several versions of the full manuscript as it developed.

This book relies on dozens of interviews, both with people cited by name and with others who contributed valuable information and ideas but wished to remain anonymous. I thank all of them again for putting up with me and for taking the time and having the patience to describe and explain their work. In particular, I would like to thank William Sweeney and Sandra Perlmutter, who showed unfailing patience and generosity with their time and ideas in the early stages of this project.

Finally, I thank Chatham House/Seven Bridges Press for their support throughout. Ed Artinian provided tremendous encouragement at critical times, and I wish he could be here to see the finished product. I particularly thank Kathy Paparchontis for her masterful copyediting, Ilana Kingsley for indexing, and Bob Kern for his help and patience in the final production work.

I of course take full responsibility for any omissions or errors of fact or interpretation.

I dedicate this book to my family. Thank you Wendy, Sam, Ike, and Nell for your love, support, ideas, insight, humor, creativity, and sheer stubbornness. The boat is finally out of the basement.

Let's go fishing.

David Menefee-Libey
Claremont, California
April 1999

1

Parties, Elections, and American Democracy

This then is life.

Here is what has come to the surface after so many throes and convul-
sions.

—Walt Whitman, "Starting from Paumanok"

Ross Perot's off-again, on-again presidential campaign in 1992 provided political pundits one last opportunity to spout the waning conventional wisdom of an era. The quirky Texas billionaire could make a credible independent run, they said, because loyalty to the major national parties had declined since the 1960s. Perot gained public support because candidates—Democratic, Republican, and otherwise—now stood at the center of our campaigns and elections. Voters would decide, the pundits proclaimed, on the basis of personality and issues rather than party loyalty—and Perot could be the next president.

As it turned out, the pundits and their conventional wisdom were wrong. Voters in 1992 made their decisions on the basis of personality, issues, *and* party. Brushing aside Ross Perot, they elected Bill Clinton president and gave Democrats control of the United States Congress. Two years later, in 1994, millions of new Republican voters frustrated with Clinton's performance turned out and elected a Republican congressional majority for the first time in a generation. Each of these elections offered voters clear partisan alternatives, and voters made partisan choices that mattered. By 1996, the conventional wisdom of party irrelevance had nearly vanished from the world of media commentary.

That waning conventional wisdom had started to disappear from academic writing on elections nearly ten years before. Beginning in the 1960s and with increasing force throughout the 1970s, most political scientists agreed that "the golden age

1

l passed. They argued that the two major American parties had declined
longer perform their essential functions: control nominations, frame
ntrol campaign money and personnel, and deliver the votes on election
day. The Democrats, the dominant party of the New Deal era, had fallen especially far
because of factional fighting and sweeping reforms in their presidential nominating
process. But Republicans had fallen as well, driven to near-oblivion by the Watergate
scandal.[1]

In the absence of strong national parties, the academics argued, elections centered on candidates, their issues, and their personalities. Entrepreneurial candidates
could ignore the parties' former power brokers and gain nomination in primary
elections or even by petitioning onto the ballot as Perot did in 1992 and as John
Anderson had done in 1980. The candidates chose their issues, organized their own
campaigns, and hired their own campaign managers and staff. The mass media, especially television, presented these candidates to an increasingly nonpartisan electorate by broadcasting news coverage and paid campaign commercials. And voters
grew increasingly willing to make separate decisions about each office—split their
tickets—based on their perceptions of candidate personalities and issue positions.[2]

This conventional "party decline" wisdom, faced with powerful countercur-
rents, waned in the 1980s.[3] Ronald Reagan led Republicans back from their Watergate
exile and helped redefine their party as one of solid conservatism. The decline of
voter partisanship slowed, and a solid majority of American voters remained loyal
to the major parties. Democrats and Republicans in Congress increasingly voted
along party lines throughout the 1980s and into the 1990s. National party organizations played a growing financial and strategic role in elections. All of these developments culminated in 1994, when Representative Newt Gingrich of Georgia and
his fellow Republicans presented the Contract with America as a partisan national
campaign platform, and their party swept into power in both the House of Representatives and the Senate.[4]

By 1996, the media commentators had figured out what most party scholars,
candidates, and campaign operatives already knew, and a new conventional wisdom emerged: though their role had changed, political parties had recovered from
their decline to become vital participants in American elections.[5] Their organizations now recruited candidates, contributed money and steered contributions to
campaigns, offered an array of professional services to candidates and campaigns, as-
sisted sympathetic consultants and campaign managers, and helped develop campaign themes and strategies. Indeed, supposedly scandalous fundraising success by
the parties provoked some to wonder whether they had become *too* strong.

What happened? How did the role of parties change so dramatically? How did
American elections change so quickly? The answers to these simple questions are

complex, but in essence I argue in this book that the shifting conventional wisdom about American elections reflects some profound truths. American political parties have indeed changed dramatically, though the changes we now recognize have been under way for decades. Electoral politics has been radically transformed through the past half century in ways we are now coming to understand, and the parties have struggled desperately to adapt to that transformation. We have witnessed the emergence of a dramatically different electoral order, one in which the political foundations of our representative democracy have been transformed into something entirely new: campaign-centered politics.

Representation, Deliberation, and Choice

If we are to understand this "something new," I argue that we must develop a new way of thinking about American electoral politics. We must begin with the premise that *campaigns and elections are important because they offer our society's approximation of representative democracy.* To carry out campaigns and elections, we develop processes and organizations that mediate between citizens and those who would represent them in government. Based on this premise, campaigns and elections are about *representation, deliberation,* and *choice.*[6]

Campaigns and elections in any society reflect the quality of representative democracy in that society. We understand that one-party states, or societies that restrict ballot access for candidates or suffrage for citizens, or governments that censor political speech during campaigns, or governments that abrogate electoral outcomes cannot legitimately claim to be representative democracies.

In legitimate representative democracy, campaigns and elections must offer citizens opportunities for representation, deliberation, and choice. The ballot must be open enough so that citizens of different ideologies, issue concerns, groups and sectors of society can be represented by the candidates and parties running for office, or by the issues placed on the ballot.

Further, political speech must be open and unregulated enough so that candidates, parties, and citizens can openly discuss, debate, and deliberate how they will vote and work to convince others to vote with them. Finally, suffrage rights must be broad, voting must be accessible and secret, and the outcomes of voting must be carried out; all citizens must have the opportunity to make uncoerced and consequential choices in keeping with their own considered interests and values.

For those who would represent the citizens, conversely, democratically legitimate campaigns and elections must offer opportunities to represent, to lead deliberation, and to gain power. The representatives, whether organized into parties or not, must have the opportunity to present their views and programs, to interact with the citizenry during a campaign, and to hear what citizens think and believe. Further, candidates and parties representing the political diversity of the society must have a democratically appropriate chance of winning on election day, or representation will have no meaning. They must also be able to present their views widely to frame the voting choices available to citizens and persuade citizens to deliberate and support their candidacies and positions. Finally, the election itself must offer the opportunity for decisive choice of who will gain the power to control government.

This same logic applies to the more directly democratic practices of initiative and referendum. Those who wish to legislate through elections must have reasonable access to the ballot if their views are to be fairly represented. Just as in campaigns for office, individuals and groups with competing views on an issue must have the opportunity to organize and advocate their views in public. They must have a democratically appropriate chance of winning, and the legislative decision made on election day must be enacted decisively.

These electoral dimensions of representative democracy offer a new way of thinking about the historical development—and the current state—of electoral politics in America. They allow us to ask a series of consistent and practical questions about the conduct of elections, questions that help to develop a richer analysis of American politics. Table 1.1 summarizes those questions in a format that will recur throughout this book.

We can further refine this new thinking if we look beyond the isolated actions of individuals involved in elections and focus instead on what makes the whole system work. Which people or organizations mediate or coordinate relations between ordinary citizens and those who would represent them? In what public settings do citizens deliberate about their interests and values, and what patterns can we find in deliberative interactions among citizens and leaders? What organizations or institutions coordinate the act of voting, in which citizens conclusively express their electoral preferences? In short, who mediates the practices of representation, deliberation, and choice? Answers to such systemic questions enable a fuller and clearer understanding of "how politics works" in America.

Campaign-Centered Politics and American Parties

Starting from these premises, we can draw conclusions somewhat different from the conventional wisdom that contemporary American politics is candidate centered. On election day, the foundations of our electoral politics are actually government centered. That is, the government mediates the "choice" stage of American elec-

Table 1.1
Electoral Dimensions of Representative Democracy

Representation	Are citizens of different ideologies, issue concerns, groups, and sectors of society represented by candidates, parties, or issues placed on a ballot? How? Do leaders present their views and programs, interact with citizens, and hear what citizens think and believe? How?
Deliberation	Do citizens freely and openly discuss and debate their political interests and values? How and where? Do leaders present their views and programs to *frame* voting choices available to citizens and to persuade citizens? How and where?
Choice	Do citizens have broad suffrage rights? Is voting accessible and secret? Are the outcomes of votes enacted? Do leaders who gain the required plurality take office?

tions—regulates our registration, protects the secrecy of our vote, counts our ballots, and enforces our choices—thanks to reforms won by early-twentieth-century Progressives and others. But for the weeks and months of campaigning that lead up to election day, on the important dimensions of representation and deliberation, contemporary American politics is *campaign centered*. It is coordinated and mediated by campaign organizations.

It was not always so. American elections were once party centered. The transformation from party-centered politics to campaign-centered politics over the decades after World War II carried sweeping implications for the quality and character of representative democracy in the United States. It also radically disrupted Americans' understanding of their own political system, and challenged them to develop new paradigms—new ways of thinking—about politics. It presented the most profound challenge to the parties themselves because it threatened to render them obsolete and irrelevant to American elections. That challenge, and the parties' response to it, is the principal focus of this book.

In the most limited sense, this historical study of party organizations—principally the Democratic National Committee's headquarters organization (DNC), and the Democratic Congressional and Senatorial Campaign committees (DCCC and DSCC), but also their Republican counterparts (RNC, NRCC, and NRSC)—provides a valuable lens through which to view the emergence of a "new politics" during the contemporary electoral order. As they were displaced, party activists and professionals struggled to understand the changes that had swept them aside. Democratic Party activists in particular, reluctant to let go of the New Deal era in which they had dominated American government at all levels, at first struggled to resist the tide. Later activists took a more promising approach by adapting to the new politics and seeking to establish a new role for parties. The actions and fortunes of these activists and their organizations help us to see more clearly the nature and force of the contemporary social and political transformation from a perspective that shows more than voter surveys or election results can.[7]

This study is warranted in a broader sense as well. Throughout the period that this book covers, Americans have witnessed a transformation of U.S. society and politics. Historically, American political parties have been at the center of such transformations. Andrew Jackson's Democratic Party ushered in universal white male suffrage and the (relative) democratization of American economic opportunity in the 1830s. The newly emergent Republican Party served as the catalyst for secession and civil war in the 1860s and for Reconstruction in its aftermath. The Democratic Party ended Reconstruction, and Republicans encouraged the industrial revolution of the late nineteenth century. In the twentieth century, Democrats created America's welfare state and Republican administrations presided over the end of the Cold War. In each of these instances, party politics was central to wide-ranging political, economic, and social change.

The emergence of the new politics since World War II has been no exception. Even as they were displaced and struggling, the parties played an important role in the changes of postwar America. As late as 1968, national party organizations exercised narrow but direct influence in electoral politics: the parties' national headquarters coordinated the conventions that decided presidential and vice-presidential nominations and provided organizational umbrellas for decentralized presidential campaigns, while Capitol Hill campaign committees supported the reelection campaigns of incumbent members of Congress.

Over the next thirty years, the Democratic and Republican Parties' national organizations did not simply step into a national version of the state and local parties' former role. Instead, they eventually asserted a broader, more diffuse influence in electoral politics and pulled the agents of campaign-centered politics into their own orbit. Democratic Party organizations in particular helped to shape nomination processes and participants, campaign coalitions, campaign strategy and tactics, even the personnel who run the new politics. Republican organizations in particular helped to professionalize the business of campaigning and to develop a standard array of services to campaigns and standard fundraising practices to pay for them. In short, though parties no longer stood at the center of electoral politics, their national organizations gained important influence over patterns of representation and mediation in our representative democracy.

This book explores the development of both parties' national organizations, but it focuses especially on Democratic Party organizations for two reasons. First, recent party scholarship has already devoted substantial attention to the Republican Party organizational transformations that began in the late 1970s.[8] Second, and more important, Democratic leaders and activists considered a broader set of alternatives in their struggles to survive the emergence of campaign-centered politics. The range of their debate from the 1950s well into the 1990s allows a richer exploration of the contours and strength of the campaign-centered electoral order.

Plan of the Book

This book offers a narrative and analysis of party and electoral politics since campaign-centered politics (or "the new politics"—I will use the terms interchangeably) emerged in the 1950s. The next two chapters lay the analytic foundation for the narrative. Chapter 2 offers a brief historical survey of American electoral politics, then argues for the analytic value of considering that history as a sequence of "electoral orders," periods demarcated on the basis of patterns in the ways representation, citizen deliberation, and choice are organized and practiced. It then presents evidence that the campaign-centered politics that emerged after World War II constitutes a distinct electoral order and sketches the contours of that order. Chapter 3 further develops this analysis of the contemporary electoral order and its historical setting, arguing that campaign-centered politics developed in an increasingly suburban, affluent, and mobile postindustrial society and economy that strongly shaped it.

Chapter 4 begins the analytic narrative by reexamining the old party-centered electoral order as it withered during the 1950s and 1960s. It briefly describes the displacement of state and local parties from electoral control during that period, along with the impact of the nationalization of American politics on parties. The chapter then turns to the central motif of the book: that party weakness produced a profound crisis in many Americans' understanding of how politics worked, a crisis that led to a search for alternative paradigms or ways of explaining the political world. This chapter also looks at the first paradigm proposed to enable major party adaptation to the new politics. Party leaders and activists, focusing on conventional or "textbook" party concerns of patronage, distributive legislation, and control of nominations, tried to create national parties on a model developed at the state and local level.

Chapter 5 explores and reinterprets perhaps the most complex period of intra-party conflict in American history, from 1965 through 1975. It opens with an account of President Lyndon Johnson's brief trial and abandonment of a Textbook Party paradigm, then shows how liberals' factional challenges to Johnson in 1968 introduced a second paradigm for change: a Reform analysis of party-centered politics built around open decision making and proportional representation. The early and mid-1970s were dominated by efforts to reconcile factional and paradigmatic struggles in both parties—ultimately, by introducing the rough outlines of a third, Accommodationist paradigm—as Republicans gained strength and the Democratic coalition splintered.

The next three chapters explore the emergence and eventual triumph of the third paradigmatic response to the campaign-centered order: abandoning party-centered politics and accommodating the new order by servicing and brokering among professionalized campaigns. Chapter 6 explores the convergence of national party organizational strategies around the Accommodationist paradigm, as party activists and leaders eventually reconciled themselves to the new politics in the 1980s. Chapters 7 and 8 focus on Capitol Hill campaign committees and show how adoption of the Accommodationist paradigm aided their integration into the Washington establishment.

Chapter 9 presents an overview of the new conventional wisdom about party organizations, arguing that despite their displacement from centrality and dominance, such organizations have come to exercise a surprisingly strong influence over the shape of the contemporary electoral order. It then surveys party activity during the watershed 1994 election, the remarkably conventional 1996 campaign, and the contentious 1998 midterm election. Chapter 10 returns to the opening themes of the book, and argues that campaign-centered politics, though probably inescapable, is a decidedly mixed blessing for both the parties and the American people. Though representation and deliberation have never approached democratic ideals at any time in American history, the patterns of the contemporary electoral order raise increasingly serious doubts about our representative democracy. The American people have responded with disdain through repudiation of "the Washington establishment" and demands for campaign finance reform and term limits. Despite this disdain, however, the core dynamics and participants of the campaign-centered order remain adaptive and resilient and will be with us for the foreseeable future.

In addition to its analysis and argument, this study offers two principal sets of empirical findings about the campaign-centered electoral order. First, based on original research, interviews, and observation, it discerns three competing paradigms that leaders and activists proposed to analyze and ground national party responses

Parties, Elections, and American Democracy

to this order, exploring the content and implications of each paradigm. Second, it documents the development of national party responses to the contemporary order, which culminated in the common political practices of the 1980s and 1990s. By demonstrating the confluence of factional politics with arguments over paradigms of analysis and action, it shows that the historical developments of the campaign-centered order have emerged from intensely political processes, without any obvious or preordained outcome.

Analytically, the book's central value is in outlining a new way of thinking about American electoral politics, one that may offer a fuller, more comprehensive analysis than the piecemeal "party system" and "party decline/resurgence" approaches. By investigating the interrelated components of the contemporary electoral order—professionalized campaigns, struggling parties, competitive and often "split-level" elections, a fragmented and changing electorate, and so on—we can better understand America's troubled version of representative democracy.

NOTES

1. Jeff Fishel, ed., *Parties and Elections in an Anti-Party Age: American Politics and the Crisis of Confidence* (Bloomington: University of Indiana Press, 1978); Everett Carll Ladd, *Where Have All the Voters Gone? The Fracturing of America's Political Parties*, 2d ed. (New York: Norton, 1982); and William J. Crotty and Gary C. Jacobson, *American Parties in Decline* (Boston: Little, Brown, 1980).

2. Barbara G. Salmore and Stephen A. Salmore, *Candidates, Parties and Campaigns: Electoral Politics in America*, 2d ed. (Washington, D.C.: CQ Press, 1989); Alan Ehrenhalt, *The United States of Ambition: Politicians, Power, and the Pursuit of Office* (New York: Times Books, 1991); Martin P. Wattenberg, *The Rise of Candidate Centered Politics: Presidential Elections of the 1980s* (Cambridge, Mass.: Harvard University Press, 1991).

3. See, for example, David Price, *Bringing Back the Parties* (Washington, DC: CQ Press, 1984); Xandra Kayden and Eddie Mahe Jr., *The Party Goes On* (New York: Basic Books, 1985); Larry J. Sabato, *The Party's Just Begun* (Glenview, Ill.: Scott, Foresman/Little, Brown, 1988); and Paul S. Herrnson, *Party Campaigning in the 1980s* (Cambridge, Mass.: Harvard, 1988).

4. Philip A. Klinkner, ed., *Midterm: The Elections of 1994 in Context* (Boulder, Colo.: Westview, 1996).

5. See, for example, Daniel M. Shea and John C. Green, eds., *The State of the Parties: The Changing Role of Contemporary American Parties* (Lanham, Md.: Rowman & Littlefield, 1994); and James A. Thurber and Candice J. Nelson, ed., *Campaigns and Elections American Style* (Boulder, Colo.: Westview, 1995).

6. Lawrence C. Dodd and William E. Hudson have independently developed similar democratic standards. See Dodd, "Congress and the Politics of Renewal: Redressing the Crisis of

9

Legitimation," in *Congress Reconsidered,* ed. Lawrence C. Dodd and Bruce I. Oppenheimer, 5th ed. (Washington, D.C.: CQ Press, 1993), 418f; and Hudson, *American Democracy in Peril,* rev. ed. (Chatham, N.J.: Chatham House, 1997), chap. 5. The importance of deliberation to democratic legitimacy has drawn particular attention in recent years, exemplified by Seyla Benhabib, "Toward a Deliberative Model of Democratic Legitimacy" and other chapters in *Democracy and Difference: Contesting the Boundaries of the Political,* ed. Seyla Benhabib (Princeton, N.J.: Princeton University Press, 1996).

7. Indeed, John Aldrich argues that these party organizations—rather than voter coalitions or electoral "alignments"—are *the* defining elements of the now-transformed parties. See Aldrich, *Why Parties? The Origin and Transformation of Political Parties in America* (Chicago: University of Chicago Press, 1995), 269–74.

8. See, for example, the excellent coverage of Republican Party activities in A. James Reichley, "The Rise of National Parties," in *The New Direction in American Politics,* ed. John Chubb and Paul E. Peterson (Washington, D.C.: Brookings Institution, 1985); Kayden and Mahe, *The Party Goes On;* Sabato, *The Party's Just Begun;* and several chapters of John C. Green, ed., *Politics, Professionalism, and Power: Modern Party Organization and the Legacy of Ray C. Bliss* (Lanham, Md.: University Press of America, 1994).

2

The Campaign-Centered Electoral Order

*It is not the decline of the political party which we have witnessed but
the emergence of new individual and institutional relationships to the
larger world for which parties are far less appropriate than are other
mechanisms.*

—Samuel P. Hays

Current patterns of electoral politics emerged gradually in the decades following
World War II, shaped by political institutions and practices established long before.
This chapter will briefly sketch the development of those institutions and practices,
then survey the emergence of the new, campaign-centered politics and evolving efforts
to understand its meaning.

The Historical Development of American Electoral Politics

In a populous and diverse society such as the United States, the messy and complicated business of electoral politics does not happen automatically. It requires some
kind of infrastructure; something or someone must coordinate and mediate the representation, deliberation, and choice that enables the possibility of representative
democracy.[1] Historian Joel Silbey and others argue that such coordination and mediation have followed distinct patterns in each of four eras of American history: (1)
a pre-party era from colonial times into the 1830s; (2) an intensely partisan era from
the 1830s until the turn of the century; (3) a transitional, reformed but still party-
centered era from the 1890s until the 1950s; and (4) a dealigned, fragmented,
nearly postpartisan period since the 1950s.[2] In each of these "electoral orders," as

Byron Shafer has called them, a distinct set of agents has coordinated and mediated electoral politics.[3]

The Pre-Party Electoral Order

During the colonial period and the first decades of nationhood, Americans practiced only a very limited form of representative democracy (see table 2.1). Voting was often restricted to white male property holders, most local elective offices were held by men of wealth, and many presidential electors were chosen indirectly by state legislatures. Richard L. McCormick has written that parties existed in a primitive form during this period, but that they are better understood as *factions*, "shifting networks of elites who cooperated on some causes and parted, often explosively, on others, who never wrote political platforms, who relied on the deference paid them in their local communities, and who only intermittently cultivated followings in the electorate."[4]

Table 2.1
Dimensions of the Pre-Party Electoral Order, Colonial Era–1830s

Representation	Few established channels of direct representation. Most voters viewed "partisan" advocacy of interests as corrupt and destructive. Most officeholders were local aristocrats who did not normally consult others to discover their views.
Deliberation	Only limited public discussion and debate in most places, often limited to public broadsides or speeches. Nonelite citizens typically deferred to leaders.
Choice	Suffrage often limited to white male property holders. Voting often preempted by uncontested nominations and elections. When voting did occur, it was visible and public, subject to coercion.

Representation worked on three levels. Members of the "shifting networks of elites" gained direct representation through local groupings around legislative factions, connections among notable families, Southern courthouse "juntos," and ad hoc caucuses.[5] Nonelite white male property holders gained indirect representation through those they voted for, but deference to elites and distrust of partisanship often restrained them from holding public officials accountable to their particular interests or values. The rest of the population—women, slaves and other nonwhites, and most nonproperty-holding white males—found no representation at all.

Deliberation on public matters often occurred in private, within the factions, juntos, and caucuses of the local political elites. Silbey reports that conflictual public discussions frightened or disgusted many Americans during this period because of "the still-potent eighteenth-century fear that recurrent internal conflict endangered all republics."[6] There were exceptions, for example, in the often raucous town meetings of Boston and other New England towns. But most voters apparently looked to local leaders on public matters and deferred to the cues those leaders gave in printed broadsides or public addresses to—rather than conversations with—the voters.[7]

The practices of voters expressing their choices varied widely around the small nation. Nominations to office were often uncontested, so voter choice was often irrelevant. "In many cases in the early years there was little campaigning, and candidates were local 'notables,' prestigious and well-known figures in their communities, who simply 'stood' for election more often than they 'ran.'"[8] In both nominating and general election contests, voting was a public act. A voter expressed his choice by speaking up or raising his hand at a public meeting, or by publicly casting a visibly marked ballot. Such voting invited both subtle influence and direct coercion. For example, some candidates threw drunken parties for voters, and landlords were known to march their tenants to the polls and watch them vote under threat of eviction. William Chambers reports that in "rougher wards" of New York City, "mobilization...was often reinforced by local 'bruisers.'"[9] Put simply, the young United States fell far short of democratic ideals.

The Golden Age of Parties

Silbey writes that, beginning around the time of Andrew Jackson's presidency in the 1830s, "the entire texture and structure of the political world shifted markedly."[10] State legislatures had amended their constitutions to mandate universal white male suffrage and virtually direct election of American presidents. Improvements in transportation and communication permitted broad expansion of the national economy, raising public expectations and drawing citizens into public debates over government policy. And stable, organized parties finally emerged as central and widely accepted players in electoral politics.[11]

The emergence of parties as the focus of American politics transformed patterns and channels of representation (see table 2.2, p. 14). Parties penetrated deeply into both political and social life, organizing people on "ethnic, religious, communal, occupational, and sectional" lines in towns and cities throughout the country.[12] Partisans attended meetings, rallies, and parades in addition to voting at conventions and at the polls. Parties developed substantive policy platforms for local, state, and national government, and fostered deep and lasting loyalties among voters. In cities, parties organized powerful "machines" that mobilized voters and rewarded supporters with patronage jobs and distributive government policy.

Table 2.2

Dimensions of the Party-Centered Electoral Order, 1830s–1890s

Representation	Parties mediated and coordinated most political participation, focused at the state and local level. White males gained wide and diverse opportunities to organize politically and to express their interests and values in public settings.
Deliberation	Public political discourse became less elite focused, more visible. Improved transportation and communications technology enabled wider audiences for discussion and debate.
Choice	Suffrage opened to virtually all adult white males, and political participation and voting increased radically. Frequent, contested partisan elections for large numbers of public offices. Voting remained public, and parties systematically mobilized voters.

Public deliberation over electoral alternatives also changed dramatically as growing numbers of Americans no longer deferred to political and economic elites. Public speeches and debates reached broader audiences. Partisan newspapers emerged as the first American mass media. And issues of concern to ordinary people—the building of public roads and canals, slavery, Civil War pensions, government regulation of business, the creation of public schools—drew broad discussion and participation. Voters were of course still vulnerable to manipulation and shallow, symbolic campaigns, but American political discourse grew more democratic during this period.[13]

Expanded suffrage (though still excluding women and nonwhites[14]), the democratization of political participation, and the increasing frequency of elections led to an explosive growth in voting and other expressions of political choice. Electoral politics and partisanship remained intense throughout this period. Two-party politics emerged as the norm as major parties—first the Whigs against the Democrats, then the Democrats against the Republicans—contested unprecedented numbers of offices across the country, presenting voters with genuine alternatives. Citizens responded eagerly, although voting was still a visible public act and voters remained vulnerable to manipulative mobilization and coercion. Walter Dean Burnham reports consistent voter turnouts of 75- to 80-plus percent in presidential elections and 60-plus percent in off-year elections between 1840 and 1896.[15]

The Reformed Party-Centered Electoral Order

Serious challenges to party power, driven by several forces, gained strength late in the 1890s. As the United States developed into an urban industrial nation, public concern grew over concentrated power—and its attachment to party—in both the business sector and government. A devastating depression in the early 1890s triggered a regional realignment of the Republican and Democratic Party coalitions that dramatically decreased the number of competitive state and local elections. New Progressive coalitions throughout the nation inaugurated sweeping political reforms from the 1890s through the 1920s that deeply undercut the parties' monopoly control of American elections.[16]

Choice was the most striking dimension of change during this period (see table 2.3, p. 16). In the most wide-ranging expansion of democracy in American history, the Nineteenth Amendment granted women the vote in 1920. An array of other reforms was directed at reducing party influence. Many offices, particularly local offices, became "nonpartisan," denying parties the opportunity to nominate candidates and signal endorsements to partisan voters.[17] Initiative, referendum, and recall enabled nonpartisan means of direct voter influence. Even nominations to many partisan offices, once controlled by party conventions, were opened to direct voter control through primary elections. Elections became less frequent, as reformers consolidated or "unified" election days, thus reducing the frequency of party contacts with voters. Almost every state passed laws taking control over voting away from parties: state governments took over the business of registering voters and printing ballots, and state governments and local police forces guaranteed the secrecy of voters casting those ballots. Many voters still demonstrated strong allegiance to parties, but "split-ticket" voting increased and voter turnout declined precipitously at the turn of the century and in the decades that followed.[18]

Progressive reform and other developments broadly influenced patterns of representation. The years from the 1890s through the 1950s are best described as a transitional period: parties continued to mediate and coordinate many channels of representation, but other important channels emerged as well. In particular, shifts in government policymaking practices spurred the emergence of interest groups as central players in elections and policymaking. In a shift strongly reinforced by Franklin D. Roosevelt's New Deal in the 1930s, parties increasingly shared their representational role with labor unions, trade and industrial associations, ethnic and religious organizations, other groups, and even agencies of the federal government.[19] Though they continued to control most statewide and national nominations and elections, the parties became coalitions of progressively autonomous groups.

Table 2.3

Dimensions of the Reformed Party-Centered Electoral Order, 1890s–1950s

Representation	Parties continued to mediate and coordinate political participation, but they increasingly shared that role with specialized interest groups. Parties came to organize as coalitions of interest groups.
Deliberation	Transportation and communications technology continued to improve, and nonpartisan newspapers and radio reached wide audiences. Parties and interest groups were two among many channels for public discussion and debate.
Choice	Voting rights expanded to include women. Nonwhites remained largely disenfranchised. Sweeping reforms in the mediation and practice of voting: nonpartisan offices, direct primary nominations, government regulated registration, secret ballots, "unified" elections. At the same time, steep declines in voter turnout and "straight-ticket" voting.

Practices of public debate and deliberation also entered a transitional period. Public political discourse continued to be mediated in part by the parties, as local party organizing and activity continued—though at a reduced level—throughout the period. But as nonpartisan (often antipartisan) daily newspapers and then radio emerged as widely accessible mass media, the parties lost their dominant role in informing Americans about elections and public policy. Interest groups asserted an autonomous role in shaping public views of candidates, politics, and government, as did some agencies within the federal government. Growing segments of the public started to "redefine politics as a detached search for objective, and therefore correct, policies—a search unrelated to the passions, rituals, self-interest, and deception connected with political parties."[20] After a period of wide acceptance and power, parties faced growing doubts about their legitimacy and power to shape public deliberation.

The Campaign-Centered Electoral Order

The electoral order that emerged in the 1950s is the focus of the remainder of this book. However, a brief survey of its contours here (see table 2.4, p. 18) will allow some comparison with its predecessors.

As chapters 3 and 4 demonstrate, many of the remaining party-centered aspects of representation were displaced in the 1950s and 1960s by the emergence of "the new politics": extra-party candidate recruitment and nomination, professional campaign management, and issue-oriented campaigns conducted through independent organizations and the mass media. That displacement was further reinforced by an almost simultaneous shift in the focus of American politics to the national level. American parties had never organized effectively at the national level, and they proved incapable of adapting quickly to such sweeping social and political change.

By the mid-1960s, extra-party interest groups and political organizations offered far more compelling channels for representing citizens' interests and values. Citizens' views were also expressed in summary form through growing numbers of public opinion polls. Candidates seeking to represent those citizens increasingly used the methods and strategies of the new politics to gain power, as did those who placed initiatives and referenda on ballots across the country. Even officeholders resorted to new politics methods for communicating with voters, adopting a strategy that journalist Sidney Blumenthal aptly called "the permanent campaign."[21] Chapters 5 through 8 show how the parties struggled and ultimately succeeded in regaining a collaborative role in this representational system by the mid-1980s.

Parties were also further displaced from their deliberative role, both for elites and for an increasingly mobile, educated, and well-informed citizenry. Martin Wattenberg has shown the decline of party as a force shaping public thinking about elections and public policy during the Television Age, although W. Russel Neuman and others demonstrate that substantial numbers of Americans still look for cues from partisan leaders and activists in developing their own voting preferences.[22] A decisive minority of citizens now make their decisions based on their assessments of individual campaigns rather than party labels, which has in turn diminished many candidates' and initiative writers' interest in framing their campaigns in partisan terms.[23] In the most important development of this period, autonomous candidate and initiative campaign organizations emerged as the central actors shaping the issues under consideration and the terms under which they would be considered. Again, the parties responded to this displacement partially by collaborating with individual campaign organizations and partially by sustaining a remnant of their former role in shaping public issues and opinion.

Reform continued to alter the mediation of voting and other expressions of political choice during this period, although the public grew increasingly frustrated with their options. The Civil Rights Act of 1964 finally removed most legal barriers to African-American voting. A series of voting rights acts in 1965 and thereafter mandated the redrawing of jurisdictional lines to guarantee opportunities for minority representation (although recent Supreme Court decisions may bring an end to such districts). The Twenty-Sixth Amendment in 1971 lowered the legal voting age to eighteen. Broad reforms in the Democratic and then in the Republican presidential nominating processes during the 1970s (see chapter 5) led to widespread changes in candidate nominations and public political participation, principally by making primary nominations nearly universal. Despite these reforms, voter turnout continued to decline throughout the 1970s and afterward, with only a brief respite in 1992 and 1994. During the 1980s, voters and scholars grew increasingly convinced that real electoral choices were thwarted by entrenched incumbents,[24] though that argument has had little credence since the victories of Bill Clinton in 1992 and the Republican congressional majority in 1994.

Table 2.4
Dimensions of the Campaign-Centered Electoral Order, 1950s–Present

Representation	Representation principally mediated by interest groups and autonomous campaign organizations. Even officeholders resort to "permanent campaign." Parties shift to a collaborative role in this system.
Deliberation	Increasingly mobile, educated, and well-informed citizens rely on various sources of information in developing their political views. Interest groups and campaigns shape public opinion with increasing intensity and skill.
Choice	Full voting rights extended to nonwhites and citizens eighteen and older. Most nominations now determined in primary elections. Yet, voter frustration grows and turnout declines throughout the 1970s and afterward.

The distinct patterns of each electoral order have in some ways reflected the developments of their times. But the reverse is also true: the forms and practices of representation and deliberation have shaped politics and democracy in profound ways. Consider in greater detail the emergence of the new politics in our own time.

The Contemporary Transformation of American Politics

By 1968, most Americans understood that their political world was changing. Postwar economic growth, suburbanization, geographic mobility, and increasing social equality had cut away many of the roots of the New Deal political era. A new "postindustrial" economy—based on information and services rather than manufacturing—began to transform people's work lives.[25] Suburbia and freeways sprawled around America's declining cities, and the Sun Belt started its slow climb toward economic development. The children of the baby boom were reaching adulthood, and the youth culture was emerging in full force to challenge the nation's values and leaders. Despite urban riots and the assassination of Martin Luther King Jr., the civil rights revolution now carried the force not only of court decree but also of legislation, and it was beginning to show results in housing, education, and employment.

Economic and social change was matched in political arenas. Progress on civil rights had brought a backlash against racial liberals in both major parties and fueled George Wallace's 1968 "states' rights" presidential bid. Lyndon Johnson's Great Society legislation met growing opposition as well in the public and in Congress. The Vietnam War became a polarizing magnet, drawing committed activists into politics but offering no resolution of differences. Supreme Court-mandated reapportionment changed the memberships of Congress and state legislatures in the South and across the nation, shifting political power toward growing cities and suburbs. New political movements and organizations emerged throughout the country, and old movements and organizations, civil rights groups, feminist groups, environmental groups, public interest lobbies, single-issue groups, and candidate organizations, were transformed.[26]

Some of the most striking changes came in electoral politics, as developments challenged the way Americans practiced and thought about representative democracy. First, because of the substantial growth of the national government begun during the New Deal and World War II, American politics and elections grew increasingly national in their focus. More and more important governmental decisions—from social welfare and economic policy to law enforcement and the ways local schools would be run—were made directly by the national government, or required the approval of the national government.[27] The decentralized, regional and factional partisan politics of the 1930s and 1940s gave way to a more consistently liberal Democratic party and a more consistently conservative Republican Party nationwide. Following Dwight Eisenhower and John Kennedy's lead, the nation's presidential, then senatorial, gubernatorial, and even House campaigns and elections slipped from the control of state and local parties and political organizations.[28]

As those state and local parties lost control of elections and office holders, a new kind of politics arose that built on the broad social change of the era. A more educated, affluent, and mobile citizenry saw "amateur" activists enter politics around issues and causes rather than partisan competition.[29] Politicians drew on this volunteer base—and an emerging group of professional consultants who could blend it effectively with partisan politics—to support their campaigns as they ran for office, gaining party nominations through open primaries, and running personal campaigns with little regard for party tickets. Growing numbers of candidates presented their campaigns and personal issue positions to voters through radio and television in "spot" commercials.[30]

This "new politics" first gained broad attention in the mid-1960s as an ideological phenomenon. Left-leaning candidates such as John Lindsay for New York City mayor in 1966 and Eugene McCarthy for president in 1968 used these tactics to defeat the "old guard" of New Deal liberals who controlled the Democratic Party in so many cities and states across the country. When Lindsay won and McCarthy scared President Lyndon Johnson out of his reelection campaign, the new politics looked like the wave of the future in a changing country.

Still, the changes under way in 1968 remained incomplete, and the old system remained clearly visible. Vice-President Hubert H. Humphrey—the favorite of the old liberals—won the Democratic nomination without risking his fortunes in a single primary. The campaign styles of Lindsay and McCarthy remained the exception rather than the rule, as most candidates still ran traditional campaigns through partisan groups and party organizations at the state and local level. Republican former Vice-President Richard Nixon won the presidency in 1968 even as Democrats retained control of Congress, restoring the divided government pattern established in the 1950s under Eisenhower. And although Walter Dean Burnham warned about split-ticket voting and other changes sweeping through Americans' voting behavior, the two parties still commanded wide support, and party identification still explained most voting.[31]

More than a generation later, the political changes Americans recognized in the 1960s now seem nearly complete. The new politics of candidates, consultants, issues, and mass media appeals, although it first drew attention as a left-wing Democratic tactic, gained broad acceptance in the 1970s and 1980s as a means of winning elections for candidates of every ideological stripe. Since 1972, both major parties' presidential nominations have been decided in a long sequence of primary elections, and the fall campaigns have been waged almost entirely on television. Since the mid-1980s, every presidential candidate, virtually every congressional and statewide candidate, and many candidates for local office have built professionalized personal campaign organizations and polished their images and issue positions with voters, while party organizations have mostly serviced whoever won nomination. The practice even goes beyond campaigns for office: those working on behalf of most statewide and many local ballot initiatives use the same kinds of organizations and strategies. What had been a novelty is now the norm.[32]

In short, campaigns and elections for both candidates and ballot initiatives today look very different from those of the 1930s and 1940s. Their transformation reflects and is a part of broader changes in American society during the post-World War II period. The new politics methods used by Bill Clinton and his successors—and by virtually every other candidate for president and Congress to at least some degree—are now "the American way" in a nation of suburbs, freeways, single-family homes, and cable television.

Political Science and the New Politics

Beginning in the mid-1960s, media pundits and academics alike realized that the American electoral system had changed, and they struggled to understand what it was changing into. Three things shaped their early analyses: the scholarship of V.O. Key Jr., ideals about the central role of parties in democracy, and the emergence of sophisticated survey research.

Key, dean of American electoral research and author of a standard American politics textbook used from the 1940s through the 1960s, argued that American parties and elections were best understood in periods and pieces. Based on aggregate election data, he was the first to observe and systematically explain American electoral history as a series of party alignments and realignments.[33] In explaining that history, he argued that voters, who made up the "parties in the electorate," could be considered separately from the campaigning "party organizations," which were distinct from "parties in government."[34] Following his lead, scholars performed specialized investigations of the new system's components.

One approach, focusing on the "party organization" dimension of Key's scheme, was to compare the new system with the old system. As noted in chapter 1, political scientists developed a "party decline" school in the 1970s, which argued

al way of understanding the new era was to recognize that "the golden
" had passed. Their research showed that the two major American par-
what the scholars viewed as their core political functions: their ability
to control nominations, set the issues for campaigns, provide the money and personnel for campaigns, and deliver the votes on election day.[35] This was no small
matter for these scholars who argued that political parties performing these functions "are indispensable to the realization of democracy. The stakes are no less than
that."[36] Though this party decline school was often right in describing what had
been lost, it lacked a framework for describing and exploring the new system that
was unfolding.

As survey research and computers grew in sophistication, voting studies often
displaced party decline analyses in working toward a description and explanation
of the new system. In recent years, as a result of that research, attention to individual voters often dominates our thinking about American electoral politics. When
we place our era in an historical context, we talk in terms of *voter* alignments and
realignments (and dealignment). Our discussions of particular campaigns focus on
voter preferences, issue orientations, partisanship, and turnout. We consider candidates in terms of their demographic categories, popularity, and public image. Our
most often cited research tools are surveys, polls, and focus groups.

The conventional wisdom that emerged in the 1960s about the new system—
and still at times predominates in contemporary discussions of electoral politics—
grew from this attention to voters. In describing American elections before the 1950s,
scholars noted that most voters framed their deliberations and choices in terms of
their partisan loyalties. Thus, scholars embrace the custom of describing that system in voting behavior terms, as "*party* centered." During the 1960s, as the decisive
voters' deliberations and choices came to focus on candidates, scholars began to describe U.S. politics as "*candidate* centered."

This label and this conventional wisdom, however, can have misleading consequences Key would never have intended. It focuses almost exclusively on what is
going on inside citizens' hearts and minds and offers no description of changing
patterns of political organization and institutional power. Its narrow focus deflects
attention from the practices of real politics, from understanding the real coordinators and mediators of representation, citizen deliberation, and choice in contemporary elections.

The prior electoral order was party centered not only because of voter partisanship, but also because state and local parties coordinated and mediated most
representation and deliberation during that time. Thinking of the current electoral
order exclusively as candidate centered neglects broader dynamics and practical is-

sues of representative democracy in contemporary America. The current order
candidate centered, but it is *also* campaign centered. They are two inseparable sides
of the same coin.

But how does a campaign-centered analysis improve our understanding of
current politics? To gain a sense of perspective, consider an historical comparison.
Campaign-centered politics has a long history in America, dating back at least to
the pre-party electoral order of the late eighteenth and early nineteenth centuries.
George Washington was a practitioner in his 1758 campaign for the Virginia House
of Burgesses, when his campaign organizers arranged a drunken festival to draw local Virginia farmers into town to hear their campaign pitch on election day. While
Washington was off defending Fort Cumberland from hostile Indians, his friends
organized and campaigned:

> George William Fairfax and John Carlyle agreed to visit the Valley and to
> assist in lining up their tenants. James Wood, the most influential man in the
> County, was wholeheartedly for Washington....Lieut. Charles Smith, then in
> command at Fort Loudoun, assumed responsibility with innkeepers and mer-
> chants for the beverages that were to be served voters on the day of the election...
>
> In Washington's stead, James Wood had sat on a bench while voters de-
> clared their preference and he had thanked those who had voted for the absent
> candidate...
>
> The expense had been considerable, because the drinkables consumed by
> voters on a July day had been incredible. Three hundred and ninety-one voters
> and unnumbered hangers-on who possessed no franchise had accounted for...a
> total of 160 gallons [of liquor], or something more than a quart and a half per
> voter. Washington's bills from the various inns and tippling houses, including a
> dinner for his special friends, was £39, 6s.[37]

Consider the details of the Washington campaign in contemporary terminology. Its
organization, fundraising, targeting, outreach, mobilization, and victory are simultaneously strange and familiar to the present-day reader as campaign-centered politics before American parties or mass media existed. The organized campaign, run by
Fairfax, Carlyle, Wood, and Smith, coordinated and mediated who would be represented in the election, and they guided the (mostly drunken) voters' deliberation
and choice to Washington's advantage and victory. The campaign organization
stood at the center of the practical business of representative democracy.

Many candidates today are far more directly involved in their campaigns than
George Washington was in 1758. Nevertheless, in most conventional late-twentieth-
century campaigns, individual candidates do *not* stand at the center of the electoral
process, even from many voters' perspectives. In most cases, citizens seeking representation do *not* work with individual candidates personally during election cam-

1ere are too many such citizens for the candidates to meet
s deliberating what an election is about today may look to candi-
or issue positions, but their exposure is often *not* to the candidate
personally. In initiative and referendum campaigns, candidate-
; not even possible. The voters may consider a measure on its
merits, weigh the content of advertising received through various channels, or base
their decisions on the visible advocates and opponents of the measure.

Candidates, of course, are the *focus* of most electoral politics, and they play a
crucial role in it. Their names appear on the ballots usually because they initiated
personal campaign coalitions. They personally solicit some of the financial contributions (or use their own money). Often they hire and fire campaign organization
staff. They help choose the issues of the campaign, and they give most of the
speeches. Candidates meet and talk with many voters, both one-on-one and before
large audiences, and give many of the media interviews. They are in the voters'
minds on election day. Most importantly, the candidates are the ones who assume
office after a successful campaign.[38]

Yet much of this was true of candidates in prior electoral orders as well, and
no one before the contemporary era argued that American elections were candidate
centered. Candidates were important in the two prior electoral orders, but they
worked within a political system mediated and coordinated by political parties. As
party-centered politics began to wither in the 1950s, candidates did not personally
take over the parties' role mediating and coordinating representation, deliberation,
and choice. They turned that role over to campaign organizations, usually staffed
by professional political operatives.

At the state and national levels in America today, election contests with
prominent candidates, contests with less prominent candidates, and initiative and
referendum contests with no candidates at all usually follow a common set of broad
patterns of representation and deliberation. Autonomous, often professionalized
campaign organizations handle the process of getting candidates and issues onto
the ballots, thus shaping who or what will be represented in elections. These campaign organizations raise funds, hire staff, and shape the messages presented to voters. They establish contacts with citizens either directly or through the media, and
in doing so, broker representation, guide deliberation, and frame the choices available to voters.[39]

American politics scholars Barbara and Stephen Salmore describe contempo-
rary state and national election contests as following a consistent, three-step process.
First, each campaign organization works to gain public recognition of its candidate.
Second, each tries to shape the terms of the contest, "the criteria by which both its

candidate and the candidate's opponent are to be judged by the public."[40] Finally, each campaign works to convince citizens to vote for its candidate or against its opponents on election day.

Except in those rare cases in which a candidate handles all of these tasks, candidates are not the ones who make contemporary American elections work the way they do. Even billionaire Ross Perot, who apparently wished that he could control and manage every aspect of his own presidential campaigns, was not up to that task.[41] *In most contemporary contests for national and statewide office, professionalized campaign organizations—not the parties, and not candidates themselves—coordinate and mediate the most important aspects of our electoral politics.* Just as in the "pre-party" days of George Washington, when his associates bought the beer and put up the flyers and herded in the crowds to hear the endorsement speeches, in the "post-party" age the professionals and the consultants package their candidates and present them to the citizenry. The social context is dramatically different, but the central logic is strikingly similar.

Most candidates, party insiders, and campaign operatives figured out this new context as it emerged in the 1960s and 1970s, as did a small number of journalists and American scholars studying elections. A growing number of scholars recognized this phenomenon as they continued to study campaign organizations and electioneering and struggled to define its broader implications. It was not until the late 1980s and early 1990s, however, that most scholars in the field of parties and elections agreed on the new politics.

Barbara and Stephen Salmore were among the first to offer a compelling analysis of the contemporary political order as centered on campaigns rather than parties or candidates. They described campaign organization and strategy and the ways organized campaigns interact with citizens in mediating representation and voter deliberation.[42] Paul Herrnson, in his studies of congressional campaigns, describes national party organizations brokering services between professional consultants, donors, and candidates' campaign organizations.[43] In collaboration with Kelly Patterson and John J. Pitney Jr., Herrnson outlines the emergence of this politics at the parties' national committees.[44] And John Aldrich has couched an explanation of the contemporary transformation in his broader analysis of parties.[45] Scholars at the Center for Responsive Governance have written about the ways California initiative campaigns resemble candidate campaigns and suffer from similar abuses.[46] Perhaps the two most consistent sources of excellent scholarship on political parties are edited volumes. One is Sandy Maisel's *The Parties Respond* series.[47] The other is the series of volumes edited by John Green and others on behalf of the American Political Science Association's Political Organization and Parties Section and the Ray

Bliss Institute of Applied Politics at the University of Akron.[48] The list, though short, is growing.[49]

Another set of scholars has written about the nonparty people who run campaign-centered politics. These professionals and consultants have drawn scholarly and media attention since the late 1950s, when some viewed the arrival of Madison Avenue public relations and advertising in campaigns as a scandal.[50] As noted earlier, the emergence of political consulting as an important and lucrative profession in the 1970s prompted one journalist to proclaim that we live in the age of the "permanent campaign."[51] Academic research on the field has been limited by the reluctance of campaign professionals to expose their secrets to public view and criticism, not to mention to their competitors. Yet a growing number of scholars in recent years have begun to investigate and write about campaign consultancy.[52]

In short, after some initial difficulty, scholars have explored the broader logic of the current age, in which campaigns have replaced parties as the focus of our national elections. Their findings have helped to develop a new conventional wisdom about how American elections work. We live in a *campaign-centered* political era, during a time when parties no longer provide the central organizing logic of our representative democracy. Professionalized, autonomous campaign organizations now coordinate and mediate representation and deliberation for most Americans in most elections. Those who serve in elective office are chosen through this campaign-centered process, and ordinary citizens increasingly make binding legislation through initiatives and referenda decided through the same process.

So What?

But so what? What are the implications of this analysis?

Representative democracy built around campaigns—rather than parties or even candidates—raises broad concerns about the health of our political system. First, consider the professionalized campaign organizations that mediate and coordinate the representation and deliberation of this new system. They are usually ad hoc aggregations of autonomous (though partisan) professionals with various specialties, such as campaign management, advertising, survey research and polling, voter identification and turnout, and so on. These ad hoc aggregations combine, dissolve, and recombine with different participants in each campaign. From the candidate's perspective, these professional campaign organizations may do their job very well.

From a voter's perspective, however, the arrangements of campaign-centered politics are not nearly so satisfying. Despite the central role of these professionals in the current system, citizens seeking representation or deliberating on their choices rarely know who the professionals are. And though the professionals may have mediated a citizen or group's representation to the candidate in a prior campaign, once the candidate is in office or starts a new campaign, the mediating organization may vanish completely. In the case of initiatives and referenda, the coalitions sponsoring and opposing the ballot measures almost always dissolve after the election, without even leaving an officeholder as a point of citizen contact. Thus, the transient mediators and coordinators of campaign-centered politics offer a far less promising foundation for representative democracy than the former party-centered system, even when we recognize the abuses common in that old system. If the contemporary system were organizationally candidate centered, it would at least offer a consistent practical means of gaining representation or coordinating deliberation.

This analysis suggests the leverage we gain from recognizing the campaign-centered nature of the contemporary electoral order. We can integrate what we already know from a Key-style piecemeal analysis of voters, campaigns, and government into a broader empirical and normative exploration of American politics. For example, on the empirical side, this analysis offers a more fundamental basis for explaining the fragmentation of contemporary government and policymaking.[53] If we begin with the notion that our electoral politics is candidate centered, we explain the fragmentation by looking at the incentives for each elected official to be, in Morris Fiorina's phrase, "responsive but irresponsible."[54] Those incentives are indeed present, but our campaign-centered system offers no means for establishing consistent representative or deliberative relationships *even if* a candidate or officeholder wanted to do so.

The normative implications are also striking. In the eighteenth century, relatively few Americans were troubled by the way campaign-centered politics insulated elected elites such as George Washington from their constituents. Now the near absence of two-way communication between citizens and those elites seems understandable, but far more difficult to justify in democratic terms.

NOTES

1. My thinking on coordination and mediation has been helped substantially by ideas raised in Robert H. Wiebe, *The Segmented Society: An Introduction to the Meaning of America* (New York: Oxford University Press, 1975); Peter Berger and Richard John Neuhaus, *To Empower People: The Role of Mediating Structures in Public Policy* (Washington, D.C.: American Enterprise Institute, 1977); Samuel P. Hays, "Politics and Society: Beyond the Political Party," in *The Evolution of Party Systems*, ed. Paul Kleppner et al. (Westport, Conn.: Greenwood, 1981); and Byron Shafer, "The Notion of an Electoral Order," in *The End of Realignment? In-*

terpreting American Electoral Orders, ed. Byron Shafer (Madison: University of Wisconsin Press, 1991).

2. Lee Benson, Joel H. Silbey, and Phyllis F. Field first presented this analysis in "Toward a Theory of Stability and Change in American Voting Patterns," in *The History of American Electoral Behavior,* ed. Joel H. Silbey, Allan G. Bogue, and William H. Flanigan (Princeton, N.J.: Princeton University Press, 1978). For development, see Joel H. Silbey, "From 'Essential to the Existence of Our Institutions' to 'Rapacious Enemies of Honest and Responsible Government': The Rise and Fall of American Parties, 1790–2000," in *The Parties Respond: Changes in the American Political System,* 3d ed., ed. L. Sandy Maisel (Boulder, Colo.: Westview, 1998); and Richard L. McCormick, *The Party Period and Public Policy: American Politics from the Age of Jackson to the Progressive Era* (New York: Oxford University Press, 1986).

3. Shafer, "Notion of an Electoral Order."

4. McCormick, *Party Period,* 145. For a slightly different account, see John H. Aldrich, *Why Parties? The Origin and Transformation of Party Politics in America* (Chicago: University of Chicago Press, 1996), chap. 3.

5. William N. Chambers, *Political Parties in a New Nation: The American Experience, 1776–1809* (New York: Oxford University Press, 1963), chap. 1.

6. Silbey, "From 'Essential to the Existence of Our Institutions,'" 6.

7. In "Politics and Society," Hays challenges these historians' assertion of deference, arguing instead that while citizens certainly acted on their political interests, "individuals could carry out their demands upon government rather effectively without" parties or other methods contemporary Americans use (p. 250).

8. Chambers, *Political Parties in a New Nation,* 22.

9. Ibid., 23.

10. Joel H. Silbey, "Beyond Realignment and Realignment Theory: American Political Eras, 1789–1989," in Shafer, *End of Realignment?* 9.

11. On the Jacksonian transformation and its aftermath, see also McCormick, *Party Period*; Lee Benson, *The Concept of Jacksonian Democracy* (Princeton, N.J.: Princeton University Press, 1961); Joel H. Silbey, *The American Political Nation, 1838–1893* (Stanford, Calif.: Stanford University Press, 1991); and Aldrich, *Why Parties?* chap. 4.

12. McCormick, *Party Period,* 164.

13. Silbey, *American Political Nation.*

14. The Fourteenth and Fifteenth Amendments granted suffrage to male former slaves and other African-American men after the Civil War, but the collapse of Reconstruction after 1876 sharply restricted black voting well into the next century.

15. Walter Dean Burnham, "The Turnout Problem," in *Elections American Style,* ed. A. James Reichley (Washington, D.C.: Brookings Institution, 1987), table 5-2, p. 113.

16. Silbey, "From 'Essential to the Existence of Our Institutions'"; Paul Kleppner, *Continuity and Change in American Politics, 1893–1928* (Westport, Conn.: Greenwood, 1987); Grant McConnell, in *Private Power and American Democracy* (New York: Knopf, 1966), chap. 2; Hays, "Politics and Society."

17. Samuel P. Hays, "The Politics of Reform in Municipal Government in the Progressive Era," in *American Political History as Social Analysis,* ed. Samuel P. Hays (Knoxville: University of Tennessee Press, 1980).

18. Silbey, "From 'Essential to the Existence of Our Institutions'"; Kleppner, *Continuity and Change*; Burnham, "Turnout Problem."

19. McConnell, *Private Power;* Theodore Lowi, *The End of Liberalism,* 2d ed. (New York: Norton, 1979). On the establishment of administrative agencies as channels of representation, see Sidney M. Milkis, *The President and the Parties: The Transformation of the American Party System Since the New Deal* (New York: Oxford University Press, 1993).

20. Silbey, " From 'Essential to the Existence of Our Institutions,'" 13.

21. Sidney Blumenthal, *The Permanent Campaign,* rev. ed. (New York: Touchstone, 1982).

22. Martin P. Wattenberg, *The Decline of American Political Parties, 1952–1996* (Cambridge, Mass.: Harvard University Press, 1998); W. Russel Neuman, *The Paradox of Mass Politics* (Cambridge, Mass.: Harvard University Press, 1986); Edward G. Carmines and James A. Stimson, *Issue Evolution: Race and the Transformation of American Politics* (Princeton, N.J.: Princeton University Press, 1989).

23. Russell J. Dalton and Martin P. Wattenberg, "The Not So Simple Act of Voting," in *The State of the Discipline II,* ed. Ada W. Finifter (Washington, D.C.: American Political Science Association, 1993).

24. See, for example, Benjamin Ginsberg and Martin Shefter, *Politics by Other Means: The Declining Importance of Elections in America* (New York: Basic Books, 1990).

25. For an early analysis, see Daniel Bell, *The Coming of Post-Industrial Society* (New York: Basic Books, 1973).

26. Allen J. Matusow, *The Unravelling of America: A History of Liberalism in the 1960s* (New York: Harper and Row, 1984); and Godfrey Hodgson, *America in Our Time: From World War II to Nixon* (New York: Random House, 1976).

27. Milkis, *President and the Parties.*

28. Robert Agranoff, ed., *The New Style in Election Campaigns,* 2d ed. (Boston: Holbrook Press, 1976); and William N. Lunch, *The Nationalization of American Politics* (Berkeley: University of California Press, 1987).

29. James Q. Wilson, *The Amateur Democrat* (Chicago: University of Chicago Press, 1962).

30. Jeff Fishel, ed., *Parties and Elections in an Anti-Party Age: American Politics and the Crisis of Confidence* (Bloomington: Indiana University Press, 1978).

31. Walter Dean Burnham, "The Changing Shape of the American Political Universe," *American Political Science Review* 59 (March 1965):7–28.

32. Barbara Salmore and Stephen Salmore, *Candidates, Parties and Campaigns: Electoral Politics in America,* 2d ed. (Washington, D.C.: CQ Press, 1989); James A. Thurber and Candice J. Nelson, ed., *Campaigns and Elections American Style* (Boulder, Colo.: Westview, 1995); and Ron Faucheux, ed., *The Road to Victory 2000: The Complete Guide to Winning Political Campaigns—Local, State and Federal* (Dubuque, Iowa: Kendall/Hunt, 1998).

33. V.O. Key Jr., "A Theory of Critical Elections," *Journal of Politics* 17 (February 1955):3–18; and "Secular Realignment and the Party System," *Journal of Politics* 21 (May 1959):198–210.

34. V.O. Key Jr., *Politics, Parties and Pressure Groups,* 5th ed. (New York: Thomas Y. Crowell, 1964). Key developed these distinctions from an analysis first presented in Ralph M. Goldman, "Party Chairmen and Party Factions, 1789–1900," Ph.D. diss., University of Chicago, 1951.

35. See, for example, Fishel, *Parties and Elections in an Anti-Party Age;* Everett Carll Ladd, *Where Have All the Voters Gone? The Fracturing of America's Political Parties,* 2d ed. (New York: Norton, 1982); and William Crotty, *American Parties in Decline,* 2d ed. (Boston: Little, Brown, 1984).

36. Committee on Party Renewal, "Statement of Principles" (September 1976), as quoted in Everett Carll Ladd and Regina M. Dougherty, "On the Need for Parties 'Strong' and 'Great': A Dissent," in *The Politics of Ideas: Intellectual Challenges to the Party after 1992,* ed. John K. White and John C. Green (Lanham, Md.: Rowman & Littlefield, 1995), 28.

37. Douglas Southall Freeman, *George Washington: A Biography,* vol. 2, *Young Washington* (New York: Scribner's Sons, 1948), 318, 320–21.

38. Linda L. Fowler, *Candidates, Congress, and the American Democracy* (Ann Arbor: University of Michigan Press, 1993) offers a definitive discussion of candidates.

39. The best portrait of the evolving state of professional campaign organizations and their work can be found in *Campaigns and Elections* magazine, or in the anthology compiled by the magazine's editor, Ron Faucheux, *Road to Victory 2000.* A sampling of books on the subject includes Ann DeLaney, *Politics for Dummies: A Reference for the Rest of Us* (Foster City, Calif.: IDG Books Worldwide, 1996); Stephen J. Wayne and Clyde Wilcox, eds., *The Quest for National Office: Readings on Elections* (New York: St. Martin's, 1992); and Edward Schwartzman, *Political Campaign Craftsmanship: A Professional's Guide to Campaigning for Public Office,* 3d ed. (New Brunswick, N.J.: Transaction, 1989).

40. Salmore and Salmore, *Candidates, Parties and Campaigns,* 14.

41. For an insightful discussion of how Perot tried to run his own campaign in 1992, see James Ceaser and Andrew Busch, *Upside Down and Inside Out: The 1992 Elections and American Politics* (Lanham, Md.: Rowman & Littlefield, 1993), chap. 4.

42. Salmore and Salmore, *Candidates, Parties and Campaigns.*

43. Paul S. Herrnson, *Party Campaigning in the 1980s* (Cambridge, Mass.: Harvard University Press, 1988); and *Congressional Elections: Campaigning at Home and in Washington,* 2d ed., (Washington, D.C.: CQ Press, 1998). See also Paul S. Herrnson and David J. Menefee-Libey, "The Dynamics of Party Organizational Development," *Midsouth Political Science Journal* 11 (Winter 1990):3–30; and Paul S. Herrnson and David Menefee-Libey, "The Transformation of American Political Parties," paper presented at the annual meeting of the Midwest Political Science Association, Chicago, April 1988.

44. Paul S. Herrnson, Kelly D. Patterson, and John J. Pitney Jr., "From Ward Healers to Public Relations Experts: The Parties' Response to Mass Politics," in *Broken Contract? Changing Relationships between Americans and Their Government,* ed. Stephen C. Craig (Boulder, Colo.: Westview, 1996).

45. Aldrich, *Why Parties?* See also John A. Aldrich and Richard D. Niemi, "The Sixth American Party System: Electoral Change, 1952–1992," in Craig, *Broken Contract?*

46. California Commission on Campaign Financing, *Democracy by Initiative: Shaping California's Fourth Branch of Government* (Los Angeles: Center for Responsive Government, 1992).

47. L. Sandy Maisel, *The Parties Respond: Changes in American Parties and Campaigns* [three editions] (Boulder, Colo.: Westview, 1990, 1994, 1998).

48. These volumes include Daniel M. Shea and John C. Green, eds., *The State of the Parties: The Changing Role of Contemporary American Parties* (Lanham, Md.: Rowman & Littlefield, 1994); John K. White and John C. Green, eds., *The Politics of Ideas: Intellectual Challenges to the Party after 1992* (Lanham, Md.: Rowman & Littlefield, 1995); and John C. Green and Daniel M. Shea, eds., *The State of the Parties,* 2d and 3d eds. (Lanham, Md.: Rowman & Littlefield, 1996, 1999).

49. Denise Baer offered an early review of this literature in "Who Has the Body? Party Institutionalization and Theories of Party Organization," *American Review of Politics* 14 (1993): 1–38.

50. Stanley Kelley, *Professional Public Relations and Political Power* (Baltimore: Johns Hopkins University Press, 1956).

51. Blumenthal, *Permanent Campaign;* see also Larry Sabato, *The Rise of Political Consultants: New Ways of Winning Elections* (New York: Basic Books, 1981).

52. For an excellent survey of the literature, see James A. Thurber, "The Study of Campaign Consultants: A Subfield in Search of Theory," *PS: Political Science and Politics* 50 (June 1998): 145–49, and the articles that follow.

53. This kind of analysis is precisely what John J. Coleman calls for in his essay, "Resurgent or Just Busy? Party Organizations in Contemporary America," in Shea and Green, *State of the Parties.* His effective attempt at such an analysis is *Party Decline in America: Policy, Politics and the Fiscal State* (Princeton, N.J.: Princeton University Press, 1996).

54. Morris P. Fiorina, *Congress: Keystone of the Washington Establishment,* 2d ed. (New Haven, Conn.: Yale University Press, 1989).

3

The Foundations of
Campaign-Centered Politics

Tear down a tree and put up a parking lot.

—Joni Mitchell, "Big Yellow Taxi"

The foundations of campaign-centered politics lay in the transformation of the American society and economy after World War II, rather than in any particular campaigns or parties.[1] For at least the last three decades, both scholars and the public have recognized the outlines of this new politics and the problems it presents. Yet we have not done a good enough job of explaining why the politics is as it is or what role parties have played in its development.

This chapter explores those broader themes in order to lay the groundwork for later chapters. It begins by sketching contemporary problems of representation, deliberation, and choice that have drawn public and scholarly concern. It grounds those problems in the social and economic developments of post–World War II America and begins to link them to the development of party politics during this same period. Finally, this chapter describes a transformation in group politics during this period that presents troubling implications for representative democracy in the United States.

Electoral Politics That Doesn't Work

Americans often express disappointment with electoral politics in contemporary America, arguing that it simply does not work very well as a means of enabling popular control of the national government.[2] The fall of the Soviet Union and its satellites makes this especially ironic. It is now commonly observed that though citizens of nations around the world have deposed their dictators and embraced western democracy, people in the largest western democracy have doubts about its success here.[3] Those doubts concern all three of the political dimensions raised by this book: representation, deliberation, and choice.

Public confidence in political representation has been undermined by the serious fragmentation of group identifications that defined our political culture under the prior electoral order, with viable alternatives to replace them emerging only slowly. This change was signaled in the 1960s, when many members of traditionally partisan social groups—white southerners, union members, Roman Catholics, WASPs, and so on—scattered into collections of increasingly unpredictable individuals on election day.[4] Today, African Americans and to some extent Jews stand alone as the only large, cohesive, and predictably partisan groups of voters left in national elections.[5] We may have seen the emergence of a reliably Republican vote among white Evangelical Protestants in elections since 1992, but that group has proven quite dynamic over the past fifteen years.[6]

The organization of representational activity has, if anything, fragmented even more dramatically. Despite (or perhaps because of) the splintering of partisan social groups, organized interest groups have exploded over the past generation.[7] These numerous and newly dominant groups take a profoundly different approach to politics from the "old" partisan social groups. They participate in both elections and policymaking, but most of them do so with far narrower objectives.

One of the defining characteristics of the "old politics"—New Deal–era party politics—is coalition building through "logrolling," with diverse sets of people bargaining over an array of policy questions, seeking to build majoritarian platforms and coalitions. As noted in chapter 2, a central purpose of party politics under the prior electoral order was to provide arenas for such bargaining. But when interests organize on narrower grounds, and among people with little in common beyond a specific issue, the process becomes untenable and representative democracy has a difficult time maintaining legitimacy. Frank Sorauf saw the beginnings of the problem in the early 1960s, when he wrote that interest groups increasingly bargained with candidates and officeholders outside of party settings.[8] By the late 1970s, Anthony King questioned whether such bargaining and coalition building were even possible over the long term.[9]

Today, most candidates for national office make only limited use of the party coalition strategy. Instead they build campaign organizations that can establish some kind of direct relationship with their own electorates. They try to secure their electoral fortunes through campaign-centered politics.[10] The campaign organizations that now act as intermediaries between ordinary citizens and candidates have replaced parties and interest groups at the center of this politics. Unlike the old intermediaries, however, these campaign organizations often come and go quickly and carry no obligation to bargain or build lasting coalitions. Such a politics undermines officeholders' accountability and representative democracy. Ironically, as later chapters show, party organizations increasingly view their mission as serving practitioners of that campaign-centered politics.

These developments are closely tied to what many see as pathology in public deliberation over politics and policy. We encounter increasingly powerful arguments that national policymaking exists in a world only indirectly shaped by elections. Sam Kernell has argued persuasively that presidents often preempt bargaining and instead manipulate images of policy and brief bursts of public opinion to intimidate opponents and get their way.[11] Other research demonstrates that members of Congress and even interest groups have learned to imitate this presidential tactic quite effectively.[12] The problem with this approach to policymaking, however, is that it is shallow and incoherent; it works best when unrestrained by continuing obligations to constituencies or concern with coherent election platforms. Without lasting intermediaries to connect them with ordinary citizens, it enables an insulated set of officeholders, "experts" in policy networks, and the specialized media to make most important decisions about policy.[13]

This vision of policymakers as agents who seek and achieve autonomy from electoral politics has been advanced most forcefully by Benjamin Ginsberg and Martin Shefter, who have proclaimed "the declining importance of elections in America."[14] They argue that consistently divided government—a common feature of the contemporary electoral order—means that no candidate or party can be held accountable for current policy or governmental problems.[15] Instead, *decisive* political conflict has shifted from elections into the mass media, courts, congressional investigations, and even impeachment. And, consequently, the public now finds only rare opportunities to deliberate over and make serious decisions about the course of government. This argument must acknowledge the restoration of united government under President Bill Clinton and congressional Democrats in 1992 and the return of divided government with the Republican take-over of Congress in 1994. But even when such decisive choices are available, the public often finds that interest group politics presents polarized and unpalatable alternatives or that elected politicians overreach their mandates.[16]

As a result of these and other developments, public confidence in the value of political choice in the contemporary electoral order has eroded. Data on individual political behavior paint a bleak picture. In the most direct sense, elections are faltering because large numbers of Americans abstain from voting. Though turnout rose slightly in 1992 and 1994, it declined afterward and remains substantially below the levels of thirty years ago. We might hope that such abstention reflects a basic satisfaction among those who choose to not vote, but we have increasing evidence of the opposite: abstention for most is a sign of alienation.[17] Martin Wattenberg has demonstrated the partisan aspects of this trend, showing that a substantial number of Americans are not simply independent; they do not care about parties one way or the other.[18]

Further, surveys indicate public disgust with the mechanics of campaigning for national office, with its dependence on shallow negative advertising and special interest financing. Markle Commission and Pew Center studies suggest that abstention is becoming even more profound, as Americans—especially younger Americans—increasingly ignore basic information about major issues of politics and government. The authors of the Markle Commission report went as far as to proclaim "citizen abdication of the electoral process."[19]

The campaign-centered electoral order thus shows troubling signs on all three of its central dimensions. None of the preceding should be surprising to any moderately well-informed observer of American politics, but we should be concerned about the cumulative effect of these broader developments. They give credence to the real doubts Americans express not only about whether elections *do* serve as a means to assert public control over the national government under the contemporary order, but whether they *can*. These doubts seem even more legitimate when we recognize why we are in our current fix.

Post-Industrial Society and the Transformation of Group Politics

The conditions described above arose from two simultaneous and interconnected developments during the post–World War II era. One is the United States's shift from a mostly urban, industrial society to a mostly suburban, postindustrial society.[20] The second, which we will return to later, is the concurrent development of social science expertise and the technology to use it politically.

People recognized signs of an emerging postindustrial society as early as the 1950s, when John Kenneth Galbraith and Daniel Bell began writing about it.[21] The American economy's center of gravity shifted in the 1950s and 1960s from goods production to services. For our purposes here, the central importance of this lies not just in the tremendous economic growth of those years, but also in the growth of employment in service and white-collar professional occupations, which gradually outstripped manufacturing as the largest employers of American workers. The value of such "knowledge-based" occupations to workers is that their skills are more portable, enabling the increased mobility that was a hallmark of the postwar boom, a mobility that continued even in the more stagnant economy of the 1970s, 1980s, and early 1990s.[22]

Most obviously, the boom and its occupational revolution enabled increased social mobility among Americans. Along with educational opportunities provided under the GI Bill, the economic expansion meant that millions of Americans could live dramatically better material lives than their parents. Moving from blue-collar to white-collar jobs implied social advancement and autonomy from dehumanizing mechanical labor. In most cases, the move also brought increased wages and an improvement in living standards.[23] But white-collar service and professional jobs also meant separation from the neighborhoods, mill towns, and unions that had offered some political coherence to industrial America during the prior electoral order. Although citizens became increasingly affluent and well educated after World War II, they were also becoming increasingly disconnected from the social groups that had shaped their political culture, ideas, and behavior.[24]

Affluent Americans were not only more occupationally and socially mobile. They were also more geographically mobile in two broad senses. First, they accelerated the move from city to suburb that had begun at the turn of the century, leaving behind dense urban neighborhood living for privacy and single-family homes. With the help of mass automobile ownership and freeways, the demographic balance tipped. By the 1980 census, more Americans were living in suburbs than in central cities.[25]

Perhaps even more profoundly, Americans continued to move frequently throughout the postwar period.[26] These shifts in residence and residential stability are essential to any understanding of the contemporary electoral order. Attachments to long-standing ethnic or residential communities, religious affiliations and congregations, and even broad social or value commitments are far less likely to survive in suburbia. The whole ethos of suburban America is dominantly antipolitical; it is about mobility and freedom from extensive group entanglements and seeking private solutions for public problems.[27]

Geographic mobility during the post–World War II era was regional as well as metropolitan, with sweeping political repercussions. Urban scholars realized at least thirty years ago that occupational shifts and increased mobility would have broad consequences for the whole country. The 1990 Census showed a continuation of the trend that has now become familiar: population migration to and growth in the

South and Southwest at the expense of the Northeast and Midwest. More colloquially, the post–World War II era has seen the growth of suburbs and the Sunbelt (and their politics) and the decline of cities and the Rustbelt (and their politics).[28]

With this economic and demographic transformation in mind, consider the earlier discussion of social and political groups in America. The social, occupational, and geographic mobility that the transition enabled helps explain the fragmentation and dissolution of the "old politics." As noted earlier, that politics was built primarily around bargaining and logrolling among representatives of definable groups in U.S. society. For the Democratic Party, leaders of groups participated in and their members voted for the party because it offered them explicit governmental action (or inaction) that appealed to their interests in exchange for their votes. For white southerners, the Democratic Party meant public works, economic development policies, social insurance and, for a time, the protection of white supremacy. For union members, the Democratic Party offered governmental support for collective bargaining and an array of supportive social policies. For ethnic Catholics, the Democratic Party meant cultural identity and tolerance as well as public investment in the cities where most of them lived. The list goes on, and a similar list can be provided for the WASP, suburban, and small-town voters who voted Republican during the period.

During the prior electoral order, these partisan group attachments constituted both myth and reality. Myth arose in the idea of broad groups as political monoliths: all union members as Democrats, all northeastern Protestants as Republicans, and so forth. Recent analysis of survey data spanning the post–World War II period suggests that people within these groups never marched in lockstep. Group identities concealed diverse interests and values. Nevertheless, the foundations of the old politics were the clear majorities within each of these groups that behaved as party leaders expected. As those majorities evaporated for many groups, so did the old politics.

The "dealignment" of the 1970s and 1980s may be understood better as a weakening of group solidarity, or perhaps a period of transition to alternative configurations of group solidarity. Table 3.1 (p. 38) shows that partisan group attachments have not vanished entirely. For blacks, who still tend to live in strikingly segregated residential areas, the attachments are stronger than ever. Most union members and most Jews still vote Democratic. Similarly, most WASPs still vote Republican, and white conservative Christians appear to be developing into a complex and consistent political force. But these are the exceptions rather than the rule in contemporary America.

The reality of partisan group attachments during the prior electoral order ran deeper than group voting on election day, however. It suffused the representative and deliberative politics of the period. Leaders of these groups and constituencies—Walter Reuther of the United Auto Workers, Governor Strom Thurmond of South Carolina, and others—claimed to speak for their followers and bargained on their behalf at presidential conventions and in the halls of Congress. We should not romanticize this group politics, whose groups were often optical illusions that manipulative elites sustained for less than democratic ends.[29] But we also cannot ignore its centrality to the old politics.

Table 3.1
Voting in 1998 U.S. House of Representatives Election by Selected Groups (in percentages)

By Race/Ethnicity	Democratic	Republican
Whites	42	55
Blacks	88	11
Hispanics	59	35
Asians	54	42
By Religion/Denomination		
Catholic	51	45
Jewish	78	21
Protestant	37	60
White religious right	24	73
By Union Membership		
Union member in household	61	35

Source: 1998 Voter News Service exit poll data from www.cloakroom.com (17 November 1998).

A transition to the "new politics" of our electoral order happened in part because such partisan group attachments declined to where they no longer decided elections, and everyone knew it. In our *mostly* suburban, postindustrial society, these groups have become less important both because they are less cohesive and because they are increasingly outnumbered by Americans who do not think of themselves centrally as group members. The transition to postindustrial America has increasingly made the old group politics obsolete.

A new kind of group politics, made possible by the increased mobility of the post–World War II period, has become the norm. This new group politics is grounded more in ideological and membership-based interest groups than in partisan social and demographic groups. Such groups have, of course, been active in America for centuries in one form or another, but their importance dramatically increased in the post–World War II period. Most are membership based or corporate groups, organized around products, services, professions, or specific policy interests. As noted earlier, these more numerous and fragmented groups participate in elections and policymaking with far narrower objectives than the "old" groups, and are far more willing to work outside the bounds of partisan politics. For many, their very existence can be attributed to the increased independence and affluence of Americans, many of whom routinely give a few (or many) dollars to an issue-oriented group that solicits them.[30]

The implications of narrower interest groups providing the primary means of representation for most citizens are profound. Political scientists throughout the twentieth century have documented the abuses and distortions of interest politics in America, which the current electoral order seems only to exaggerate.[31] In the simplest terms, such groups can only represent their members on a narrow set of issues because that is all that their members know about them. (Set aside the obvious and important problem of representation for those who lack the money or information to participate in politics at all.[32]) The lack of partisan social groups to check the specialized interest groups produces a bewilderingly fragmented system of representation, with no apparent means for individuals to reconcile the positions of the diverse groups they may wish to join. Such fragmentation undermines any possibility that even members of such groups can use electoral politics to control the national government. Recent research demonstrates that some groups work to develop informational networks and find "lead PACs" to guide their alliance and contribution decisions, but even those practices have proven difficult to sustain.[33] Unless some kinds of intermediaries to enable ties between broad coalitions of groups and partisan slates exist, no citizen can clearly know whether a candidate is accountable to anyone.

But these more fragmented groups cannot easily step beyond their narrow missions and build coalitions. If they do, they almost certainly move beyond their legitimacy and succumb to domination by their own unaccountable elites and staffs. Consider two examples from earlier in the contemporary period. First, many corporate political action committees that solicited and received contributions from their own employees on the promise of advocating the firm's interests in 1980 established programs of ideological contributions to conservative candidates and causes that had little to do with the firms.[34] On the other end of the ideological spectrum, when Common Cause president Fred Wertheimer wanted his organization to join a national coalition lobbying against the B-1 bomber in 1976, many of his members objected that the organization "had no business getting involved in defense issues." Wertheimer contributed Common Cause resources to the lobbying effort and "simply stopped informing its members about the activity."[35] No one can bargain legitimately under such conditions.

A product of the postindustrial transition—the highly educated political managers and technicians who populate the upper echelons of our increasingly bureaucratic society—staffs the growing numbers of Washington offices of these interest group–based organizations. Economist Joseph Schumpeter predicted the emergence of such a "new class" almost fifty years ago, and there was a brief flurry of writing about it during the 1970s but, like the postindustrial revolution, it has since become a commonplace.[36] All of us have encountered this class; indeed, many who will read this book are a part of it. The important point to note here is that such people usually reflect the postindustrial society that produced them: possessing portable (often intellectual) skills, socially and geographically mobile, usually secular, not particularly attached to ethnic or geographic origins.[37] In other words, disconnected not only from the roots of the "old" electoral order, but also from the lives of most ordinary people.

Our insular national policymaking processes are also increasingly run by members of this new class, which helps explain how and why the processes have become more insular. Later chapters demonstrate that our political parties are increasingly staffed by the same kinds of people—those who approach elections having personally encountered only a narrow segment of America's increasingly diverse citizenry. Jeane Kirkpatrick explored these issues during the 1970s and raised some questions that need to be revisited.[38] Surveys and public commentary surrounding the 1994 election demonstrated that the public understands the phenomenon and is disgusted by it.[39] We need to ask how political operatives and candidates think about the citizenry and the groups within it in the wake of the first broad development of the post–World War II period: the emergence of a mostly suburban postindustrial society.

From Groups to Categories: Politics and Marketing

This requires that we consider the second broad development of that period: sophisticated social science and the affluence and technology to use it politically. Survey research of individual attitudes and behaviors, and the statistical methods to carefully analyze the results, have become integral to electoral politics over the past generation. Consultants and other specialists have developed tools far beyond the old horserace polls and turnout models of the 1950s and 1960s. Combining the results of academic research in politics, sociology, and psychology with computerized statistical packages and marketing research, they have provided the essential tools for candidate-centered politics.[40] In doing so, they have enabled professional campaigns to mediate representation and deliberation for citizens.

The raw materials of this new political technology are packages which combine broad behavioral information with U.S. Census data. The best known and most widely used, PRIZM (Potential Rating Index for Zip Markets), is a good example. Claritas Corporation developed PRIZM in the 1970s and sold it first as a marketing tool for private businesses. The database contains detailed economic, consumer, behavioral, and attitudinal information about Americans and can give demographic profiles on those dimensions down to the zip code, even down to the census tract. Claritas divided neighborhoods into forty categories with catchy titles, from the most affluent (Blue Blood Estates, Money & Brains) to the poorest (Public Assistance, Hard Scrabble). These categories continue to evolve, but their purpose remains the same. If you ask about a specific location, Claritas can tell you a great deal about the people who live there: what cars they drive, what foods they eat, what music they listen to, what they do for recreation, and so forth.[41]

Claritas is only one of many such analytic databases. SRI International has developed VALS (Values and Lifestyles) that focuses on value systems and personality types as well as consumer behavior. Their eight types include "Actualizers," "Achievers," "Strivers," and "Strugglers," among others, categories that do not necessarily correlate with income.[42] The Times Mirror media conglomerate developed a more public-affairs oriented typology in the mid-1980s as background for its coverage of elections. Its eleven types—which have since been adopted and updated by the Pew Research Center for The People and The Press—include "Enterprisers," "Moralists," "Seculars," and "New Dealers," among others.[43] There are several other typologies as well, most of which have been integrated with census data to provide profiles of specific places and constituencies. Perhaps more important, newer "Geographic Information System" (GIS) software such as ESRI's ArcView or Wessex's First Street enables users to construct their own custom typologies and analyses with census and other data.

In a nation whose elected officials represent districts and states, such information has tremendous political value. Combined with frequent polls, these databases and analytic tools allow candidates and officeholders to "know" what different categories of citizens think without even talking with them.[44] To a great extent, they can at times render group politics, both old and new, unnecessary. Anyone with an organized campaign and the money to pay a consultant can now have access to a filtered version of what potential voters think and want, by whatever kind of group breakdown they like. In some narrow ways that they can control, candidates and officeholders have far better information about the citizenry than their predecessors did. But they are also more insulated and isolated from the people they must represent.[45]

Ironically, when social scientists began to develop such data in the late 1950s, probably the first thing that they discovered was the diversity and complexity of stereotypically homogeneous groups noted earlier in this chapter. Partisan social groups had been less than monolithic all along, and campaigns with better information no longer needed to bargain with self-proclaimed group leaders unless those leaders truly had followers. Otherwise, the campaign could approach citizens in ways that better served a campaign's purposes. Candidates and political parties caught on to this and used it in devising direct-mail fundraising and targeted political advertising, as later chapters will show.

One illustration of the usefulness of data came in the 1984 presidential election, when polling began to reveal a sizable "gender gap," with women 5 to 10 percent less likely than men to support President Ronald Reagan's reelection. In response, Richard Wirthlin, Reagan's chief survey researcher, commissioned an extraordinarily large survey of 45,000 women voters, then grounded campaign strategy on this rich data pool.

> "We realized that all women weren't the same," says Wirthlin. "So we broke women down into 64 different categories, depending on age, whether they were married or single, working or nonworking." Not surprisingly, Reagan had different strengths and weaknesses with each group....
>
> The 64 groups were later compressed to eight....Using data that showed each group of women's concerns, Republicans targeted messages at each in their television ads, direct mail and campaign appearances.[46]

Thus, the Reagan-Bush campaign organization framed the election choice in various ways that they chose, not as organized groups of citizens—particularly women's organizations such as the National Organization for Women—might have preferred. By election day, the gender gap had shrunk to half its former size, and Reagan won in a landslide.

This illustration suggests the ultimate political power of advanced social science and the technology to use it. As E.E. Schattschneider remarked, "the definition of the alternatives is the supreme instrument of power."[47] Survey-style communication between elites and citizens can only be initiated by elites—citizens cannot ask to be polled—and the framing of the communication is almost completely under the control of the people doing the survey. The whole point of the clustered categories is that they break people out of standard social groupings, capitalizing on what

Schattschneider called "cross-cutting cleavages." If some fraction of the electorate still has some old-fashioned (say, urban industrial) group attachments that do not fit the emerging electoral order, a campaign does not need to negotiate with or seek accommodation with organized groups that claim to represent those citizens. Instead, it can look for "wedge" issues to divide members from the group, to undermine the social cohesion that has previously shaped those citizens' worlds, and to move them from group to mere category.

Framing issues in ways that unite supporters and divide the opposition has always been central to political success in America, but new technology allows the tactic to be taken to extremes. The more fragmented a society is, the more effective the tactic can be. In this context, it is no wonder that large numbers of people in the current electoral order abstain from electoral politics; they probably recognize how fragmented, chaotic, and manipulative it really can be.

If these databases do not do the trick, the marriage of social science and marketing has helped produce another alternative to group politics: instant or artificial groups, called "focus groups." Social researchers and campaign consultants construct such groups—usually ten to twenty people—by paying selected people to sit down and participate in a guided discussion for an hour or two. Focus groups provide the social interaction that surveys cannot and allow elites to hear how ordinary people talk and think about the issues that are raised in the discussion.[48] Most important, focus groups provide a surrogate for the real social groups that have fragmented in the transition to a suburban postindustrial society.[49] But focus groups are no less manipulative and elite controlled than surveys; again, a citizen with ideas or a grievance cannot ask to participate in a focus group.

With the availability of the new social science and technology, any campaign organization faces a series of strategic choices about its relationship to citizens. What kind of representation and deliberation does it want to mediate and coordinate? Does it want to engage in group politics at all? If so, what kinds of groups are most important in the given district or state: "old" partisan social groups or "new," more fragmented interest groups? Can one set be approached at the expense of the other? Both can provide important sources of money and support, but there are always strings attached. Group politics, however, does have the virtue of parsimony—much of the organizational expense of representation is borne by the groups rather than the campaigners—so many underdogs' and challengers' campaigns work this way by default. A campaign based exclusively on group politics today, however, is presumed to be either unsophisticated or "indebted to special interests."

Most often during the current electoral order, campaigns balance their citizen contacts between group politics and "category" politics, using whatever survey research based information they have the money to buy. A whole campaign consulting industry has emerged in the past thirty years to provide the core services of category politics.[50] This politics is also best known today because we see it everywhere. The mass media—television, radio, direct mail—are particularly powerful vehicles for the products of category politics, because they can reach people individually in their homes, away from distracting social groups.

Category politics is the dominant method of the campaign-centered electoral order. It is also a method that enables the insulation raised earlier in this chapter. When mediation between citizen and candidate or government official is primarily controlled by the latter, policymaking elites gain autonomy from electoral pressures. And to the extent that our political parties engage in this kind of politics, they may be hastening their own destruction.

NOTES

1. Everett Carll Ladd and Charles D. Hadley, *Transformations of the American Party System,* 2d ed. (New York: Norton, 1978) were the first to explore effectively the changes of this period and their implications for parties.

2. Such sentiments may have peaked in 1994, but they still remain quite strong. See the Pew Research Center for The People and The Press's survey, "Compared to 1994: Voters Not So Angry, Not So Interested," http://www.people-press.org/june98rept.htm (15 June 1998). See also Everett C. Ladd, "American Society: Where Are We Headed?" and later articles in a special edition of *Public Perspective: A Roper Center Review of Public Opinion and Voting,* February/March 1997; and Fred Steeper and Christopher Blunt, "Distrusting Government's Actions: Public Concerns Center on the Lack of a Proper Ethical Base," *Public Perspective,* October/November 1998, 46–49. For earlier discussion, see The Harwood Group, *Citizens and Politics: A View From Main Street America* (Dayton, Ohio: Kettering Foundation, 1991); and Richard Jensen, "The Last Party System and the Decay of Consensus, 1932–1980," in *The Evolution of Party Systems,* ed. Paul Kleppner et al. (Westport, Conn.: Greenwood , 1981).

3. For an insightful example, see Jean Bethke Elshtain, *Democracy on Trial* (New York: Basic Books, 1995).

4. Ladd and Hadley, *Transformations;* John R. Petrocik, *Party Coalitions: Realignments and the Decline of the New Deal Party System* (Chicago: University of Chicago Press, 1981).

5. "The American Electorate in Campaign 1998," *Public Perspective,* April/May 1998, 2–24.

6. Lyman A. Kellstedt, John C. Green, James L. Guth, and Corwin E. Smidt, "Has Godot Finally Arrived? Religion and Realignment," *Public Perspective,* June/July 1995, 18–22.

7. Robert H. Salisbury, "The Paradox of Interest Groups in Washington: More Groups, Less Clout," in *The New American Political System,* ed. Anthony King, 2d version (Washington,

D.C.: AEI Press, 1990); Salisbury, *Interests and Institutions: Substance and Structure in American Politics* (Pittsburgh, Pa: University of Pittsburgh Press, 1992).

8. Frank J. Sorauf, *Political Parties in the American System* (Boston: Little, Brown, 1964).

9. Anthony King, "The American Polity in the Late 1970s: Building Coalitions in the Sand," in *The New American Political System*, ed. Anthony King (Washington, D.C.: American Enterprise Institute, 1978).

10. Ironically, Franklin D. Roosevelt may have been the first skilled practitioner of such politics, but the first national campaign built this way was John F. Kennedy's. For detail, see Theodore H. White, *The Making of the President, 1960* (New York: Athenaeum, 1961).

11. Samuel Kernell, *Going Public: New Strategies of Presidential Leadership*, 2d ed. (Washington, D.C.: CQ Press, 1993).

12. Jeffrey M. Berry, *The Interest Group Society*, 3d ed. (Reading, Mass.: Addison Wesley, 1997). The health-care reform debate of 1993–1994 offers many examples of such politics; see Haynes Johnson and David S. Broder, *The System: The American Way of Politics at the Breaking Point* (Boston: Little, Brown, 1996).

13. One exploration of this argument is John W. Kingdon's *Agendas, Alternatives, and Public Policies* (Boston: Little, Brown, 1984). See also Hugh Heclo, "Issue Networks and the Executive Establishment," in King, *New American Political System*. One may reasonably doubt that this system is any worse than the old system of "iron triangles" described, for example, in Grant McConnell, *Private Power and American Democracy* (New York: Vintage, 1966).

14. Benjamin Ginsberg and Martin Shefter, *Politics by Other Means: The Declining Importance of Elections in America* (New York: Basic Books, 1990).

15. For a fuller discussion, see David J. Menefee-Libey, "Divided Government as Scapegoat" and other essays in *PS: Political Science and Politics* 24 (December 1991):643–46.

16. E.J. Dionne Jr., *Why Americans Hate Politics: The Death of the Democratic Process* (New York: Simon and Schuster, 1991); James Q. Wilson, "The Government Gap," *The New Republic*, 3 June 1991, 35–38. A pointed illustration of this problem arose in 1995, when surveys showed American voters simultaneously satisfied that Republicans had won control of Congress and dissatisfied with many of the conservative policies those Republicans were pursuing ("Polity Watch," in *Public Perspective*, June/July 1995, 59). For an excellent analysis of partisan "overreaching," see Margaret Weir, "Political Parties and Social Policymaking," in *The Social Divide: Political Parties and the Future of Activist Government*, ed. Margaret Weir (Washington, D.C.: Brookings Institution, 1998).

17. Walter Dean Burnham, "The Turnout Problem," in *Elections American Style*, ed. A. James Reichley (Washington, D.C.: Brookings Institution, 1987). For a powerful rebuttal to this pessimistic interpretation of abstention, see Everett Carll Ladd and Regina M. Dougherty, "On the Need for Parties, 'Strong,' and 'Great': A Dissent," in *The Politics of Ideas: Intellectual Challenges to the Party after 1992*, ed. John K. White and John C. Green (Lanham, Md: Rowman & Littlefield, 1995).

18. Martin P. Wattenberg, *The Decline of American Political Parties, 1952–1996* (Cambridge, Mass: Harvard University Press, 1998). For a fuller discussion, see Russell J. Dalton and

Martin P. Wattenberg, "The Not So Simple Act of Voting," in *The State of the Discipline II*, ed. Ada M. Finifter (Washington, D.C.: American Political Science Association, 1993).

19. The Markle Commission on the Media and the Electorate, *Key Findings* (New York: Markle Commission, 1990); and Kimberly Parker and Claudia Deane, "Ten Years of the Pew News Interest Index," paper presented at the annual meeting of the American Association for Public Opinion Research, May 1997.

20. The writings of Everett Carll Ladd and Charles Hadley serve as the starting point for much of this discussion of postindustrial politics. See in particular Ladd and Hadley, *Transformations of the American Party System;* and Ladd, "The Shifting Party Coalitions from the 1930s to the 1970s," in *Party Coalitions in the 1980s,* ed. Seymour M. Lipset (San Francisco: Institute for Contemporary Studies, 1981).

21. John Kenneth Galbraith, *The Affluent Society* (Boston: Houghton Mifflin, 1958); Galbraith, *New Industrial State* (Boston: Houghton Mifflin, 1967); and Daniel Bell, *The Coming of Post-Industrial Society* (New York: Basic Books, 1973).

22. Frank Levy, *Dollars and Dreams: The Changing American Income Distribution* (New York: Norton, 1987); Robert Reich, *The Work of Nations: Preparing Ourselves for 21st Century Capitalism* (New York: Knopf, 1991).

23. An important challenge to the notion of white-collar jobs as a panacea was offered in the 1980s by University of Massachusetts professor Ralph Whitehead, who argued that most white-collar workers were little better off than their blue-collar counterparts. See, for example, Scot Lehigh, "New Collar: I Have Seen the Future, And It Doesn't Work in a Three Piece Suit," *Chicago Reader*, 6 December 1985,1, 14–25

24. A furious debate emerged over arguments such as this in 1995 after the publication of Robert D. Putnam, "Bowling Alone: America's Declining Social Capital," *Journal of Democracy,* January 1995,65–78. Putnam elaborated on the argument in "Tuning In, Tuning Out: The Strange Disappearance of Social Capital in America," *PS: Political Science & Politics 40* (December 1995):664–83. For a rebuttal, see Everett C. Ladd, "The Data Just Don't Show Erosion of America's 'Social Capital'" and accompanying articles in a special issue of *Public Perspective,* June/July 1996; and Andrew Greeley, "The Other Civic America: Religion and Social Capital," *The American Prospect,* May–June 1997, 68–73.

25. Richard Wade, "The Suburban Roots of the New Federalism," *New York Times Magazine,* 1 August 1982. For an excellent recent discussion, see Rhodes Cook, "Suburbia: Land of Varied Faces and a Growing Political Force," *Congressional Quarterly Weekly Report*, 24 May 1997, 1209–17.

26. Larry H. Long, *Migration and Residential Mobility* (New York: Russell Sage Foundation, 1988); Sam Roberts, "U.S. Census Study Reveals a Nation of Rolling Stones," *New York Times,* 12 December 1994, A14.

27. Although the authors might disagree, I think this is the central thrust of Robert Bellah et al., *Habits of the Heart: Individualism and Commitment in American Life* (Berkeley: University of California Press, 1985). For discussion, see William Schneider, "The Suburban Century Begins," *Atlantic Monthly,* July 1992, 33–44. For an excellent survey of suburban voting behavior in the 1996 elections, see Cook, "Suburbia: Land of Varying Faces And a Growing

Political Force", and accompanying articles in *Congressional Quarterly Weekly Report,* 24 May 1997, 1209–29.

28. Sam Roberts, *Who We Are: A Portrait of America Based on the Latest U.S. Census* (New York: Random House, 1993). For earlier analysis, see Kevin Phillips, *The Emerging Republican Majority* (Garden City, N.Y.: Doubleday, 1970); Kirkpatrick Sale, *Power Shift: The Rise of the Southern Rim and Its Challenge to the Eastern Establishment* (New York: Vintage, 1975); and George Sternlieb and James W. Hughes, eds., *Post-Industrial America: Metropolitan Decline and Inter-Regional Job Shifts* (New Brunswick, N.J.: Rutgers University Press, 1975).

29. See, for example, McConnell, *Private Power and American Democracy.*

30. Berry, *Interest Group Society.*

31. The literature is rich. For the best of it, see E. Pendleton Herring, *Public Administration and the Public Interest* (New York: McGraw-Hill, 1936); McConnell, *Private Power and American Democracy;* and Theodore J. Lowi, *The End of Liberalism: The Second Republic of the United States,* 2d ed. (New York: Norton, 1979).

32. See Sidney Verba, Kay Lehman Scholzman, and Henry E. Brady, *Voice and Equality: Civic Voluntarism in American Politics* (Cambridge, Mass.: Harvard University Press, 1995).

33. Robert Biersack, Paul S. Herrnson, and Clyde Wilcox, eds., *Risky Business: PAC Decision-making in Congressional Elections* (Armonk, N.Y.: M.E. Sharpe, 1994).

34. See, for example, Thomas Byrne Edsall, *Power and Money* (New York: Norton, 1988).

35. Nick Kotz, *Wild Blue Yonder: Money, Politics, and the B-1 Bomber* (New York: Random House, 1988), 154–55.

36. Joseph A. Schumpeter, *Capitalism, Socialism and Democracy,* 3d ed. (New York: Harper and Row, 1950); B. Bruce-Briggs, ed., *The New Class?* (New Brunswick, N.J.: Transaction, 1979).

37. Reich, *Work of Nations.* See also Ronald Inglehart, *Culture Shift in Advanced Industrial Society* (Princeton, N.J.: Princeton University Press, 1990).

38. Jeane J. Kirkpatrick, *The New Presidential Elite* (New York: Russell Sage Foundation, 1976); Kirkpatrick, *Dismantling the Parties: Reflections on Party Reform and Party Decomposition* (Washington, D.C.: American Enterprise Institute, 1978).

39. Ladd and Dougherty, "On the Need For Parties, 'Strong,' and 'Great': A Dissent," 33–43. Such opinions also emerged in a survey the Hart/Teeter polling firm performed in March 1995, "A National Public Opinion Survey Conducted for the Council for Excellence in Government," which the author obtained privately from the Council for Excellence in Government.

40. Susan Herbst, *Numbered Voices: How Opinion Polling Has Shaped American Politics* (Chicago: University of Chicago Press, 1993). See also Robert Westbrook, "Politics as Consumption: Managing the Modern American Election," in *The Culture of Consumption,* ed. Richard Wrightman Fox and T.J. Jackson Lears (New York: Pantheon, 1983).

41. As of January 1999, Claritas' World Wide Web site for PRIZM is at http://www.claritas.com/seg_nbr.htm. For an early survey, see Michael Weiss, *The Clustering of America* (New York: Harper and Row, 1988).

42. As of January 1999, SRI's World Wide Web site for VALS is at http://future.sri.com/vals/valsindex.html. For an early survey, see Arnold Mitchell, *The Nine American Lifestyles: Who We Are and Where We're Going* (New York: Macmillan, 1983).

43. Times Mirror Center for Press and Public Policy, *The People, the Press, and Politics* (Washington, D.C.: Times Mirror Foundation, 1987). This typology, and surveys based on it, are now coordinated by The Pew Research Center for The People and The Press, which as of January 1999 maintains a World Wide Web page at http://www.people-press.org.

44. David Beiler surveys the history of such tactical uses of geodemographics in campaign politics in "Precision Politics," *Campaigns and Elections,* February/March 1990, 33–36, 38. For a reconsideration of geodemographics, see Hal Malchow, "The Targeting Revolution in Political Direct Contact," *Campaigns and Elections,* June 1997, 36–39.

45. Nelson Polsby makes a similar argument in *The Consequences of Party Reform* (New York: Oxford, 1983), 75.

46. Bill Peterson, "Reagan Did Understand Women: While Democrats Slept, The GOP Skillfully Captured Their Votes," *Washington Post,* 3 March 1985, C5. For discussion of Wirthlin's work on other demographic groups, see Evan Thomas, "Every Region, Every Age Group, Almost Every Voting Bloc: How a Coast-to-Coast Victory Was Forged," *Time,* 19 November 1984, 42.

47. E.E. Schattschneider, *The Semisovereign People: A Realist's View of Democracy in America* (Hinsdale, Ill.: Dryden, 1960), 66.

48. For an introduction to how focus groups work, see David L. Morgan, ed., *Successful Focus Groups: Advancing the State of the Art* (Thousand Oaks, Calif.: Sage, 1993); and Richard A. Krueger, *Focus Groups: A Practical Guide for Applied Research,* 2d ed. (Thousand Oaks, Calif.: Sage, 1994). For a brief discussion of their early use by campaign consultants, see Larry Sabato, *The Rise of Political Consultants: New Ways of Winning Elections* (New York: Basic Books, 1981), chap. 3. For a broader discussion of their implications for democratic representation, see Kristi Anderson and Stuart J. Thorson, "Public Discourse or Strategic Game? Changes in Our Conception of Elections," *Studies in Political Development* 3 (1989):263–78.

49. See, for example, the first Clinton/Gore campaign's use of focus groups, described in Peter Goldman and Tom Mathews, "'Manhattan Project,' 1992: With Dial and Focus Groups, Clinton's People Recast his Campaign in Midcourse to Reach a National Audience," *Newsweek,* November/December 1992, 40–56.

50. Sidney Blumenthal, *The Permanent Campaign,* rev. ed. (New York: Simon and Schuster, 1982); and Sabato, *Rise of Political Consultants.*

4

Campaign-Centered Politics
Leaves the Parties Behind

The dogmas of the quiet past are inadequate to the stormy present. The occasion is piled high with difficulty, and we must rise with the occasion. As our case is new, so we must think anew, and act anew. We must disenthrall ourselves, and then we shall save our country.

Fellow citizens, we cannot escape history.

—Abraham Lincoln, "Annual Message to Congress," 1862

The social and political changes surveyed in chapters 2 and 3 first became visible in presidential politics. General Dwight Eisenhower, after being courted by both major parties, declared himself a Republican and ran for president in 1952. His campaign, however, was run by a group called Citizens for Eisenhower as much as by party organizations. He carried in a Republican Congress on his coattails, but that unified party government vanished with the election of a Democratic congressional majority in 1954.

Democrats' problems began in 1948, when South Carolina Governor Strom Thurmond led southern segregationists out of the party to the right, and former Vice-President Henry Wallace led his followers out to challenge President Harry Truman from the left. In 1956, Senator Estes Kefauver defied Democratic leaders and ran for the party's presidential nomination in primaries rather than by courting party elites in state caucuses. That move spurred the party's 1952 nominee, Illinois Governor Adlai Stevenson, to win voter support for his renomination in 1956. That summer, delegates to the Democratic National Convention nominated Stevenson and Kefauver to the same ticket. Open nomination contests, increasingly beyond party leaders' control, have remained the norm ever since, as have factional and ideological battles.

By the late 1960s, academics and journalists alike looked at the post–World War II patterns of candidate- and campaign-centered politics and divided government as signs of national party decline.[1] Yet, as sophisticated observers of the time recognized, a reexamination of the 1950s and early 1960s yields a more complex verdict: instead of declining at the national level, the parties were left behind at the state and local level by the emergence of the campaign-centered electoral order. This chapter shows that *the parties were displaced from their former dominance at the state and local level, the prior locus of American electoral politics*. Their displacement was compounded by the nationalization of government and elections that shifted politics to broader arenas in which parties had never established themselves.

National party decline was more perception than reality. As the new electoral order emerged, many Americans expected political parties to somehow evolve and adapt to this new order automatically and play the same role in national politics as they had in state and local politics. When the parties could not control nominations to national office, shape issues to be debated in campaigns, provide substantial money and resources for campaigns, or deliver voters in November, most observers described these failures as "decline." It would be more accurate to say that *the national parties, though they had changed little, had declined relative to raised public expectations*. Still, whether perception or reality, the result was the same: as the campaign-centered order gained clear dominance in the 1960s, the parties played only a peripheral role in national elections.

Anomalies, Crises, and the Emergence of New Paradigms

This transformation was profoundly disorienting to formerly successful party leaders and activists entrenched in the "old" politics. Under the rules of the old electoral order, Eisenhower and Kefauver's strategies—bypassing local party structures, ignoring established group alliances, and building campaign coalitions from scratch—should have proven disastrous, shunned by leaders and voters alike. Instead, Eisenhower won and Kefauver gained a place on the Democratic ticket. Though at first dismissed by some as anomalies, these successes became models for the future. The world of American elections was changing, challenging party leaders and activists to understand and respond or face irrelevance and extinction.

Party leaders' and activists' confusion in the face of such historic political change compares in many ways with scientists' confusion in the face of dramatic discoveries. Scientists were no less disoriented after Copernicus convinced them that the earth revolved around the sun, or after Albert Einstein convinced them that nuclear fission could transform matter into energy. Thomas Kuhn explored such dramatic leaps in his book, *The Structure of Scientific Revolutions,* and his analysis offers valuable guidance for understanding the emergence of the contemporary electoral order.[2]

Scientists rely on theoretical paradigms or worldviews to explain the world they explore. Pre-Copernican astronomy, for example, assumed that the stars and planets revolve around the earth. When scientists find that the world does not conform to their paradigm—as when planetary orbits do not follow predicted paths—they initially dismiss their findings as anomalies or mismeasurements. But when consistent anomalies accumulate, scientists must eventually recognize them as unexplained puzzles or problematic facts that present a crisis for accepted paradigms or worldviews.

What follows for scientists, Kuhn discovered, is a struggle to solve the puzzles, to develop new paradigms that can explain this newly recognized and different world so that scientific inquiry can resume. Innovators may promote competing alternative paradigmatic explanations, forcing scientists to test and debate the merits of each. But such new paradigms rarely gain unquestioned and immediate acceptance. On one hand, institutions—universities, scientific disciplines, research communities—that were built around the explanatory legitimacy of the prior paradigms remain. The leaders of such institutions many times resist a new paradigm because its acceptance renders their authority obsolete. On the other hand, advocates of other new paradigms often compete vigorously for their own prescriptions for future inquiry. Kuhn argued that the success of any important new paradigm can therefore best be described as a "scientific revolution." It overturns the old order and redefines the scientific field in its own image.[3]

Similarly, this chapter will show how developments in the 1950s and 1960s revealed a political world that radically challenged the understanding of experienced party leaders and activists. Campaign-centered politics, initially thought to be an anomaly, emerged as the defining feature of a revolutionary new electoral order, a new puzzle to be solved. Some party leaders and activists tried to resist the emerging electoral order and protect their own waning power. Others struggled to find new paradigmatic explanations for the changing world around them and to develop corresponding paradigmatic strategies for responding to those changes. Those struggles began at the state and local level.

Displacement from State and Local Dominance

In 1952 V.O. Key Jr. argued that the Democratic and Republican Parties were best understood nationally as "coalition[s], rather than hierarch[ies]."[4] In the standard college textbook on American party politics, Key explained that "instead of being subject to commands from above, state and city committees, leaders, and bosses occupy positions of power in their own right. The party nationally tends to be an alliance of state and city leaders who work together most faithfully during a presidential campaign." Even the parties' national organizations—national committees and Capitol Hill campaign committees—reflected this reality. Their members gathered from around the country as "sovereigns to negotiate . . . with each other" rather than as subordinates to some national organization.

Key's description surprised no one; as noted in chapter 2, American parties had been organized like this for more than a hundred years. Just as the pre-party campaign-centered order of the late eighteenth and early nineteenth centuries had focused on local and sometimes state elections, the parties during the following electoral order organized primarily at the local level. This tradition of local organization and strength continued well into the twentieth century. But as the post–World War II years went by, the new politics increasingly threatened the parties.

Consider this prominent example: Representative Mike Kirwan of Youngstown, Ohio chaired the Democratic Congressional Campaign Committee—the national vehicle for assisting Democratic campaigns for the U.S. House of Representatives—from 1947 until he died in 1970. Kirwan's work with that committee epitomized the old politics. In his 1964 memoirs, Kirwan relates that when he took over the committee in 1948, a pollster approached him. The pollster offered to develop statistical profiles of the nation's 100 most competitive congressional districts. For $75,000, he said, Kirwan's committee could use the demographics and voting patterns of each district to develop an effective campaign for the following year's election.

Kirwan turned him down, but not because he doubted the value of information and strategic campaigning. On the contrary, Kirwan insisted that "knowledge in detail of the issues in a particular campaign, and how these issues may be used either for or against a particular strategy, is vital." Kirwan stuck with his "instincts" and doubted that a pollster could offer any helpful information that local party people did not already have. He scoffed at the early rudiments of new politics technology and explained that

> mathematics and probability have validity when they are applied to a controlled situation. But when the situation becomes fluid, as in a political campaign, the mathematical probabilities tend to disappear and in their place come situations that are human in scope and nonnumerical and therefore less subject to computation . . . . Judgement is still the base of successful politics.[5]

Kirwan's trust in the state and local base of the 1948 parties was rewarded. That November, President Harry Truman surprised the pollsters by winning reelection over Republican Thomas Dewey, and Democrats swept back into power in Congress. Kirwan kept his job that year and held onto it for a generation.

Yet, as he wrote memoirs sixteen years after dismissing that pollster, Kirwan admitted that "three of four candidates for Governor, two of three candidates for Senator, and one of ten candidates for the House of Representatives used surveys in their 1962 campaigns for election."[6] He hated to admit it, but from his vantage point at the national committee, he could see the growing displacement of the local parties' strategic role in congressional elections.

This displacement followed diverse paths across the country because local politics in America was (and is) diverse. Alan Ware, in a brilliant study of party politics during this period, demonstrates that even in the 1950s, state and local parties assumed diverse forms. Local parties ranged from tightly controlled patronage-based hierarchies in cities such as New York and Chicago, through a variety of leadership and activist organizations, to the already campaign-centered politics of California. "Each state was different, and the variations in the relationships reflected differences in electoral laws, history, and political culture."[7]

Despite this diversity, state and local parties faced a fairly consistent set of challenges, paralleling the national trends outlined in the last chapter. One challenge came as citizens established organizational alternatives to parties. For those excluded from power in many cities around the country, Saul Alinsky's model of community organization provided a valuable nonpartisan alternative.[8] But increasing numbers of mobile and affluent citizens also established more conventional political organizations that reflected their own interests and values. James Q. Wilson documented the emergence of local Democratic "clubs" in the late 1950s and early 1960s, organized around liberal reform or other issues and causes and staffed by white-collar "amateur" volunteers, yet still committed to working with parties at election time.[9] His colleague John Kessel found a similar effort at independent yet partisan grassroots organization by conservative Republicans a few years later.[10]

Ware observed the emergence of these groups as a common factional problem for state and local parties. The groups' members left party politics throughout the 1960s, drawn to work as amateurs with the campaign organizations of ideologically attractive candidates. Some of these activists left electoral politics altogether, as social movements and advocacy groups offered them purer opportunities to further their causes.[11] As noted in chapter 3, the representational and organizational base of politics changed and fragmented during these years, striking parties at their base and leaving little for many local parties to build on.

The new politics reinforced this displacement as campaign professionals offered candidates many of the resources state and local parties had formerly provided. New social scientific tools, backed by new technology, further strengthened the professionals' appeal. Additionally, pollsters and public relations professionals visible on the national scene presented their services to candidates for governorships, mayoralties, and other important offices. They raised money; managed volunteers and professional staff; produced advertising for television, radio, and newspapers; sent direct mail to voters' households; and turned out voters on election day. By 1967, Frank Sorauf wrote that "the political party no longer monopolizes the important political skills or manpower. . . .Indeed, it is possible to 'rent' a private enterprise 'political party'—such as Spencer Roberts in California—which will do everything that any party organization can do, and a great deal more than most are capable of."[12] This development, combined with earlier Progressive reforms that sharply limited patronage in most state and local governments and the survey research sophistication and computers that emerged in the 1970s, made it virtually impossible for state and local parties to recover their former role.

The Nationalization of Elections

The other powerful factor that reinforced state and local party displacement was the growing nationalization of politics and elections. This nationalization pervaded all dimensions of political life: representation, deliberation, and the governmental institutions that grew from Americans' political choices.

Political representation through parties, interest groups, and other channels revealed emerging national patterns by the end of the 1950s. Electronic media drove this most powerfully, with the nationwide establishment of first radio and then television networks that could broadcast political information into virtually every American home.[13] As Americans saw politicians from all parts of the country, state and local parties found it difficult to sustain autonomous identities and agendas. Increasingly, the Democratic and Republican Parties moved toward internal ideological homogeneity, and their elected officials found their fortunes shaped by national party fortunes and partisan policy agendas.[14] Interest and advocacy groups also established themselves at the national level, pressing the growing national government to respond to their constituents.[15]

The deliberative focus of individual attitudes and behavior also shifted increasingly to the national level.[16] Party loyalties began to decline across the nation, as did election turnout.[17] Growing numbers of those who remained partisan defined their partisanship in terms of national, rather than local, issues and policies. Faced with conflicting signals among partisan local, state, and national politicians and national policy issues not yet clearly defined in partisan terms, increasing numbers of mobile and educated voters declared their independence from party labels. Many based their votes not on party, but on their impressions of the qualities and issue positions of individual candidates, thus giving rise to the conventional wisdom that formerly "party-centered" politics was becoming "candidate centered."

In the institutions that grew from Americans' political choices, the national government increasingly coordinated and directed all sectors of public policy. National economic policy followed the initiatives of the New Deal and reflected the Keynesian revolution.[18] Social welfare policy remained broadly federal—containing national, state, and local components—but subject to national regulation.[19] Housing and urban development policy became more national, driven by direct national government spending and grants.[20] With *Brown* v. *Board of Education* in 1954, the 1957 Civil Rights Act, and the Little Rock confrontation in 1957, civil rights policy shifted from state to national control.[21]

This nationalization looks obvious now, as does the displacement experienced almost simultaneously by state and local parties throughout the nation. So does the emergence of the campaign-centered electoral order, for that matter. But these developments stymied Democrats and Republicans all over the United States, and left academics and journalists wondering about party decline.

Even in the face of this displacement and nationalization, most *party* electoral activity remained focused at the state or even local level. A national study of campaigns from 1952 through 1964, despite documenting the growing pervasiveness of the new politics (what its authors called the New Methodology), concluded that

> The New Methodology . . . has not supplanted the time-tried techniques. The personal handshake, the neighborhood tea, the rally, the precinct captain and the carpool are still very much with us. Getting out the vote still depends greatly on state and local organizations.[22]

The state and local parties, and many individual campaigns, were slow to recognize and respond to the changing world around them. Their reluctance came partly because the old politics often still worked, especially if unchallenged by newer methods. But their reluctance also came partly because state and local party activists could not imagine any other way to retain an electoral role for parties. Walter Dean Burnham observed this delay at the time and expressed surprise that "the organizational structures and functions of the major parties themselves remained largely unchanged."[23]

In short, party leaders and activists struggled to understand and respond to the changing world around them, much as fifteenth-century astronomers struggled to understand the paths of the planets. Their paradigmatic world views failed them.

The failure and confusion created an opening for the development of new paradigms—new world views and strategies—that could solve the puzzle and spur party change and adaptation. During the 1950s and 1960s, three such paradigms would emerge.

The Academics Begin to Sketch a New, "Textbook" Paradigm

The first signs of such paradigmatic thinking came almost by accident from the academic world. In 1950 the Committee on Political Parties of the American Political Science Association (APSA) published a profile of American parties along with prescriptions for reform. That report, *Toward a More Responsible Two-Party System,* began with conventional wisdom:

> Historical and other factors have caused the American two-party system to operate as two loose associations of state and local organizations, with very little national machinery and very little national cohesion. As a result, either major party, when in power, is ill-equipped to organize its members in the legislative and the executive branches into a government held together and guided by the party program. Party responsibility at the polls thus tends to vanish.[24]

To that point, the report simply restated a common criticism of American parties offered by advocates of "responsible party government" and cohesive party policy programs.[25]

Much of the committee's prescription for change revolved around these responsible party views. Based in part on an idealized vision of British parliamentary government, they argued that truly democratic parties must create internally democratic processes of participation, platform writing, and candidate nomination, and that their nominees must run for office and govern on clear and consistent national platforms.[26] The report proposed an elaborate reorganization and reorientation of the Democratic and Republican Parties to align them with responsible party principles. Though these prescriptions would resurface in party reform debates almost twenty years later, they were widely ignored in the 1950s by politicians and the American public.[27]

But the report was more than simply a "responsible party" broadside. Blended into its conventional critique and prescription was the first academic analysis of the emerging electoral order. The authors noted that *"the main trends of American politics, especially the emphasis on national action, have tended to outflank the party system."*[28] They then surveyed trends in "the nature and scope of public policy" as well as "changes in the social structure and economy of the United States."[29] Though the authors had not yet observed and documented campaign-centered politics, the committee's report captured many other dimensions of the emerging electoral order, including nationalized government and politics, political use of the mass media, and growing affluence and suburbanization. Additionally, the report recognized some of the difficulties that such changes would create for America's already weak political parties.

The committee first sketched a paradigmatic analysis of the puzzle posed by such change, centered on the nationalization of American politics, and then pointed to a solution based on that analysis. The parties should build on their former success, the report argued, by creating national structures that shared some of the strengths of the formerly cohesive state and local parties described in the textbooks of V.O. Key Jr., and others:

> The sort of party organization needed today is indirectly suggested by the origin of the traditional party structure. This structure developed in a period in which local interests were dominant and positive governmental action at the national level did not play the role it assumed later.[30]

Though the authors did not elaborate on this aspect of their prescription, it created a possible avenue for building a more fully developed new paradigm for the parties. If the nationalization of politics was the central problem for parties that had previously been successful at the state and local level, then perhaps the solution was to create national versions of the old, familiar state and local parties.

Searching for a New Paradigm at the National Party Organizations

Despite whatever insights it may have contained, there is no evidence that the APSA Committee on Political Parties report gained wide readership among Democratic and Republican leaders and activists. Those partisans instead struggled to develop their own paradigmatic explanations of the emerging electoral order and to devise practical strategies for party survival and success in the face of change. Interestingly, their early efforts at paradigm building borrowed heavily from state and local experience as well. The first initiatives that arose looked in many ways like national efforts to revive the familiar and formerly powerful state and local parties.

Many leaders and activists focused their attention on their parties' national organizations. The oldest of these, the Democratic National Committee (DNC), had been created in 1848 as a setting in which a committee of state and local party leaders could meet and coordinate the party's presidential nomination and campaign. They elected a national chair to preside. That position later became permanent, though it usually commanded only minimal staff and the committee itself met only episodically. The DNC has sponsored an occasionally wealthy and permanent headquarters operation since the 1930s, with a frequently changing program of action and a sizable staff, but it remained subordinate to local Democratic leaders. Republicans had established a similar committee in the 1850s, with similarly decentralized intentions and results.[31]

On Capitol Hill, campaign committees were created as adjuncts to the congressional party caucuses. The Democratic Congressional Campaign Committee (DCCC) came first, created in 1866 by Democrats in the House of Representatives who supported Republican President Andrew Johnson's Reconstruction policies. House Republicans responded immediately with a similar committee of their own, which eventually became the National Republican Congressional Committee (NRCC). Creation of Senate campaign committees—the Democratic Senatorial Campaign Committee (DSCC) and National Republican Senatorial Committee (NRSC)—came quickly after popular election of senators was amended into the Constitution in 1913. These Capitol Hill committees, supervised parochially by House and Senate members, waxed and waned with the campaign seasons until the 1940s and 1950s, when they established permanent staff organizations.[32]

All six national organizations served a single simple purpose: to win elections and enable their decentralized parties to take over and run the national government. This remained an almost entirely aggregate enterprise into the 1950s, as congressional candidates minded their own local business while state and local Democratic and Republican leaders loosely coordinated their parties' presidential efforts into semblances of national campaigns. But the puzzle posed by the emerging electoral order led some party leaders to seek new initiatives at the national organizations.

Those organizations were unlikely leaders of party renewal in the 1950s and early 1960s. For one thing, party scholar Hugh Bone found that "most national committeemen seldom visit the national office, and they have no clear conception of the work being done by the staff."[33] They mostly left the chairs to carry out each organization's business and develop its programs. Further, the chairs supervised staffs that expanded and contracted like accordions throughout the 1950s, according to Bone, who conducted the first academic research on post–World War II national party organization. The Democratic National Committee, for example, had about 50 paid staff at its headquarters except during presidential election years, when it expanded to about 200. The wealthier Republican National Committee (RNC) maintained a steadier size, which peaked at about 250 during presidential years, but similar to the DNC, suffered from high staff turnover. The congressional campaign committees had much smaller staffs, ranging from the NRCC's 30 down to a half-dozen or fewer at each of the other three.[34]

The chairs of these relatively small and turbulent organizations struggled throughout the 1950s and early 1960s to develop programs that parties could use to reassert a central role in American elections, but prior obligations limited their initiatives. The first responsibility of the national committee chairs and the headquarters organizations was to prepare for and manage the quadrennial presidential nominating conventions, which absorbed the largest portion of their resources. Such event coordination itself placed a heavy burden on the DNC and RNC as they struggled to adapt to the requirements of public spectacles in the television age.

Interestingly, the one initiative pressed on the Democratic headquarters organization by the national committee of this period focused on the conduct of state party delegations at those nominating conventions. After the 1948 defections of Democratic convention delegates to the independent presidential campaigns of Henry Wallace and Strom Thurmond, the national committee empowered the headquarters organization to investigate the commitment of various state party organizations and national convention delegations to support the party's future presidential nominees. After 1952 the DNC expanded this mandate to supervising state level procedures for selecting national convention delegates. Responsibility for enforcing these reforms—an extremely controversial matter because it might mean expelling a delegation at some future convention—was handed to the national committee and the headquarters organization.[35] Democratic chairs, in turn, avoided exercising these regulatory powers, leaving the conventions to struggle with them.[36]

Bone discovered in the late 1950s that party chairs preferred to focus on services instead. The chairs remained convinced that the basis of the parties' former strength needed restoration rather than regulation. "All the national party organizations are vitally interested in fostering the strongest possible state and local organizations."[37] Cornelius Cotter and Bernard Hennessy found the same pattern in the early 1960s:

> The Hill congressional and senatorial campaign] committees exist primarily to help finance state and local party activity (one should say, more accurately, candidate activity); the national committees exist to direct and administer what there is of national party activity and are financed largely by state and local party interests.[38]

Much of their activity, in short, continued in old patterns.

The chairs also worked, however, to present themselves and their staff organizations as the solution to problems posed by party displacement and nationalization. Because the parties remained grounded in diverse coalitions of state and local leaders, social groups and interest groups, the chairs asserted leadership as national brokers of those coalitions, standing above the fray and offering "a common denominator for integrating the party."[39] Both parties' Senate campaign committees developed advisory "policy committees" for this purpose. When their parties were out of the White House, both the Democratic and the Republican headquarters organized similar committees as well as regional associations of party leaders and activists.[40] Their apparent strategy was to make bargaining within national party arenas attractive to factions and interest groups who were increasingly operating on their own, and thus create a central niche for parties in national politics. If successful, the parties' national committees could give some coherence to an otherwise fragmented and chaotic electoral order.

The party organization chairs also worked to provide services to the party's national officeholders as well as to party candidates for national and state offices.[41] Many of those services mimicked state and local party activity during the prior electoral order. Just as local parties had done since the early nineteenth century, the committees worked to help party loyalists and contributors find jobs in the federal government, although the 1939 Hatch Act sharply reduced federal patronage. As the state and local parties had done for their candidates, the committees raised money from various contributors and allocated it to what they judged to be the neediest party candidates for national office. The national committees tried to consolidate those contributions into a challenge to campaign-centered politics:

> It is important to observe that both national committees discourage direct contributions to candidates and encourage donations to the committees. Institutionalization of the collection and the disbursement of campaign funds through the national office is one method of achieving this objective of contributing to a party rather than to a specific nominee.[42]

Just as local parties had been forced to build relationships with nonparty activists and professionals, the national party committees did the same by building ties with organizations such as Citizens for Eisenhower and the emerging cadres of campaign consultants.[43]

Perhaps most important, national party organization staff members established themselves as sources for campaign and policy intelligence, advice, and advocacy, based on information they gathered and analyzed from sources across the country. Initially, they based their intelligence work on policy committees and on the words of party coalition members and various "specialists in such fields as labor, agriculture, taxation, natural resources, and foreign relations."[44] Both parties' committees commissioned polling in the 1950s, however, and in the 1960s turned increasingly to formal survey research and computer analysis of electoral data.[45] So although their approach to political intelligence and analysis remained partly grounded in party coalition experience, they began to adopt the analytic methods of the new politics.

The Textbook Party Paradigm

Cumulatively, these initiatives constitute the outlines of a first paradigmatic party response to the challenge of the new electoral order. Leaders in the national party organizations developed a response to both "problems" they faced: party displacement by practitioners of the new politics and the nationalization of electoral politics away from the former locus of party strength at the state and local levels. Through trial-and-error, they developed an array of "solutions" on all three dimensions of electoral politics (see table 4.1). If successful, those solutions could enable the parties not just to survive, but also to shape broader patterns of mediation and coordination in the emerging electoral order.

Table 4.1
The Textbook Party Paradigm:
A National Version of the Old State and Local Parties

Representation	National party organizations seek to develop strong relationships with those who represent voters, and reinforce those relationships with policy and patronage. They help to broker and maintain party coalitions of social groups and interest groups. The organizations also raise and distribute money to party nominees.
Deliberation	National party organizations work to frame issues and positions for public debate, based on intelligence gathered both from coalition-member groups and from public opinion surveys, then mobilize voters.
Choice	Presidential and congressional nomination procedures and practices remain under state and local control, with little national party input.

Consider the implications of this paradigm for each of the three dimensions of representative democracy. Only the dimension of choice remained untouched by this emerging paradigm, largely because most activities on this dimension had already come under government control, as noted in chapter 3. On the other two dimensions, this paradigm proposes to do at the national level what textbooks say successful parties ought to be doing at any level of American politics: controlling nominations, setting issues for campaigns, providing money and resources for campaigns, delivering votes on election day, then making policy and distributing patronage once in power.[46]

On the dimension of representation, party activists and leaders developed programs at the national level that tried to reassert patterns established at the state and local level during the prior electoral order. During the first half of the twentieth century, parties had nursed along the regional, ethnic, and cultural group partisan allegiances formed during the prior, party-centered electoral order by bargaining to form coalitions among those social groups. As interest groups emerged, the parties worked to draw those groups into their coalitions as well, brokering policies and programs the interest groups would find attractive. During the 1950s, party chairs tried to continue and further develop those hybrid practices, working nationally to broker and maintain what Cotter and Hennessy called "new power balances among party leaders and groups."[47]

The deliberative role asserted under this emerging paradigm was similarly grounded in the parties' former state and local strength, though with some departures. The party organization staffs gathered and analyzed intelligence to frame issues and positions for public debate. State and local parties, along with partisan groups, provided much of the information. The staffs then distributed the intelligence to party officials and nominees, while party organization chairs toured the country speaking on the themes they had developed. But the national organizations moved beyond these conventional methods in the 1950s, drawing on polls and social scientific analyses of public opinion to guide issue development and campaign strategy. All this intelligence and issue work served a single purpose: to assert a national party role in shaping public deliberation over electoral politics.

This overall vision, rather than the APSA Committee on Political Parties' more academic model, emerged as the basis for the Textbook Party paradigm, the first real alternative party paradigm for understanding and responding to the emerging electoral order. Party initiatives within this paradigm were clearly rooted in real experience, yet by the end of the 1950s, they still only amounted to a sketchy response to the campaign-centered order. The extent to which the analysis underlying this emerging paradigm adequately explained the world, *and* the extent to which the program prescribed by this paradigm could survive real politics, would be tested severely during the Kennedy and Johnson presidencies.

NOTES

1. Walter Dean Burnham, "Party Systems and the Political Process," in *The American Party Systems: Stages of Political Development,* ed. William Nisbet Chambers and Walter Dean Burnham (New York: Oxford University Press, 1967); David S. Broder, *The Party's Over: The Failure of Politics in America* (New York: Harper and Row, 1971).

2. Thomas S. Kuhn, *The Structure of Scientific Revolutions,* 2d ed. (Chicago: University of Chicago Press, 1970).

3. Ibid., 103.

4. V.O. Key Jr., *Politics, Parties and Pressure Groups,* 3d ed. (New York: Thomas Y. Crowell, 1952), 350. All quotations from Key in this paragraph come from the same page.

5. Mike Kirwan and John M. Redding, *How to Succeed in Politics* (New York: McFadden Books, 1964), 28–29.

6. Ibid., 30.

7. Alan Ware, *The Breakdown of Democratic Party Organization, 1940–1980* (New York: Oxford University Press, 1985), 3.

8. Robert Bailey Jr., *Radicals in Urban Politics: The Alinsky Approach* (Chicago: University of Chicago Press, 1972); David J. Menefee-Libey, *The State of Community Organizing in Chicago* (Chicago: Center for Community Research and Assistance, 1985).

9. James Q. Wilson, *The Amateur Democrat* (Chicago: University of Chicago Press, 1962).

10. John H. Kessel, *The Goldwater Coalition* (Indianapolis: Bobbs-Merrill, 1968).

11. Ware, *Breakdown of Democratic Party Organization,* chap. 4.

12. Frank J. Sorauf, "Political Parties and Political Analysis," in Chambers and Burnham, *American Party Systems,* 54.

13. Doris Graber, *Mass Media and American Politics,* 5th ed. (Washington, D.C.: CQ Press, 1996); William G. Mayer, "Trends in Media Usage," *Public Opinion Quarterly* 57, no. 4 (Winter 1993):593–611.

14. Everett Carll Ladd, *American Political Parties: Social Change and Political Response* (New York: Norton, 1970).

15. Theodore J. Lowi, *The End of Liberalism* (New York: Norton, 1969).

16. Donald E. Stokes, "Parties and the Nationalization of Electoral Forces," in Chambers and Burnham, *American Party Systems.*

17. Walter Dean Burnham, "The Changing Shape of the American Political Universe," *American Political Science Review* 59 (March 1965):7–28.

18. Herbert Stein, *The Fiscal Revolution in America,* rev. ed. (Washington, D.C.: American Enterprise Institute, 1990).

19. James T. Patterson, *America's Struggle Against Poverty, 1900–1994* (Cambridge, Mass: Harvard University Press, 1995).

20. John H. Mollenkopf, *The Contested City* (Princeton, N.J.: Princeton University Press, 1983).

21. Edward G. Carmines and James A. Stimson, *Issue Evolution: Race and the Transformation of American Politics* (Princeton, N.J.: Princeton University Press, 1989).

22. American Institute for Political Communication, *The New Methodology: A Study of Political Strategy and Tactics* (Washington, D.C.: American Institute for Political Communication, 1967), 7.

23. Burnham, "Party Systems and the Political Process," 302.

24. Committee on Political Parties, American Political Science Association, *Toward a More Responsible Two-Party System* (New York: Rinehart, 1950), v.

25. For a thorough survey of this school of thought, see Austin Ranney, *The Doctrine of Responsible Party Government* (Urbana: University of Illinois Press, 1954).

26. Committee on Political Parties, *Toward a More Responsible Two-Party System,* 22ff. See also Ranney, *Doctrine of Responsible Party Government,* chap. 2, for an overview.

27. Evron M. Kirkpatrick, "Toward a More Responsible Party System: Political Science, Policy Science, or Pseudo-Science?" *American Political Science Review* 65 (1971):965–90.

28. Committee on Political Parties, *Toward a More Responsible Two-Party System,* 25, emphasis in original.

29. Ibid., 33, emphasis removed from original.

30. Ibid., 24–25.

31. Ralph M. Goldman, *The National Party Chairmen and Committees: Factionalism at the Top* (Armonk, N.Y.: M.E. Sharpe, 1990).

32. Hugh Bone, *Party Committees and National Politics* (Seattle: University of Washington Press, 1958), chap. 5.

33. Ibid., 18.

34. Ibid., chap. 2.

35. Cornelius P. Cotter and John F. Bibby, "Institutional Development and the Thesis of Party Decline," *Political Science Quarterly* 95 (1980):14–15. See also William Crotty, *Party Reform* (New York: Longman, 1983). Neither Bone, in *Party Committees and National Politics,* nor Cornelius P. Cotter and Bernard Hennessy, in *Politics without Power: The National Party Committees* (New York: Atherton, 1964), found these regulatory powers worth serious discussion.

36. For a survey of the resulting convention battles, see Richard C. Bain and Judith H. Parris, *Convention Decisions and Voting Records,* 2d ed. (Washington, D.C.: Brookings Institution, 1973), 286–98.

37. Bone, *Party Committees and National Politics,* 22.

38. Cotter and Hennessy, *Politics without Power,* 178.

39. Bone, *Party Committees and National Politics,* 10.

40. Bone, *Party Committees and National Politics,* chaps. 6 and 7; Cotter and Hennessey, *Politics without Power,* chaps. 10 and 11. For an important analysis of these "out-party" activities, see Philip A. Klinkner, *The Losing Parties: Out-Party National Committees, 1956–1993* (New Haven, Conn.: Yale University Press, 1994).

41. For the national officeholders' perspective and description of these services, see Charles L. Clapp, *The Congressman: His Work as He Sees It* (Washington, D.C.: Brookings Institution, 1963), chap. 8. The book is based on a 1959 series of Brookings roundtable discussions among members of Congress.

42. Bone, *Party Committees and National Politics,* 102.

43. Ibid., 27–35.

44. Ibid., 46.

45. Cotter and Hennessy, *Politics without Power,* 168.

46. Many party scholars continue to present similar lists of textbook standards to evaluate party strength. I have adapted this list from Ware, *Breakdown of Democratic Party Organization,* x.

47. Cotter and Hennessy, *Politics without Power,* 79.

5

Reform and the Search for a
New Party-Centered Politics

*Few national chairmen . . . are philosophers and theorists. Their approach,
as well as that of their staffs, is intensely practical where intelligence and
all other operations are concerned. The national headquarters, like so
many other institutions, has been shaped in a pragmatic spirit. It has
been built in a piecemeal and opportunistic fashion, unburdened with
theoretical or abstract principles.*

—Hugh Bone, 1958

A series of elections in the mid-1960s exposed the weakness of the national parties
for all to see. In 1964 Senator Barry Goldwater captured the Republican presidential
nomination, riding on a wave of grassroots conservative organizing within his own
party.[1] Despite this surge, and his party's apparent strength in presidential elections
since 1948, Goldwater went on to lose to President Lyndon B. Johnson in a record
landslide. Johnson, in turn, saw his own Great Society mandate and coalition
evaporate only two years later. His party lost forty-seven seats in the House and
three more in the Senate in the 1966 midterm election, leaving him even weaker
than he had been when he took office after President John F. Kennedy's
assassination. The Democrats' slide accelerated in 1968, as Republicans regained the
White House.

Some partisans looked to their national committees or the White House for
help, and those organizations struggled to respond. Seizing the theme of "decline,"
journalists and political scientists disparaged national party organizations as trivial
actors in American elections and the changing political scene. One prominent American politics scholar argued that "in no real sense do the American parties exist at

the national level."[2] David Broder, one of Washington's most astute political journalists, declared "the party is over" as a central actor in national elections and policy-making.[3]

Not everyone gave up on the national parties, however. Even as campaign-centered politics emerged as the dominant form of electoral politics, some Republican and Democratic Party officials and activists searched for ways to build party strength at the national level and to create a new kind of party-centered politics. Republican efforts, led by National Chair Ray Bliss from 1965 through 1968 and picked up again in the 1970s by Senator Bill Brock and others, have been well documented.[4] Developments within the national Democratic Party are less well known, in part because they have been overshadowed by the fiery politics of Democratic presidential nomination reform.[5] But late 1960s and early 1970s party politics for Democrats involved far more than presidential nominations. Beginning with President Lyndon Johnson, a series of party leaders and activists pursued several important and diverging paradigmatic visions of national party activism and influence. The failure of those efforts demonstrates both the resilience of the emerging campaign-centered electoral order and the persistence of party as a means for challenging that order.

Lyndon B. Johnson Tries and Discards a "Nationalized" Party

By the time he moved into the White House, Lyndon B. Johnson (LBJ) knew the Democratic Party's national organizations quite well. His first foray into national party politics had come in 1940, when as a junior House member he helped funnel Texas oil money into a moribund Democratic Congressional Campaign Committee and helped stave off further losses for Roosevelt's New Deal congressional coalition.[6] As Senate Majority Leader in the 1950s, Johnson worked closely with the Democratic Senatorial Campaign Committee, using it as a tool to retain majority status. After taking office as president in 1963, he looked to the Democratic National Committee for assistance.

At first, he seems to have intended to pursue the developments consistent with the Textbook Party paradigm as sketched in the previous chapter, creating a new party-centered politics built around a national version of the idealized strong state and local parties of the past. Such parties—which could organize arenas for nomination decisions, frame issues for campaigns, provide money and resources for campaigns, deliver voters on election day, and organize the government after victory—had never existed at the national level, but Johnson gave it a brief and ill-fated try. His efforts raised controversies that quickly convinced him that party organization politics now carried more risk than promise, and from early 1966 on, he turned to a more campaign-centered approach.

LBJ was confident of his own reelection in 1964, so he saw little reason to bring immediate changes to the headquarters he had inherited from President John F. Kennedy (JFK). He retained Kennedy's party chair John Bailey, continued Kennedy's practice of financing committee operations with large-donor support, and supported the consolidation of DNC financial operations with the Senate and House campaign committees.[7] The latter consolidation was part of Kennedy's program to use the headquarters to bolster his own legislative coalition, and it first helped JFK and then LBJ to firm up congressional support for the successful 1964 campaign.

In the 1964 election, the headquarters contributed significant resources both to the Capitol Hill committees and to Johnson's own campaign. The landslide that followed produced the largest presidential election majority in history and the largest Senate and House majorities since 1936 and gave Johnson confidence in his own party-building prospects at the national level. Early in 1965, he expanded the party headquarters's liaison work on Capitol Hill, hoping to use the national committee to sustain the congressional majority and its support for his political agenda. Broder described the efforts to help the seventy-seven Democrats elected to the House in 1964:

> Johnson ordered the executive agencies to help the freshmen on projects for their districts. In small groups, they were brought to the Democratic National Committee for private sessions with representatives of the White House and the domestic departments . . . .
>
> Instead of dismantling the National Committee's publicity machine after the presidential campaign, the President kept it functioning, on a slightly reduced scale, for the benefit of the freshmen.[8]

The party headquarters provided issue research and speech writing assistance to the new members and offered some preliminary help in raising funds for their reelection campaigns.

Johnson's motivation for establishing the program was both legislative and electoral, but it was always partisan. He wanted a liberal Democratic majority in the House large enough to pass his Great Society legislation, and he wanted popular incumbents running on the ticket with him when he sought reelection in 1968. His initial legislative and electoral success in 1964 and 1965 allowed him to focus on the most serious barrier to his paradigmatic vision of a strong nationalized party: its expense, both in personnel and money. As noted in chapter 4, state and local parties faced displacement because the loss of volunteers (and patronage-induced conscripts) forced them to pay for personnel to run campaigns, while competing professional consultants offered candidates streamlined organizations and fundraising skills to support them. At the national level, Johnson would have to face this same problem and find resources for serious professional and organizational development. He would soon discover, however, that such large-scale fundraising created political land mines.

LBJ planned to raise much of the money for this expanded staff activity at a series of sixty-five party events around the country in 1965 and 1966. Arthur Krim, president of the United Artists film company and chairman of the DNC-affiliated President's Club, built the fundraisers around party-sponsored premieres of several new United Artists films. Krim planned to raise $1 million selling high-priced premiere tickets and another $1 million selling $15,000-per-page, tax-deductible ads in the premieres' program book (*Toward an Age of Greatness*) to corporations, unions, and other Democratic Party supporters. The baldness of selling ads (which were publicly subsidized by tax deductions) to corporations and others doing business with the government, however, raised such an outcry from congressional Republicans that Johnson feared his public standing would be endangered. He had Krim scrap the project and put the $600,000 it had raised in escrow to avoid further controversy.

These aborted efforts in 1965 proved to be the high-water mark of Johnson's efforts to initiate a new party-centered politics through collaboration with party organizations; the "Greatness Fund" controversy apparently convinced Johnson that working closely and publicly with the DNC posed more risks than benefits for his 1968 reelection prospects. Enraged at the failure of funding for his national party initiative, Johnson shut down the entire program of headquarters services to freshmen before the end of 1965. He then ordered cuts in the organization's staff and budget and canceled its voter registration program.[9] As the year went on, he gradually withdrew from party affairs and shifted to what we now recognize as a campaign-centered strategy, raising his own money and tending to his personal campaign organization. He virtually abandoned Democratic candidates during the 1966 midterm election and did little campaigning before he left the country for a two-week trip and conference in Manila in mid-October.[10] His brief flirtation with ideas of organizing a nationalized party ended quickly. Creation of such a party— even if it were possible—demanded tremendous financial resources. Johnson either considered such fundraising too risky or decided to raise such money only for his own campaign.

This failure of the first real paradigmatic proposal for a party-centered alternative to campaign-centered politics only reinforced the growing perceptions of party decline. Yet despite Johnson's failure and abandonment of the Textbook Party paradigm, some Democratic activists retained this idealized vision of national party as a goal. It remains attractive to this day in part because it embodies many Americans' ideas of what strong parties should be able to do: broker coalitions, control nominations, frame election issues, and reward supporters with patronage and legislation. But even state and local parties, the locus of party strength for more than a hundred years, proved unable to sustain this approach through the 1950s and 1960s. It is difficult to imagine how national party organizations could pay the financial price—and the accompanying risk of financial scandal—necessary to succeed with a Textbook Party during the campaign-centered electoral order.

The Origins of Reform Politics

Johnson's departure from party affairs opened the door for other ideas about a revived party role in the emerging electoral order. Those alternatives got a further push when Democrats across the country floundered in the disastrous 1966 midterm election. Party leaders, including candidates who had run for election or reelection largely without DNC support, criticized Johnson and the headquarters organization for failing to provide resources or to work with them during the campaign.[11] Some of them focused on the headquarters as a vehicle for mounting a challenge to Johnson's leadership and for developing their own alternative proposals for party-centered politics.

The chair of the Democratic governors' caucus, Governor Harold Hughes of Iowa, took the lead in December 1966, saying that state leaders wanted to play a greater part in developing national and party policy, and calling for more "open" decision making at the committee as it prepared for future elections.[12] Hughes and others did more than focus on party organization support for their own campaigns. They also offered an early, unrefined version of the "reform" strategy that would win out in the coming years, arguing that the national party organization needed to do more than just provide services for party candidates in elections. They argued that it should embrace a whole new purpose for the party at a national level: to provide a coherent partisan alternative to fragmented, campaign-centered politics. Unlike Johnson's Textbook Party vision of national parties built on the old state and local model, these reformers developed a variant on the arguments that had surfaced in the American Political Science Association's *Toward a More Responsible Two-Party System* report nearly two decades earlier. This emerging Reform paradigm vision based a new party-centered politics on the development of new institutions and processes within the party. It proposed that the party mediate citizen representation, deliberation, and choice by providing political access and voice to Democrats as party "members" with diverse policy views.

Once Johnson withdrew from the presidential campaign in April 1968, these disputes seemed moot. But they were raised again by early summer when it became apparent that Vice-President Hubert H. Humphrey would beat Senators Eugene J. McCarthy of Minnesota and Robert F. Kennedy of New York in the contest for the Democratic presidential nomination. Because Humphrey had inherited most of LBJ's already strong coalition and campaign organization, he followed a simple strategy of picking up regular party delegate slates in the fourteen primary states and relying on party leaders to deliver the delegates chosen in the thirty-six states holding conventions. Although the power of these state and local leaders had faded dramatically during the 1950s and 1960s, party tradition and rules, nevertheless, gave them control over delegate selection—the relatively unchanged "choice" dimension *within* party politics—and thus the presidential nomination. Humphrey understood that system well and campaigned without formally entering a single primary.[13]

After delegate selection ended around the country in June, a group of McCarthy supporters and antiwar activists in Connecticut and New York decided to challenge Humphrey at the national convention. They saw themselves as leaders of an emerging "new liberal" majority rising to end the anachronistic domination of Humphrey and the "old liberals." The old liberals, representing the core constituencies of the New Deal coalition, were hawkish on the Vietnam War and more conservative on the social issues of civil rights, civil liberties, and the emerging youth culture. The new liberals (sometimes called "new politics liberals"), supporters of Kennedy and McCarthy's presidential campaigns, were doves on Vietnam, favored stronger federal action on poverty and civil rights, and embraced the social changes of the period. Pointing to broad support for McCarthy and Kennedy in primaries, the new liberals declared themselves the new majority within the party and demanded representation.[14]

The new liberals displayed a growing mastery of campaign-centered politics and success in congressional elections, but the old liberals held sway among state and local party activists and organizations that controlled presidential delegate selection for the upcoming convention. Not surprisingly, the old liberals and their state and local allies refused to surrender their last shreds of power. Once Humphrey had won the majority of the party's national convention delegates, the new liberals began looking for an alternative method to gain power commensurate with their voter support. They channeled their efforts into national party affairs, where they hoped to win full representation by strategically developing and advancing a new paradigmatic analysis of American elections and "reforming" the party's presidential nominating process. They hoped to complete the displacement of state and local party leaders from electoral politics by taking away from them the 1968 Democratic presidential nomination. Though many of the new liberals disdained the cloistered politics of party organization, they developed the Reform paradigm as a strategic means to an end: they had to engage in party politics to gain public office.

Ironically, the reformers decided to build their attack outside party arenas. Their idea was to launch a hurried public "investigation" into the closed delegate selection procedures that had allowed Humphrey to build his campaign coalition without directly appealing for voter support. They could then use the report from that investigation to reenter the party arena and challenge the seating of pro-Humphrey state delegations at the upcoming convention. Even if their efforts had no impact on the 1968 nomination, they hoped at least to change future delegate selection rules and give new liberal candidates opportunities to win the nomination in 1972.[15]

The investigation would be conducted by the ad hoc Commission on the Democratic Selection of Presidential Nominees, which had only six weeks to build its case. Iowa Governor Harold Hughes (a Johnson critic, McCarthy supporter, and U.S. Senate candidate) agreed to serve as chair, with Representative Donald Fraser (a reformist Humphrey supporter from Minnesota) as vice-chair. Of the remaining five commissioners, four came from the McCarthy or Kennedy camps. The seven members of what would be called the Hughes Commission met only once as a group, in Chicago two weeks before the Democratic National Convention. During that meeting they endorsed staff-written drafts of a preliminary report and recommendations for sweeping changes in the party's delegate selection rules. The report was expanded and published as *The Democratic Choice* one week before the convention.[16] Finally, the commission's staff obtained office space and convention floor passes from Democratic National Chair John Bailey so that they could lobby state delegations to support the report in Chicago.

The Democratic Choice, written in a few weeks by a small group of attorneys, became the blueprint of the Reform paradigm analysis and strategy. It opened dramatically by challenging the legitimacy of the convention as a democratic (with a small "d") party arena:

> This Convention is on trial . . . . To an extent not matched since the turn of the
> century, events in 1968 have called into question the integrity of the convention
> system for nominating presidential candidates.[17]

It proceeded to document some of the state and local delegate selection practices that had enabled Johnson and Humphrey supporters to build their coalitions and control the convention: closed slating meetings; delegate nomination deadlines more than a year before the presidential election; and state convention procedures that systematically gave advantages to party officials and discouraged newcomers, in the process excluding minorities, women, and young people. It also pointed out inequities in the apportionment of delegates among the states.

It closed with a sweeping set of recommended changes in the way state and local Democrats ran their party organizations and selected presidential convention delegates, changes which would transform the party's future presidential nominations. Most important were

- open election of all convention delegates and proportional representation of each candidate's voter support in state delegations;

- open participation in all party affairs, including party organization leadership selection, and the slating and selection of delegates to the national convention;

- representation of minorities, women, and young people in state party organizations and delegations; and

- apportionment of delegates and national committee members to each state by population.

In short, they proposed that the party challenge the emerging patterns of campaign-centered politics by establishing itself as mediator and coordinator of Democrats' representation, deliberation, and choice in national and state elections. They argued that the public would certainly join them in embracing reform, given the chance to directly nominate candidates for the presidency and other offices (see table 5.1). The reformers sought nothing less than to turn the tide of history and create a new party-centered electoral order.

Responsibility for enforcing these radical reforms would fall first to the national committee and its headquarters organization and ultimately to the Credentials and Rules committees at the quadrennial national convention. Such attempts at national party regulation of state and local parties had precedents. Indeed, many of the regulatory recommendations of the Hughes Commission had been raised long before, in the American Political Science Association's *Toward a More Responsible Two-Party System* report and in Democratic faction fights over civil rights noted in chapter 4.

While the APSA report and civil rights Democrats' proposals in prior years had been dismissed as ineffectual, the arguments made by the Hughes Commission in 1968 gained wide support within the growing new liberal faction. Some of that

Table 5.1
The Reform Paradigm: Party Mediation of Electoral Politics

Representation	National, state, and local parties create open arenas (e.g., committees, caucuses, conventions) and processes (e.g., primaries) for coalition building, bargaining, and decision making. All party nominees chosen and committees constituted by open vote, with proportional representation. When necessary, participants would be represented proportionally by delegates to higher level party nominating and platform-writing conventions. Resulting nominees and platforms to be presented to all voters in general elections.
Deliberation	Open and competitive party politics expected to draw wide participation from all sectors of society. Deliberation would occur within party settings, as participants decide party nominations, platforms, and committee memberships.
Choice	Universal access to "reformed" party decision making. One person, one vote, though votes in party committees and conventions not guaranteed to be secret.

support was strategic: new liberals saw the report as ammunition in their battle against the old liberals. But the Reform paradigm analysis and program of party-centered politics, broad participation, and proportional representation also resembled the early program of the New Left, a movement with which many new liberals sympathized.[18] The commission's agenda would remain central to Democratic factional conflict as reform politics unfolded over the next ten years.

At the chaotic convention in Chicago, Johnson and Humphrey supporters immediately showed that they were in control, at least in the convention hall itself: the Credentials and Rules Committees rejected the McCarthy camp's proposed rules for seating delegations that year. Even when they were certain of the nomination, Humphrey's representatives remained shaken by the bloody confrontations that had roiled in the streets of Chicago throughout the convention. While staunchly condemning the demonstrations and disorder, Humphrey supporters wanted to do as much as they could to placate the new liberals and avoid alienating voters represented by the party insurgents.

Leaders in the Humphrey camp thought they were taking an easy way out by symbolically recognizing the new liberals and agreeing to appoint a party commission to look into the findings presented in *The Democratic Choice*. Humphrey strategist Max Kampelman later explained that he thought of the concession as a throwaway at the time.[19] Humphrey, thinking only of November, saw no reason to resist. His campaign organization was firmly in control, and he had already committed himself to a different approach to party affairs. He stated publicly that he would support a more activist Democratic headquarters than LBJ had, though he was certainly talking about the Textbook Party paradigm rather than the reformists' activism under the emerging Reform paradigm.[20] Humphrey's campaign leaders encouraged their delegates to support a resolution calling for a Commission on Party Structure and Delegate Selection that would report to the 1972 convention. The measure passed easily and the matter was set aside until after the election.

This episode demonstrates the interplay between partisan factional battles and battles over competing paradigmatic understandings of the campaign-centered order, precisely the kind of politics Thomas Kuhn has described in the scientific realm.[21] But it also demonstrates the interplay between party organization politics and the broader world of American elections and how that interplay occasionally gains public attention. The new liberals, as well as candidates McCarthy and Kennedy, had initially focused their efforts at winning over American public opinion and Democratic primary voters. But, when they discovered that they were doomed because the "regular" state and local party leaders who controlled the party arenas also controlled the presidential nomination, these new liberals shifted their attack from the public arena to the party arena. They secured an important initial victory at the convention, then withdrew until the election was over.

The state and local parties, displaced and left behind by the transformation of electoral politics, joined forces through the Democratic National Committee and the convention to hold onto their residual power in presidential nominations as long as they could. To challenge that residual power, the new liberals were forced not only to develop a strategy that could win the presidential nomination, but also to create a national party-centered alternative to the emerging campaign-centered order. Even as scholars and journalists disparaged national party politics as irrelevant, factions within the Democratic Party began a fight over competing paradigms which would transform national elections.

Competing Visions in the Aftermath of 1968

The 1968 election only raised the stakes of national Democratic Party politics. Humphrey, almost hopelessly behind after the disastrous convention in Chicago, scrambled and scrapped his way through the fall campaign and almost defeated Richard

M. Nixon.[22] His close finish convinced both old and new liberals that control over the party's presidential nomination was worth fighting for. But, at least in the short term, decisions about the future would be controlled by the old liberals and their state and local allies on the Democratic National Committee.

When the DNC met in January after Humphrey's loss, they had more than reform to worry about. In addition to renewed demands for an activist headquarters operation—based on Republican success with activist organizations in 1966 and 1968—the committee faced staggering debt from the 1968 campaigns of Humphrey and Kennedy. With his underdog status crippling his personal fundraising and the committee offering little organizational or financial help, Humphrey had been forced to borrow more than $5 million to run his campaign. At the urging of Humphrey friend and DNC Treasurer Robert Short, the committee accepted the responsibility of repaying that debt, as well as $1 million owed to Kennedy campaign creditors. The resulting debt was more than twice the size of the DNC's budget for any previous presidential campaign and further limited opportunities to create expensive Textbook Party initiatives at the party headquarters.[23]

Humphrey controlled the committee's initial response to these problems.[24] Although he apparently never formulated a complete strategy for his leadership of the party, he exercised that leadership immediately after the election by naming Senator Fred Harris of Oklahoma to succeed Larry O'Brien as Democratic national chair. Harris, the co-chair of Humphrey's general election campaign, was a maverick who had also worked on Kennedy's campaign during the primaries. By all indications, he had conventional ideas about the party headquarters that perhaps leaned toward Textbook Party expansion and did not share the new liberal vision of the Reform paradigm and party-centered representational politics.

As a sitting senator, however, Harris soon found it exceedingly difficult to exercise consistent supervision and independent influence over the committee or its affairs. He hoped to rebuild the headquarters' financial base and traditional political activities, but he never established a successful fundraising program.[25] With the limited funds he could muster, Harris directed the headquarters staff to provide services to five of the seven Democratic House candidates running in special elections in 1969, four of whom ultimately won. Still, Harris had little success organizationally, and finally quit after a disastrous fundraiser in February 1970. When he departed, the organization's debt had grown to $9.3 million, destroying all hopes that it might lead the way to a Textbook Party alternative to campaign-centered politics.[26]

Ultimately, Harris's most important act as chair was to appoint a predominantly reformist commission—including Hughes Commission vice-chair Representative Donald Fraser—to fulfill the convention's mandate to investigate the Hughes Commission report. While Harris chose the reform commission members, Humphrey, in late January 1969, decided who would be the commission's chair. Defying the new liberals, who wanted the newly elected Senator Harold Hughes to return to his earlier commission role, Humphrey chose Senator George S. McGovern of South Dakota, a Kennedy supporter and antiwar activist whom Humphrey viewed as a "regular Democrat."[27] In fact, McGovern had ambitions of his own and was emerging as the most important new liberal leader in Congress. After talking with Harris, McGovern became convinced that the commission could serve as a vehicle not only for reform but also for his own leadership of the new liberal faction and its Reform paradigm vision of a new party-centered politics.[28] He accepted the position and set to work in the late spring of 1969 while Harris struggled to get the headquarters operation back on its feet.

An Old Liberal Ushers in Reform, Reluctantly

Harris's resignation as Democratic National Committee chair spurred Humphrey and a majority of the DNC to seek the return of Harris's predecessor, Larry O'Brien. Because of his thirty years of experience in national campaigns and party affairs and his ties to both the Kennedy and Humphrey camps, many viewed O'Brien as the only person who could revive the headquarters while averting a complete factional breakdown within the party. O'Brien initially refused, citing factional divisions—reformists opposed his appointment because of his long association with Humphrey and other old liberals—and the committee's financial mess. He relented, however, when the committee unanimously offered him the job and Texas businessman Robert Strauss agreed to join the committee as its chief fundraiser. New liberal leaders criticized his appointment, but the broad consensus within the DNC gave O'Brien an opportunity to try his own solutions to the Democratic headquarters' problems.[29]

O'Brien immediately focused the headquarters's agenda more clearly on financial recovery and Textbook Party strategies in response to the Republican challenge. Following the lead of Republican National Chair Ray Bliss, O'Brien made his top priority the development of an institutional capacity to provide services to national party candidates. Based on his own experience in competitive party politics in Massachusetts and in the presidential campaigns of John Kennedy, Lyndon Johnson, Robert Kennedy, and Hubert Humphrey, O'Brien believed that state and local party organization support could also be valuable in a close campaign. He realized that his survival as chair and his continued influence in party affairs and national policy depended on his ability to produce results at the national and state levels that

Humphrey and members of the Democratic National Committee could see and understand. Diving into the reform battle promised no such concrete results, but organization building did. His incentives, and the incentives of every other party chair before and since, clearly led him to focus on money, services, and party assistance.

O'Brien and Treasurer Robert Strauss began their efforts with the strong support of the members of the Democratic National Committee, who were happy to hear promises of national organization assistance after years of struggle at the state and local level. But O'Brien quickly discovered that he could not confine his attentions to organization building. The national committee had been targeted by party reform advocates for years, and the factional battle over reform came to a head shortly after O'Brien returned to lead the committee in March 1970.

While Harris and the Democratic National Committee struggled with their debt and the shuffling in the chair's office in 1969, the Commission on Party Structure and Delegate Selection—now called the McGovern Commission—was hard at work. Surviving on a shoestring budget provided by the DNC and personal loans from McGovern and others,[30] they continued the research initiated by the Hughes Commission staff and held more than fifteen hearings around the country (from April through July 1969) on the party's state organizations and delegate selection processes.

The hearings helped to develop further the political analysis of the Reform paradigm, as well as its prescriptive content. To begin with, the hearings surfaced additional evidence of undemocratic internal party practices that supported the new liberals' case for national party regulation of state and local parties and the development of representational processes within the national party. In its report, *Mandate for Reform,* the committee presented a chapter on delegate selection in 1968 that charged state and local parties with

- procedural irregularities, including failure to post public notices of meetings; illegitimate proxy voting; and the use of "the unit rule" to bind delegates to vote against their wishes;

- overt discrimination against blacks and women seeking to become delegates; and

- structural inadequacies such as scheduling delegate selection before the presidential campaign began; charging delegates excessive fees for participation; and malapportionment of delegates among states.[31]

As they revealed such problems, the hearings reinforced the Hughes Commission's indictment of the party's presidential nomination as undemocratic.

The hearings also reinforced the McGovern Commissioners' sympathy for the Hughes Commission's earlier recommendations for direct national party mandates to open up local party affairs to broader and more democratic participation, and create a party-centered challenge to campaign-centered politics. The McGovern Commission recommended explicit, written party rules governing delegate selection and other activities, including

- open, public, and well-advertised meetings for delegate selection;

- affirmative action procedures that would encourage participation by women, minorities, and young people "in reasonable relationship to their presence in the population of the State"; and

- proportional representation in the selection of all convention delegates, which would require an end to proxy voting, unit rules, and ex officio representation of party officials.[32]

These and the remaining recommendations of the commission would require a radical transformation of not just the selection of Democratic convention delegates but also the day-to-day business of all state and local Democratic parties. Most important, in practical terms, adopting these rules would mean that future Democratic presidential candidates would be nominated through a series of open primaries and caucuses beyond the control of state and local party leaders.

The McGovern Commission's hearings and final report drew media attention to the new liberal faction and served to mobilize people sympathetic to reform. It also brought increasing attention and resources to emerging new liberal candidates and campaigns forming for 1972. By the time the commission published its report in early 1970, the McGovern Commission had gone from an obscure throwaway resolution at the Chicago convention to a political force that Democratic Party leaders could not easily avoid.

Thus, a demand from McGovern was one of the first serious problems O'Brien faced when he walked into the chair's office. The senator informed him that the commission had not simply studied party structure and delegate selection and prepared recommendations for the national committee's consideration. They had also drafted a whole new set of national party policies to be enforced by the party's national headquarters organization. Without consulting the DNC, McGovern had sent copies of the guidelines to every Democratic state party chair, demanding compliance. When several of the state chairs threatened to resist this national party attack on their remaining power, McGovern presented O'Brien with a legal argument.

McGovern argued that the commission had been created by the party's national convention, whose mandates superseded those of the national committee.

The commission was therefore a duly constituted party authority whose policy rec-ommendations were binding on the state parties unless reversed by the national convention in 1972. If the state party leaders failed to comply and the headquarters did not enforce the new rules, the commission or its representatives would chal-lenge the states' delegations at the convention. Thus, McGovern offered O'Brien part promise and part threat. On one hand, if the DNC embraced what McGovern believed would be popular new policies, McGovern believed that the Democrats could win the election in 1972. On the other hand, if the committee rejected the rules, valuable people and resources would be lost to all Democratic campaign coali-tions and the party would certainly lose the presidency again.

McGovern's bold move pulled the headquarters organization into the fac-tional battle over reform and presented O'Brien with several options. He could have flatly rejected McGovern's efforts as beyond the commission's mandate, a move that would probably have gained strong DNC support (the committee, after all, was still dominated by old liberal regulars) even as it enraged the growing reform con-stituency and perhaps fueled third- and fourth-party organizing efforts.[33] He could also have simply refused to comment, which would have enraged the reformers and left noncomplying state parties to gamble on whether the convention's Credentials and Rules Committees would back the McGovern policies. Instead, he chose a third course, instructing Joseph Califano, the DNC's general counsel, to write a ruling that supported McGovern's claim to the commission's policymaking legitimacy. He then convinced the Democratic National Committee to support the Califano ruling and authorize the reforms and endorse giving the reform commission a continued mandate to help the states reach compliance.[34]

O'Brien's strategy was to take the initiative out of the reform commission arena and away from new liberal activists working outside the party sphere and to reassert the role of the national chair and the national committee in shaping party politics. A determined optimist, O'Brien refused to allow reform to play itself out as a factional fight in which one side had to lose. He recognized that both factions sought a new party-centered politics, though their paradigmatic visions led them to dramatically different ideas about how that politics could and should work.

He worked to develop ventures that would please advocates of both the Text-book Party and Reform paradigms. One was to use the headquarters organization to create and coordinate supportive arenas for policy discussion and party advocacy. Some of the arenas were formal committees or councils of the party's elected and activist leaders. For example, the Democratic Policy Council—which Fred Harris had established at Humphrey's behest in 1969—drafted resolutions challenging Nixon's economic and social policies and his handling of the Vietnam War.[35] O'Brien also encouraged the formation of an Association of State Democratic Chairmen and gave them office space and staff support at the DNC.[36] But many of the arenas were informal, with O'Brien acting as an "honest broker" bringing together representatives from opposing factions or campaigns for private discussions. These efforts were crucial in a party where debt and factional division encouraged distrust and discouraged cohesive party campaigns. In his single greatest coup, O'Brien brought together all the declared and potential rivals for the 1972 Democratic presidential nomination, along with the party's House and Senate leaders, in February and July 1971, and convinced them to concentrate on attacking Nixon rather than each other until the primary season began.[37]

In addition, O'Brien tried to finesse factional differences by emphasizing both factions' agreement that Democrats should develop their organizations and enable the party to build a new party-centered politics. He presented reform to the DNC as a party-building tool by emphasizing the way the new policies would help all Democratic campaigns by opening the party to broader participation and voter support.[38]

Nevertheless, O'Brien's observation that reform was "the greatest goddamn change since (the advent of) the two party system" was closer to the truth.[39] With the old state and local party-centered politics clearly dead, and the Textbook Party paradigm still incoherent and lacking sufficient resources, the Reform paradigm offered the first plausible party-centered response to campaign-centered politics. If the reforms worked as he hoped, the national Democratic Party could remake itself into a central coordinator and mediator of representation, citizen deliberation, and voter choice in American elections. He might be the one to usher in a new party-centered electoral order.

O'Brien's first success came late in 1971 when he convinced DNC members to enact a major reform measure. Reluctantly following the McGovern Commission's recommendations, committee members voted to give up a traditional advantage by ending their own status as ex officio delegates to the 1972 convention. Committee member John Powers of Massachusetts led regular opposition to the move, telling the committee that "to vote to give away something is to demean yourself."[40] But enough regulars were interested in defusing the factional fighting to ignore Powers and go along with O'Brien's arguments. While DNC members gained the satisfaction of publicly beating the new liberals by electing their own candidate for Credentials chair, they ratified their own demise as presidential power brokers with little public notice.

Even after the vote, O'Brien continued to be whipsawed by reformist and regular criticism.[41] After the McGovern Commission released its report and O'Brien convinced the DNC to throw its weight behind reform, however, most disputes over reform shifted from the national headquarters. Presidential delegate selection processes for 1972 were beginning in the states by then, and supporters of every candidate wanted the opportunity to unseat Nixon the following year (an opportunity, incidentally, described in detail by O'Brien in a Textbook Party–style mailing to party officials and activists around the country). Because state party responses to the commission's recommendations would strongly affect each presidential candidate's campaign organization and strategy, most activist Democrats turned their attention to the states, where they tried to shape the implementation of reform to their candidates' advantages.[42]

The remaining dispute at the national level concerned the institutionalization of the McGovern Commission's reforms in a new party constitution or "charter." When George McGovern stepped down as chair of the commission in 1970 to run for president, O'Brien passed the chairmanship to Representative Donald Fraser of Minnesota. Instead of standing pat and working to help the states implement the guidelines on delegate selection, however, Fraser moved in late 1971 to regain the initiative. He proposed to broaden the reforms of party policy by drafting a charter that institutionalized what had come to be called the McGovern-Fraser Commission reforms and then applied Reform paradigm principles to the Democratic National Committee structure itself. In early 1972, Fraser and Rules Commission chair Representative James O'Hara personally proposed a radical restructuring of the DNC along regional lines, with an expanded membership apportioned by population and elected by assemblies of dues-paying party members.[43]

In retrospect, Fraser's and O'Hara's personal proposals clearly tried to push Reform paradigm recommendations too far and in improbable directions. They were consistent with some aspects of the reform strategy, shaking loose old structures and opening up opportunities for party-mediated participation and representation. But by shifting national committee membership from a state to a regional base, the proposals would have immediately disconnected the national committee structure—and the party—from its historical grounding in state and local politics. They would have junked any remaining connection between the national party and competition for governorships and legislative seats. More important, they would have abandoned the existing presidential nomination system, a system that already drew the greatest public participation of any party endeavor. Fraser and O'Hara proposed to leap into a new world of party-centered politics without a bridge to get them there.

As it turned out, the full commissions watered down Fraser's and O'Hara's personal proposals somewhat by May 1972. They eliminated the regional plans, but still recommended

- expansion of the Democratic National Committee to 338 members to allow proportional representation of state populations;

- quadrennial national party policy conferences, held halfway between presidential elections, to write advisory platforms for Democratic officeholders; and

- making the Democratic national chair a full-time paid position, elected for four years at each policy conference.[44]

The proposals were largely lost in the din of the presidential primary campaign, but commission activists would raise them again as the convention drew near.

Accommodating the Campaign-Centered Era

As he struggled to cope with the persistent demands of party reform politics, O'Brien nevertheless succeeded at devoting some time and energy to his own ideas for the Democratic Party. Though he never committed those ideas to paper, he had clearly developed his own rough paradigmatic analysis of the campaign-centered electoral order. In the context of that analysis, he also developed a strategic vision of the party's role in national elections, a role not necessarily consistent with either the Textbook Party regulars' or the Reform paradigm supporters' visions of a future party-centered politics.

O'Brien understood and was comfortable with campaign-centered politics from his own work on several presidential campaigns, and he wanted most to build a national party headquarters that could help Democrats succeed in that new politics. Unlike those who envisioned a party-centered politics replacing campaign-centered politics, O'Brien was satisfied with working to create a party that could accommodate and survive campaign-centered politics. Republican National Committee Chair Ray Bliss had pursued such a strategy, and the Republicans now controlled the White House.[45] Cumulatively, the efforts of Bliss and O'Brien established early ideas about an Accommodationist paradigm, which focused on party survival during an inescapably campaign-centered electoral order.

Building on his long experience with the committee, O'Brien developed a clear agenda to present to DNC members when he walked in the door in early 1970. Despite the distractions of factional battling, he began several initiatives simultaneously. First, he reorganized the staff operation into several main offices that could provide services to Democratic campaigns. The Office of the Chair was the administrative center, as well as his vehicle for reestablishing the DNC as a visible partisan center, challenging President Nixon's politics and policies. The Communications Office handled publications, advertising, and coordinated the new Democratic Policy Council. The Campaigns Office, run by former Representative Stanley Greigg of Iowa, restarted the committee's voter registration program, published a new edition of O'Brien's venerable *Campaign Manual,* and provided what limited assistance it could to Democratic congressional candidates for the 1970 election.[46]

O'Brien worked with Robert Strauss to reestablish the committee's recovery from its $9.3 million debt.[47] Instead of shutting down the headquarters until the debt was gone, O'Brien ran the committee on a pay-as-you-go basis, raising enough money to fund operations without going further into debt.[48] In the short term, he fought for access to television time for party political and financial appeals.[49] For the long term, he worked for three solutions to the debt: develop telethons, dinners, and direct mail to rebuild large and small donor bases; secure the election of a Democratic president; and win public financing of presidential election campaigns.[50]

Each of O'Brien's and Strauss's initiatives—including those that built on Fred Harris's work—marked a major departure from past practice at the national headquarters under DNC Chair John Bailey. Cumulatively, they comprised an ambitious program to revitalize the Democratic headquarters and adapt it to the campaign-centered era as an important service provider for the party candidates' campaigns at all levels. O'Brien had promised such revitalization to DNC members when they had elected him to the chair, and his efforts won their approval. While his work on party reform remained controversial, Democrats of all stripes viewed the organizational development as helpful for party candidates in upcoming elections. At least on this dimension, he fulfilled his mandate with unrivaled success and began to develop his own Accommodationist paradigm vision even as reform was getting all the attention.

Reform Loses Its Steam as McGovern Wins and Loses

By the time Democrats met at the national convention in July 1972, the new liberals had gained virtually everything they wanted: reform had been implemented, opening up and democratizing delegate selection at the state level; new liberal, anti-war candidate McGovern had clinched the nomination; and new liberals controlled the Rules and Credentials committees that would, in turn, control the convention.[51] Their only concern paralleled the concerns of Humphrey supporters at the 1968 convention: that their victory would antagonize opposing factions and undermine broad support for the party's nominee. Memories of bloody Chicago demonstrations and fears of renewed conflict had already intimidated most Democratic organizational leaders. Not wanting to risk being involved in another disaster, they left convention management almost entirely to O'Brien.[52]

O'Brien took full advantage of the opportunity and presided over a surprisingly placid convention in Miami Beach. Recognizing the possibility of divisive conflict between McGovern's majority and the old liberals and regulars at the convention, he convinced the McGovern campaign's leaders to focus on the nomination and platform while compromising on internal party rules, much as Humphrey's people had done in 1968. So, instead of pressing for enactment of a sweeping new charter, McGovern's committee and floor leaders accepted a simple endorsement of the McGovern-Fraser Commission reforms already in place, along with an expansion of the DNC to accommodate the election of its members by proportional representation. After the convention, McGovern dismissed O'Brien and installed his own allies at party headquarters, and postponed the full charter debate to the 1974 midterm convention, well after the election would be decided.[53]

Reform politics and attention to party affairs waned as the disastrous McGovern campaign unfolded in August and September. Frank Mankiewicz and Gary Hart ran McGovern's general election campaign as a free-standing operation, a true product of the campaign-centered era, essentially disconnected from the Democratic headquarters operation. They virtually ignored headquarters fundraising, raising money instead—quite successfully, as it turned out—through the campaign organization. New DNC Treasurer Donald Petrie raised a half million dollars during the fall (compared with $30 million by McGovern's campaign), but he combined the money with Strauss's telethon income to halve the headquarters's debt by the end of the year.[54] McGovern's managers also ignored O'Brien's operational developments at the headquarters and chose instead to run the fall campaign for the most part with the organization they had built during the primary season.[55]

After spending so much time and effort winning over the national committee and convention to their agenda, McGovern and his new liberal coalition, once they had the nomination in hand, all but discarded their party-centered vision and the headquarters organization. Apparently, their attention to the Reform paradigm, the party, and its national organizations had been a short-term strategy focused only on 1972. They resisted taking on responsibility for the longer-term health of the Democratic National Committee and its headquarters organization, which they continued to view with suspicion. They had been drawn into party arenas because it had been the only way they could end the dominance of the old liberals. After that dominance had been destroyed, they preferred to return to work in their own campaign-centered style.

Reform politics enjoyed a small resurgence over the next few years, as Robert Strauss returned to chair the DNC with a strategy very similar to Larry O'Brien's.[56] Strauss appointed and worked with a Democratic Party Charter Commission that codified a slightly modified version of the McGovern-Fraser reforms after a brief bout of factional bickering. Such battles continued during the 1976 presidential nomination campaign and at the 1978 midterm convention.[57] But those battles never again commanded wide interest or approached the sweeping impact they had made in 1972.

Reform itself had mixed results. In the narrowest sense, reform worked for new liberals as a strategy for ending old liberal control over party machinery and nominations. More broadly, the McGovern-Fraser reforms spurred important changes in presidential nomination politics. State party leaders gave up their former influence in national politics. They opened up their internal decision making, delegate selection shifted from conventions and caucuses to primaries, and campaigns moved out of state party arenas and onto television. From that moment on, both parties' presidential nominees would be decided in a series of state primaries. Reform forced modifications in campaign-centered politics, producing what James Ceaser has called "plebiscitary politics" in presidential elections.[58]

But in the broadest sense, the Reform paradigm vision of an alternative to campaign-centered politics proved to be a complete bust. For some, the Reform paradigm offered a framework for a transformative party-centered politics that would challenge the fragmented politics of the campaign-centered electoral order. Newly mobilized citizens would seek representation and would deliberate over their choices within party arenas at all levels. The reforms did, in fact, increase access to Democratic Party decision making for minorities, women, and young people.[59] Despite that access and representation, however, citizen participation in party affairs and elections continued to decline among all but the most affluent and highly educated partisans throughout the 1970s.[60] Campaign-centered politics survived Reform paradigm efforts, resilient and unscathed, and serious reconsideration of the DNC's electoral role would be put off until the end of the decade.

NOTES

1. John H. Kessel, *The Goldwater Coalition* (Indianapolis: Bobbs-Merrill, 1968); Mary C. Brennan, *Turning Right in the Sixties: The Conservative Capture of the GOP* (Chapel Hill: University of North Carolina Press, 1995).

2. Frank J. Sorauf, *Political Parties in the American System* (Boston: Little, Brown, 1964), 39.

3. David S. Broder, *The Party's Over: The Failure of Politics in America* (New York: Harper and Row, 1971).

4. See John F. Bibby, "Party Renewal in the National Republican Party," in *Party Renewal in America: Theory and Practice*, ed. Gerald M. Pomper (New York: Praeger, 1980); M. Margaret Conway, "Republican Party Nationalization, Campaign Activities, and Their Implications for the Political System," *Publius* 13 (1983):1–17; Xandra Kayden and Eddie Mahe Jr., *The Party Goes On: The Persistence of the Two-Party System in the United States* (New York: Basic Books, 1985); and John C. Green, ed., *Politics, Professionalism and Power: Modern Party Organization and the Legacy of Ray C. Bliss* (Lanham, Md.: University Press of America, 1994).

5. See, for example, Austin Ranney, *Curing the Mischiefs of Faction: Party Reform in America* (Berkeley: University of California Press, 1975); William Crotty, *Decision for the Democrats* (Baltimore, Md: Johns Hopkins University Press, 1978); Byron E. Shafer, *Quiet Revolution: The Struggle for the Democratic Party and the Shaping of Post-Reform Politics* (New York: Russell Sage, 1983); and Nelson Polsby, *Consequences of Party Reform* (New York: Oxford University Press, 1983).

6. Robert Caro, *The Years of Lyndon Johnson: The Path to Power* (New York: Knopf, 1982), chaps. 31–33.

7. For a discussion of large-donor fundraising under Kennedy, see Herbert Alexander, *Financing the 1960 Election* (Princeton, N.J.: Citizens' Research Foundation, 1962), 79–82. For Johnson's use of such fundraising, see Herbert Alexander, *Financing the 1964 Election* (Princeton, N.J.: Citizens' Research Foundation, 1966), 76–84.

8. Broder, *Party's Over*, 60–61.

9. Ibid., 62–63; James Reston, "New York: The Democratic Party Machine," *New York Times*, 11 November 1966, 42.

10. Broder, *Party's Over*, 63–64.

11. Warren Weaver Jr., "Democrats Grope for Fresh Ideas to Rebuild Party," *New York Times*, 2 January 1967, 1. Sidney M. Milkis presents an interesting account and interpretation of this period in *The President and the Parties: The Transformation of the American Party System since the New Deal* (New York: Oxford University Press, 1993), chap. 8.

12. Warren Weaver Jr., "Governors Link Loss to Johnson," *New York Times*, 12 December 1966, 1.

13. Humphrey was initially preempted from entering primaries because his late start came after many filing deadlines. He declined to enter later primaries after discovering that he could win delegates anyway by relying on the support of Johnson's slates. Thereafter, Humphrey focused on the state conventions. It was a smart choice; a *New York Times* poll of county Democratic chairs nationwide in May found that 70 percent of them supported Humphrey (*New York Times*, 2 June 1968, 64).

14. For an excellent discussion of old versus new liberals, their characteristics and policy views, see Everett Carll Ladd, "The Shifting Party Coalitions: From the 1930s to the 1970s," in *Party Coalitions in the 1980s*, ed. Seymour M. Lipset (San Francisco: Institute for

Contemporary Studies, 1981). See also Alan Matusow, *The Unraveling of America: A History of Liberalism in the 1960s* (New York: Harper and Row, 1984).

15. This and following discussion of the reform movement build on the account found in Byron Shafer, *Quiet Revolution: The Struggle for the Democratic Party and the Shaping of Post-Reform Politics* (New York: Russell Sage, 1983).

16. Commission on the Democratic Selection of Presidential Nominees, *The Democratic Choice* (New York, 1968).

17. Ibid., 2.

18. For a discussion of the New Left, see Matusow, *Unravelling of America,* chaps. 11 and 13; and Godfrey Hodgson, *America In Our Time* (New York: Vintage, 1976), part III. Ironically, proportional representation had first been proposed in 1960 by "Boss" Jacob Arvey, the national committeeman from Illinois, as a way of allowing the old liberal or "regular" large industrial state delegations to control the national committee. See the *New York Times,* 5 July 1960, 22. Arvey bitterly opposed a similar reform in 1969 when the new liberals proposed it.

19. "There was not much attention to the Rules Committee reports. Our objective was to get a nominee. This was unimportant, except as it might have some effect on the nomination. We said to ourselves, if you're going to study it, you can control it. If you get the nomination, you'll have control of the DNC. If you have control of the DNC, you can control any study. A study commission would be a way of harmonizing the issue." Max Kampelman quoted in Shafer, *Quiet Revolution,* 34.

20. Warren Weaver, "Humphrey Takes Control of Party," *New York Times,* 31 August 1968, 1. See also Humphrey's brief discussion of the committee in his memoirs, *The Education of a Public Man* (Garden City, N.Y.: Doubleday, 1976), 364–68.

21. Thomas S. Kuhn, *The Structure of Scientific Revolutions,* 2d ed. (Chicago: University of Chicago Press, 1970).

22. Lewis Chester, Godfrey Hodgson, and Bruce Page, *An American Melodrama: The Presidential Campaign of 1968* (New York: Viking, 1969); Theodore H. White, *The Making of the President, 1968* (New York: Atheneum, 1969).

23. Herbert Alexander, *Financing the 1968 Election* (Lexington, Mass.: Lexington Books, 1971), 216–18.

24. See, for example, Warren Weaver, "Humphrey Charts Party Leadership," *New York Times,* 28 November 1968, 32.

25. He and Treasurer Robert Short announced an ambitious plan to erase the party's debt, raise $5 million for the 1970 midterm election, and raise $10 million more for 1972. They established both small- and large-donor programs to achieve these goals, including a restyled National Democratic Sponsor's club modeled on the old $1,000 per year President's Club. Alexander, *Financing the 1968 Election,* 219.

26. R.W. Apple Jr., "Democrats' Purse Starved at Fete," *New York Times,* 6 February 1970, 14; Apple, "Harris Quits Post as Democrats' Chief," *New York Times,* 7 February 1970, 1.

27. Humphrey quoted in Andrew Glass and Jonathan Cottin, "Democratic Reform Drive Falters as Spotlight Shifts to Presidential Race," *National Journal,* 19 June 1971, 1294. Humphrey had worked with McGovern in the Senate for years, and McGovern had immediately endorsed and campaigned for Humphrey after the Chicago convention.

28. Shafer, *Quiet Revolution,* 60–68.

29. James M. Naughton, "O'Brien Turns Down Chairmanship of Democrats," *New York Times,* 27 February 1970, 23; Christopher Lydon, "Fight to Lead Democrats Breaks Out in Committee," *New York Times,* 2 March 1970, 1; R.W. Apple Jr., "O'Brien Accepts Democrats' Call," *New York Times,* 4 March 1970, 1; R.W. Apple Jr., "Group of Left-Wing Democrats Assails Methods Used in Selecting National Chairman," *New York Times,* 5 March 1970, 25. See also O'Brien's memoirs, *No Final Victories* (Garden City, N.Y.: Doubleday, 1974), 271–73.

30. McGovern, his wife, and Harold Hughes lent the commission $15,000. See Alexander, *Financing the 1968 Election,* 220, for a listing of the commission's revenues.

31. Commission on Party Structure and Delegate Selection, *Mandate for Reform* (Washington, D.C.: Democratic National Committee, April 1970), 17–32.

32. Ibid., 33–48.

33. Alabama Gov. George Wallace had already mounted a third-party campaign in 1968 under the American Independent banner, and most observers expected him to do likewise in 1972.

34. Shafer, *Quiet Revolution,* 254–55.

35. See, for example, the Council's call for U.S. withdrawal from Vietnam by 1972, *New York Times,* 25 March 1971, 1.

36. Robert J. Huckshorn, *Party Leadership in the States* (Amherst: University of Massachusetts Press, 1976), 179–81.

37. R.W. Apple Jr., "Democratic Rivals Agree Not to Feud in Presidential Bid," *New York Times,* 11 February 1971, 1; Jonathan Cottin, "O'Brien Presses for Unity; Democrats Prepare for 1972 Convention," *National Journal,* 16 October 1971, 2093–94. See also O'Brien, *No Final Victories,* 285–87.

38. "I had to 'sell' the new rules to the national party as a whole and particularly to the state party leaders who would have to live with them . . . . At the same time I was aware that many of the reform advocates on the McGovern commission and its staff viewed me as an establishment figure who would somehow try to 'sell out' the party reforms. I accepted their suspicions as inevitable and felt my actions would be the best proof of my commitment to an open party. Reform was imperative and I and virtually every member of the National Committee wanted reform. What I also wanted, and what we did not achieve in

1972, was reform that led to party unity, not reform that came at the price of continuing division within the party." O'Brien, *No Final Victories,* 290–91.

39. Quoted in Andrew J. Glass and Jonathan Cottin, "Democratic Reform Drive Falters as Spotlight Shifts to Presidential Race," *National Journal,* 19 June 1971, 1293.

40. Quoted in R.W. Apple Jr., "Mrs. Harris Vows to Fight Mistrust," *New York Times,* 15 October 1971, 19. See also Jonathan Cottin, "Patricia Harris Wins Credentials Fight as O'Brien Turns Back Party Challenge," *National Journal,* 23 October 1971, 2144.

41. Ken Bode, "Turning Sour: Democratic Party Reform," *New Republic,* 10 July 1971, 19–20. See also Glass and Cottin, "Democratic Reform Drive Falters," 1304; and Shafer, *Quiet Revolution,* 298–99, 318, and 358–59. For a harsher treatment of O'Brien by *National Journal* reporter Andrew J. Glass in a more advocacy-oriented publication, see "Are the Democrats Serious About Reform?" *The Progressive,* October 1971, 14–17.

42. Glass and Cottin, "Democratic Reform Drive Falters," 1293–1304. For a note on O'Brien's mailing, see "Democratic Campaign," *National Journal,* 21 August 1971, 1780.

43. R.W. Apple Jr., "Radical Reshaping of Democratic Party is Urged by Heads of 2 Reform Panels," *New York Times,* 26 March 1972, 56; Jonathan Cottin, "Reform Units Propose New DNC Structure," *National Journal,* 1 April 1972, 583.

44. Warren Weaver, "Democrats Urge Parley to Guide Party Stands," *New York Times,* 20 May 1972, 14.

45. See note 4, above.

46. Associated Press, "Democrats Shift National Staff," *New York Times,* 17 May 1970, 43. For one example of the way resource constraints at the headquarters undercut the Democrats' 1970 campaign, see Jonathan Cottin, "Congressional Districts at Stake in Battle for State Legislatures," *National Journal,* 2 May 1970, 956–58.

47. Neal Gregory, "O'Brien as Democratic Leader Focuses on Television, Party Machinery," *National Journal,* 1 August 1970, 1639–46.

48. William Chapman, "Democrats Won't Dent Huge Debt in '70," *Washington Post,* 23 March 1970.

49. Gregory, "O'Brien as Democratic Leader," 1639–40.

50. See, for example, R.W. Apple Jr., "Democrats Fight Money Problems," *New York Times,* 15 November 1971, 1; Cottin, "O'Brien Presses for Unity," 2099–2100; Associated Press, "63 Democrats Are Named to Party Finance Council," *New York Times,* 10 February 1971, 20; R.W. Apple Jr., "Democrats Raise $900,000 at Gala," *New York Times,* 22 April 1971, 17; Steven V. Roberts, "Democrats Try to Talk Way Out of Debt," *New York Times,* 6 July 1972, 28; Associated Press, "Democrats End TV Fund Appeal," *New York Times,* 10 July 1972, 23. See also John W. Ellwood and Robert J. Spitzer, "The Democratic National Telethons: Their Successes and Failures," *Journal of Politics,* August 1979, 828–64.

51. See, for example, Marjorie Hunter, "Democratic Rules Panel Backs Sweeping Changes," *New York Times*, 25 June 1972, 30.

52. See O'Brien, *No Final Victories*, chap. 15, esp. 302–3.

53. Marjorie Hunter, "Reform Compromise Averts Floor Battle," and R.W. Apple Jr., "Triumph of Maturity: A New Involvement by the Delegates Is Reported at a Disciplined Convention," both in *New York Times*, 13 July 1972, 22. On the succession of Jean Westwood, a Utah businesswoman and McGovern campaign organizer and strategist, to DNC chair, see R.W. Apple Jr., "Democrats Name Western Woman Party's Chairman," *New York Times*, 15 July 1972, 1; and Theodore H. White, *The Making of the President, 1972* (New York: Bantam, 1973), 250–53.

54. Herbert Alexander, *Financing the 1972 Election* (Lexington, Mass.: Lexington Books, 1976), 304. See also Jonathan Cottin, "McGovern Reliance on Small Donors Aids His Chances of Party Control," *National Journal*, 4 November 1972, 1703–8.

55. See White, *Making of the President 1972*, 420–30.

56. Christopher Lydon, "Strauss Elected Democrats' Head and Vows Unity," *New York Times*, 10 December 1972, 1.

57. Richard Goodwin, "A Divided Party," *New Yorker*, 7 December 1974, 157–66; Democratic National Committee, *The Charter and Bylaws of the Democratic Party of the United States* (Washington, D.C.: DNC, 1974). For a transcript of the *Charter*, see *New York Times*, 9 December 1974, 44. For coverage of the 1978 convention, see Elizabeth Drew, "A Reporter at Large: Constituencies," *New Yorker*, 15 January 1979, 41–87.

58. James Ceaser, "Improving the Nomination Process," in *Elections American Style*, ed. A. James Reichley (Washington, D.C.: Brookings Institution, 1987), 36. For discussion, see Myron A. Levine, *Presidential Campaigns and Elections: Issues and Images in the Media Age*, 2d ed. (Itasca, Ill.: F.E. Peacock, 1995).

59. Crotty, *Decision for the Democrats*; Denis J. Sullivan, Jeffrey L. Pressman, Benjamin I. Page, and John J. Lyons, *The Politics of Representation: The Democratic Convention 1972* (New York: St. Martin's, 1974).

60. Steven J. Rosenstone and John Mark Hansen, *Mobilization, Participation, and Democracy in America* (New York: Macmillan, 1993), chap. 3.

6

Embracing Campaign-Centered Politics

Professional politicians are like chain smokers, lighting a new campaign off the butt of the old one.

—Steven V. Roberts, 1986

The 1980 election was a shattering experience for Democrats. Winning only six states and the District of Columbia from Ronald Reagan, Jimmy Carter became the first president to lose a bid for reelection since Herbert Hoover had in 1932. Democrats lost control of the Senate as well for the first time since 1954, as conservative Republicans swept aside a whole roster of senior liberals. Even control of the House of Representatives was threatened when Republicans halved the Democrats' comfortable margin in that body.

In the decade that followed, Democratic leaders and activists involved with their party's national organizations gradually agreed on a common response to the campaign-centered electoral order. Frightened by election losses and predictions of a Republican realignment, members of the Democratic National Committee elected a succession of activist national chairs to lead them back to victory. By 1988, the combined efforts of Chairmen Charles Manatt and Paul Kirk, carried out with ongoing national committee support, had dramatically shifted the headquarters's role, enabling the DNC to reenter national electoral politics as a major force in a presidential campaign. Then, after yet another loss, Chairman Ron Brown picked up where Kirk had left off and helped lead the Democrats to victory in 1992.

These Democratic initiatives, combined with extensive efforts at Republican national party organizations during the 1970s and 1980s, cumulatively defined an emerging third paradigmatic party response to the challenges of campaign-centered politics. The Accommodationist paradigm resembled prior proposals; it resulted from strategic efforts by party leaders and activists to survive and succeed in the new electoral order. Those who developed the paradigm were more interested in solving the problem of the new politics than in developing a new paradigmatic analysis and prescription. But the Accommodationist paradigm differed from prior proposals in its conception of the solution. Rather than offering the hope of a party-centered alternative to the campaign-centered order, this new paradigm accepted the campaign-centered order as inescapable and devised a means to accommodate its central features.

The Republican Challenge

Republican organizational development received growing national attention beginning in the late 1970s, first from political journalists and later from political scientists. Democrats, in control of the White House and both houses of Congress, were perhaps among the last to take it seriously.

Two facets of the Republicans' work finally drew the Democrats' collective attention. One was the sheer size and wealth of the national organizations that the Republicans built (see figure 6.1, p. 94). The Republican National Committee (RNC) headquarters, with its own Capitol Hill office building paid for and staffed with 350 employees, raised more than $77 million and spent more than $6 million directly on national candidates in 1980. In contrast, the Democratic headquarters organization under an incumbent president ended the 1980 election cycle with a full-time staff of 80 in rented offices downtown and an income under $16 million. It had spent just under $4 million directly on the Carter-Mondale campaign and virtually nothing on other candidates.

These contrasting figures are jarring, but there is more to the story of campaign finance in 1980. If only aggregate national campaign spending is considered, Democratic candidates appear to have fared quite well in 1980. In the presidential campaign, with federal limits on spending, both Reagan and Carter used their full allowance of about $34 million in public and national party funds. At the same time, however, Reagan and the Republicans put a great deal of energy into raising and spending "soft" money, which they could channel through their state and local party organizations without facing regulation under the Federal Election Campaigns Act. Through these unrestricted party services, the Republicans swamped Democratic efforts by $15 million to $4 million.[1]

The second facet of Republican organizational change that Democrats came to fear was the development of party services to supplement these cash contributions. Historically, Republicans have approached national party organization quite differently than Democrats. The Republican National Committee had always supported Textbook Party–style coalition building, and it had even shown passing interest in Reform paradigm party regulation in the early 1970s.[2] But, particularly since the leadership of Chair Ray Bliss in the 1960s, the Republicans' national organizations showed more interest in services to candidates' campaign organizations and to state and local party organizations.[3] Their development of those services in the late 1970s was striking.

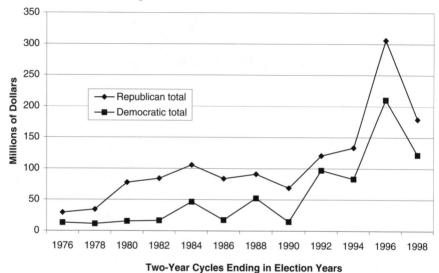

Figure 6.1
Party National Committee Receipts, 1976–96
(Note: Includes "soft" money beginning in 1992)
Source: Federal Election Commission reports

Under Bill Brock's stewardship of the RNC headquarters, Guy Vander Jagt's chairmanship of the National Republican Congressional Committee, and Bob Packwood and John Heinz's chairmanships of the National Republican Senatorial Committee, the Republicans developed wide-ranging programs of assistance to party candidates and their campaign organizations. The national party organizations provided services along three lines. First, they focused on candidates and candidate organizations. The national party staff helped state and local parties recruit promising candidates for national office as well as for important state and local offices.[4] They ran training schools for candidates and Republican campaign professionals and provided ongoing consultation on strategy and tactics during the campaign. In addition to the financial contributions outlined above, they provided a number of other services, including liaison with political action committees (PACs) and other large contributors; television and radio production assistance and advice; selective polling and issue research; and some advice on demographic and geographic analysis and targeting, as well as general political advice and intelligence. The headquarters and campaign committees did not offer these services to all Republican candidates, but they did reach a substantial majority of national and statewide candidates by 1980.[5]

The next targets of Republican national party attention in the late 1970s were the state and local parties. The national headquarters provided these affiliates with staff and financial assistance and helped them to emulate the national party's institutional development as well.[6] The presidential campaign organization was clearly the center of attention for assistance from the national headquarters, and in some cases the Republicans' Capitol Hill campaign committees used the state parties as soft money conduits to Republican congressional candidates' campaign organizations. But there was plenty of genuine assistance to the state parties for their development, especially in programs preparing Republican state activists for post-1980 reapportionment.

Third, the national Republican organizations focused on voters. The party headquarters actively developed computer records and models of voter registration and turnout across the country, and it worked with the state parties to increase Republican registration and turnout.[7] The party organizations also targeted voters through a multimillion-dollar national advertising campaign built around the theme "Vote Republican. For a Change."[8] These ads, the first national party-oriented advertising since Watergate, were placed in newspapers and magazines as well as on television and radio nationwide. Their ultimate effect on voters is impossible to assess, but their symbolic intent was clear. The Republicans produced them as a signal that their party was powerful and ready to govern.

Some analysts explained these developments as party recovery from the decline of the 1950s and 1960s, but that did not adequately describe what was happening. "Recovery" implies a return to some former healthy condition, while the strong Republican national organizations of the late 1970s bore only a passing resemblance to their former selves. Instead of simply recovering, Republican leaders and activists had built something new. They produced a new paradigmatic analysis of contemporary campaigns and elections that made sense of the campaign-centered electoral order. Then they developed a paradigmatic program of building organizations that could work effectively and gain influence in that order, accommodating to it and being competitive as a participant in it without challenging its central features.

Representation in the campaign-centered electoral order is mediated and co-ordinated primarily by interest groups and autonomous campaign organizations rather than by parties. In their Accommodationist paradigm, Republicans developed a strategy of accepting this mediation, then worked for the success of candidate organizations and campaign professionals who identified themselves as Republicans (see table 6.1). Whenever possible, national party organizations provided resources of money, personnel, and intelligence to Republican candidates to build successful campaigns and win elections by whatever means they deemed most effective.

Table 6.1
The Accommodationist Paradigm:
Party Adaptation to the Campaign-Centered Electoral Order

Representation	National parties work to support coalition building by lower level parties and partisan interest groups. They also provide money, personnel, and intelligence to support partisan campaign organization efforts to gain voter support.
Deliberation	Parties enhance the marketing sophistication and success of partisan interest groups, campaign professionals, and candidate organizations. Parties also develop issues and themes that will help persuade citizens to support partisan candidates.
Choice	Parties use marketing-style research and targeted tools to identify potential supporters, register citizens to vote, and turn out voters on election day on behalf of partisan candidates.

Deliberation has turned toward marketing during the campaign-centered electoral order, as noted in chapter 3. Some traditional public discussion of national politics and policy remains, frequently through the channels of the mass media. But in elections, interest groups and campaign organizations more frequently use surveys and computer analysis to help shape public debate in ways that enlarge their existing base. They identify potential supporters among the citizenry, then seek issues and positions that will lead those citizens to vote for the party's candidates. The strategy developed for the Accommodationist paradigm in this context was to produce a cadre of partisan professionals, provide issue research on effective campaign themes, then raise money that would enable Republican campaigns to publish targeted advertising on those positions through television, radio, direct mail, and other media.

Party influence over citizens' electoral choices is also sharply constrained in the campaign-centered electoral order. As noted in chapter 2, Progressive reform in the early twentieth century had already dealt parties a severe blow on this dimension. Reforms of the Democratic presidential nominating process reinforced this transformation, opening channels of public participation and increasing the use of primaries to select party nominees. Still, Republicans devised an Accommodationist paradigm response: use marketing-style research to identify and register Republican voters, then use focused tools such as direct mail and phone banking to help get out the vote on election day.

Seeking a Democratic Response

In the aftermath of the 1980 landslide, members of the Democratic National Committee were only too aware of the developments and ideas at Republican headquarters. Their diverse reactions to this organizational challenge strongly shaped the party debate that followed.

Demands for change had begun even before the 1980 returns were counted, and they continued for months after.[9] Party and issue activists joined Democratic candidates, both winners and losers, in calling for action to "rebuild the party," a single phrase with a multitude of meanings. As the election cycle ended and Democrats began to look to the future, a recurrent theme emerged. Anne Campbell, former head of the Association of State Democratic Chairs, stated the argument bluntly: "The 1980 election was a referendum on national party structure. We were outspent, out-targeted, and outpolled. The RNC did a superlative job. The Democratic Party should hold its head in shame."[10] Like Campbell, members of the DNC understood and regretted the impact of the old liberal–new liberal factional battles and the committee's four-year standoff with President Jimmy Carter, during which the party's national headquarters organization had been virtually drained of resources and programs.

Still, old arguments and rivalries stubbornly remained.[11] New liberals (many of whom had supported Senator Edward Kennedy the previous spring) offered several arguments. A few argued that the real problem had been the party's weak presidential ticket and that no major change was necessary. A somewhat larger faction, still clinging to the now-discredited Reform paradigm analysis that the Democratic Party could build an internally representative majoritarian politics, called for another round of party delegate selection reform. After ten years of such struggles and the concurrent decline in the party's electoral fortunes, however, the number of Democrats who viewed reform as a transformative tool for revival was shrinking.

But many new liberal Democrats remained committed to one component of the Reform paradigm strategy—using the Democratic Party as a vehicle for issue and ideological conflict and decision making—and this time they focused on the party's platform. In essence, they wanted to work within party arenas to continue and resolve the factional policy schisms of the 1960s and 1970s, hoping to expand the party's commitment to such objectives as racial and economic equality, feminism, and disarmament. Some southern and old liberal "regulars," many of whom still clung to Textbook Party hopes of party-brokered coalitions, also supported the idea, agreeing that Democrats had to settle these issues if they wanted to offer voters a clear program and remain competitive in national elections.[12] Each side supported this approach, believing that their own faction would win a fair and open debate and, as a result, win the party's future presidential nominations.

Leery of another round of divisive and probably inconclusive policy debate, some new liberals and most old liberals on the national committee instead embraced the Accommodationist paradigm as embodied in the Republicans' electoral challenge. They looked at the work that powerful Republican organizations had done and concluded that, in comparison, Democrats lacked an analysis and strategy likely to win. They argued that Democratic Party support for its candidates and campaigns was too scattered and uncoordinated to provide much help in elections. These DNC members echoed Democratic officials, led by House Speaker Tip O'Neill, outgoing Senate Majority Leader Robert Byrd, and former National Chairman Robert Strauss, who called for more attention to the "nuts and bolts" of winning campaigns and less attention to the political issues that divided Democrats.[13] The Republicans had developed superior political tools, the argument went, and it was time the Democrats developed some tools of their own.

These arguments did not fully embrace the Accommodationist paradigm analysis, which held that it was pointless to hope for party-centered politics, so parties should instead adapt and develop tools to enable their candidates to be competitive in campaign-centered politics. But no matter what their factional stripes, all members of the national committee agreed that they could benefit from services to their candidates and campaigns in 1982 and 1984.

Arguments about these two approaches continued for months after the election without resolution, and to some extent they continue today. But just as the 1980 losses had led some DNC members to reconsider their fixation on the Textbook Party and Reform paradigms as compelling explanations of how the world did—and could—work, the landslide also brought an important shift in the balance of national committee support for issue debates and campaign-centered services. Those calling for the development of party services gained support, while some issue activists apparently decided that their candidates and campaign organizations had little to gain by winning ideological control of a resource-poor headquarters.

Charles Manatt's Dual Strategy: Build Both Party and Campaign

Several candidates ran for the job of leading the Democratic National Committee and the national party after the 1980 loss, voicing variations on the themes that committee members had developed. But only National Finance Chair Charles Manatt produced a well-organized and financed campaign. A former California Democratic chair and unsuccessful candidate for the national chairmanship in 1972, Manatt had been involved in national party affairs since the 1960s and had been a very active and successful party fundraiser since 1976.

Manatt won over DNC members with an agenda for the headquarters organization, drawn largely from his own experience and from ideas already being debated publicly by Democrats. His agenda was a protean blend of all three paradigms.[14] He incorporated both issue-oriented and campaign-centered ideas in building his program for organizational change, and he offered programs appealing to all factions.

Perhaps most important, Manatt proposed the paradigmatically agnostic strategy of expanded fundraising—initially from large donors but increasingly from direct mail—to build a stable financial base for the headquarters and allow the development of a strong and permanent organization capable of doing all these things. In short, he offered proposals that would not only expand the headquarters organization but also dramatically reorient its division of labor and resources.[15] He won election to the DNC chair by presenting himself to members less as an innovator than as someone who could draw together existing ideas into a coherent and manageable program that would please all factions.

Manatt recognized that, as the 1984 presidential race drew nearer, resources for his program would become more limited and attacks from factions within the party would become more likely. In that context, his apparent strategy was not to focus on one approach to institutional development and work it through. Rather, he quickly set to work on all four of his proposed initiatives simultaneously, perhaps hoping that the appearance of vitality in the organization would please the national committee and stimulate public donations to support the vitality.

One early diversion illustrates just how difficult Manatt's job would be. Before he could work on his own ideas, Manatt first had to follow a 1980 convention mandate and appoint a new Commission on Presidential Selection. The commission, chaired by North Carolina Governor James Hunt, produced a report recommending shortening the primary season and allotting one-seventh of the next convention's seats to members of Congress as "superdelegates," and restoring DNC members' former status as automatic delegates to presidential nominating conventions. Not surprisingly, the DNC praised Manatt and Hunt's work and endorsed the commission's recommendations, but the episode had consumed months of precious time.[16] With these matters acted upon, Manatt set to work. His first, and most striking, organizational initiative was a Textbook Party effort that fulfilled a promise to various issue activists: he turned the party headquarters itself into an arena for factional coalition building. Within his first year as chair, Manatt provided staff support to the three constituency-based DNC vice-chairs who represented blacks, Hispanics, and women. He also opened similar "caucus offices" for other constituency groups—gays and lesbians, business professionals, Asian Americans, and liberals—whose leaders he wanted to draw into the party's presidential coalition. He built this caucus structure expecting these constituency group leaders to influence members of their groups and provide organizational and voter support for Democratic candidates on election day. And, by the spring of 1984, the caucus offices were a major fixture of the headquarters staff organization, run by leaders of each of the groups and doing outreach to, providing services for, and representing the interests of their constituencies.

Keeping his promises to Democratic officeholders, Manatt also followed a Textbook Party approach as he moved to establish and coordinate conferences and committees that would draw elected officials back into party affairs and engage them in discussions on elections and public policy. For example, he set up a Democratic Strategy Council of national, state, and local officeholders that would meet and talk about policy issues as well as election strategies and local events.[17] Modeled on the earlier out-party Democratic Advisory Council (1956–1960) and Democratic Policy Council (1969–1976), the commission served as an arena for party leaders to develop a unified party voice on national policy issues. But unlike its predecessors, the Strategy Council was composed entirely of elected officials. As the headquarters Executive Director Eugene Eidenberg described it, "the thought was that these people have to run for office every few years and their views and policies and personal styles embody what the Democratic Party stands for. The accumulated acts and positions of these standard-bearers are the real content of the party."[18] In a Textbook Party fashion, Manatt and Eidenberg seemed to be working to gather a kind of Democratic party-in-government that could offer a coherent programmatic response to the resurgent Republicans.

Manatt also used this approach to control a potentially more divisive event left over from the 1970s reform era. The "midterm conference" was an innovation new liberal activists had developed in the early 1970s to gain influence in the party prior to presidential campaigns. But while Carter's White House had downplayed the 1978 conference by rescheduling it until after the midterm election, Manatt moved the 1982 conference up to June, gave national committee members and elected officials clear control, and converted it into a campaign kick-off event. With this increased participation of the party-in-government, this Philadelphia conference focused on the "nuts and bolts" of winning elections, with campaign training and issue workshops, strategy sessions for congressional campaigns, and showcase speeches for Democratic presidential candidates.[19]

Manatt had also promised to emulate the Republicans' campaign-centered initiatives, and he began to deliver on them by shifting headquarters resources toward a broad program of services for Democratic candidates as well as for state and local parties. Despite a decline in financial contributions to the party after the 1980 landslide, he started several programs early in the 1981–82 election cycle. He began by providing financial assistance and strategic advice to Democratic nominees in five special House elections held in mid-1981. Democrats won three of the five, dampening talk of a sweeping national Republican realignment.[20] Yet this modest start signaled a modest future: the ongoing services and contributions to congressional candidates continued throughout Manatt's chairmanship but remained limited to little more than $100,000 in each of the 1982 and 1984 election cycles.[21]

In addition to direct campaign assistance, the headquarters sponsored the founding of a Democratic National Training Academy in Des Moines to help develop cadres of sophisticated partisan campaign professionals. The academy's staff traveled around the country over the next three years, putting on seminars and training more than 5,000 Democratic candidates and campaign workers in the methods and skills of modern elections. They worked with campaign organizations at all levels, from Congress to state legislatures.[22]

Manatt also initiated a program of services to state and local Democratic parties in 1982, following the Republicans' lead in enabling state and local parties to develop within the Accommodationist paradigm. Directed by DNC staff member Brian Lunde, "The State Party Works!" program initially focused on New Mexico as a laboratory for state party organizational development with national party assistance. Building on the Republicans' successful model of gathering, integrating, and interpreting voting, survey, and other poll data into a statewide financial appeal and campaign strategy, the New Mexico program helped Democrats build a strong base of coordinated resources and support for campaigns across the state. Despite New Mexico's landslide 1980 vote for Reagan, in 1982 the Democrats won a U.S.

Senate seat (Jeff Bingaman) and the governorship (Toney Anaya), and they held majorities in both houses of the state legislature. After this successful pilot effort, Lunde expanded the program to reach more than twenty state parties in 1984. Unfortunately, he was only able to obtain about $1 million for the project, which amounted to a token effort averaging $50,000 per state.[23]

Finally, Manatt began some longer-term projects to strengthen the headquarters' service capabilities. He convinced the DNC to join the Democratic Congressional Campaign Committee in sponsoring the development of a multimillion-dollar media center. The center, completed in January 1984, provided television and radio facilities for the campaigns of Democratic candidates and officeholders at below-market costs.[24] The most important symbolic initiative of the period, however, was the construction of a $7 million building on Capitol Hill to house the headquarters staff and the senatorial and congressional campaign committees under one roof.[25] When the three organizations moved in after the 1984 election, at the end of Manatt's tenure, they served notice that they had become permanent participants in national campaign politics.

All these scattered initiatives cost money, and fundraising drew Manatt's closest attention. He established an array of special "councils" that large donors could join in exchange for regular contact with elected party leaders.[26] Recognizing the unpredictability and political liabilities that such large-donor fundraising had created for the Democrats in the past, Manatt also followed the Republicans' lead and initiated a direct-mail program to build a predictable small-donor base for the organization. Direct mail is an expensive enterprise to begin, however, and the Democrats had neither the skills nor the computer equipment to run a major operation in-house. So, rather than build one slowly, Manatt took a monumental risk and borrowed $2.4 million to start a large-scale operation quickly. He hired the direct-mail consulting firm of Craver Matthews Smith & Co., had them send out a million fund-raising letters in August 1981, and instructed them to reinvest half of the earnings from the operation into further mailings. Such continuous "prospecting" is expensive, but because the rate of return on individual direct mailings is small, repetition is necessary to develop a large and consistent list of donors.[27]

Manatt's direct-mail gamble paid off. In 1981, the DNC mail program began with an active list of about 65,000 donors (compared with the 300,000-name list the McGovern campaign had compiled in 1972 and the 2 million names the Republicans had in 1980). At that time, it provided about 20 percent of the headquarters income. With the money from the Craver Matthews mailings, the start-up loan was repaid within two years, and by the end of 1984, the Democratic list had grown to almost 600,000 names. This expanded roster of small donors brought in more than $500,000 each month, nearly half of DNC income.[28]

In contrast with these successes, Manatt made mistakes as chair. Many arose because he tried to move too quickly, to push the organization in too many directions at once, perhaps because he lacked a clear paradigmatic vision of how electoral politics worked in the campaign-centered period and a prescription for how the party could adapt to that politics. Most notably, his attempt to revive the annual Democratic telethon over the 1982 Memorial Day weekend was a disaster, and the headquarters-sponsored speaking tour of Democratic presidential candidates in late 1983 never came together.[29] When his fundraising efforts failed to reach their targets, he was forced to cut back the headquarters's programs at awkward moments.[30] The Training Academy, symbolically placed in Des Moines as a signal that the party headquarters was reaching out beyond Washington, was eventually closed and run sporadically out of the headquarters itself.[31] And the ambitious assistance program for state and local party organizations dwindled by early 1984 to little more than a series of strategy sessions and a cooperative voter registration drive with other political groups.

Nevertheless, the Democratic National Committee ratified Manatt's initiatives at every opportunity. Although his efforts had not gelled into a coherent headquarters program, he had substantially reduced the factional polarization that had plagued the committee in the 1970s, and he had developed an array of noncontroversial services for a wide range of Democrats. After four years under Carter, when the national committee had suffered through a tense and occasionally confrontational relationship with Democratic chairs and the headquarters organization, Manatt's low-key, collaborative style was welcome. By the time presidential nomination politics began to heat up in late 1983, Manatt was presiding over an organization that bore little resemblance to the one he had taken over in January 1981. By August 1984, the DNC worked as a valuable adjunct to the Mondale-Ferraro organization through the general election.[32]

As in every Democratic presidential campaign since 1964, the Mondale-Ferraro campaign welcomed the DNC headquarters's support, but disdained any pretensions of party-centered politics. Such a dominant role for the Mondale-Ferraro organization had one ironic benefit for Manatt's headquarters. As President Ronald Reagan rolled to a landslide reelection in 1984, few Democrats blamed the DNC or the headquarters for the loss. The only aspect of the campaign with serious implications for the organization was the "special interest" charge raised against Mondale first by presidential hopeful Senator Gary Hart in the primaries and then by Reagan in the general election. In essence, they charged that Mondale's traditional style of organizing his Democratic campaign coalition around the leaders of interest and constituency groups tainted the party and guaranteed that Mondale could not govern fairly or impartially.[33] After the landslide, some members of the Democratic National Committee argued that Manatt's constituency projects at the headquarters were vulnerable to the same charge. But the issue was never fully debated: Manatt announced his intention to step down in January, leaving his work at the committee unfinished.[34]

Paul Kirk: Embracing the Accommodationist Paradigm

Despite efforts since 1981, Democrats in late 1984 faced conditions similar to those in the aftermath of the 1980 election. The party's presidential ticket had been humiliated nationwide, and the Republicans retained control of the U.S. Senate. Many Democratic organizations and candidates had been outspent and out-organized by their Republican opponents, and Democratic Party supporters feared for the future. Republicans held the White House, the Democrats' national chair was stepping down, and the members of the committee still lacked any clear paradigmatic analysis to explain what the party should do next. The barrage of demands on the members of the national committee was similar—just as broad, just as contradictory, but perhaps more urgent—and the members proved just as interested in changing the headquarters in response. Democrats wanted more money, more services, clearer policy positions, different delegate selection procedures, and more voter outreach. But most of all, they wanted to win again, and they hoped the headquarters organization could play a role in victory. As they had in 1980, the members of the national committee again used the election of its chair as a means to set the future course of the headquarters organization.

The winner this time was Paul Kirk, the sitting DNC treasurer and former Kennedy presidential campaign aide from 1980, who had campaigned with variations on the themes Manatt had embraced four years before.[35] He pledged to continue Manatt's strategy by creating organized opportunities for party and coalition building and to avoid factional divisions over changes in party rules. He promised to spend most of his energies, however, on campaign-centered projects, developing technologically advanced and politically useful services to Democratic candidates and organizations at the state and local level in preparation for the 1988 presidential election.[36] To accomplish this, he promised to continue strengthening the organization's financial base through large donors and direct mail.

Recognizing the limited window of opportunity for initiating changes before presidential election politics overshadowed party organizations, he worked quickly. Programmatically, most of Kirk's early work went to paring down the headquarters' commitment to Manatt's Textbook Party internal coalition building and Reform paradigm party rule-making. Kirk took two actions in 1985 that dramatically signaled his intentions to end Manatt's institutionalized generosity to the party's liberal issue activists and to shift strongly toward a new, campaign-centered Democratic strategy. Within weeks after taking office, Kirk first eliminated the headquarters support Manatt had provided for "caucus" offices representing particular constituency groups. He explained the move as a response to the "special interest" label Reagan had slapped on the party, saying that

> our party has traditionally mirrored the diversity of America. But lately we seem to have turned our diversity from a strength into a weakness. We have allowed the parts to grow bigger than the whole . . . .The Democratic party cannot be perceived as a retail broker of programs and patronage for each caucus and constituency.[37]

He would use the headquarters to support Democratic candidates and campaigns, he said, but he would not let the headquarters be used as a platform for constituency leaders to advance the interests and cohesion of their own groups. Eliminating the offices backfired briefly, bringing political demands for reversal from such prominent Democrats as the Reverend Jesse L. Jackson and AFL-CIO president Lane Kirkland. But the DNC's executive committee endorsed the action at its May meeting.[38]

His efforts to downplay party reform began less controversially in two of the traditionally conflictual DNC-coordinated arenas created by and for new liberal issue activists. The Fairness Commission, yet another delegate-selection reform exercise mandated by the 1984 convention, worked quietly and recommended minimal change in the presidential nomination process set up by the Hunt Commission in 1982.[39] The Democratic Policy Commission, a successor to Manatt's Strategy Council, held public hearings in an effort to reconnect the party leadership with grassroots problems and "mainstream" ideas on domestic and foreign policy. The commission released its centrist report early in the summer of 1986, and the most stinging criticism it drew was for its dullness.[40] But Kirk's decision to cancel the 1986 midterm convention drew stronger challenges, as he urged that the DNC permanently discard such conventions and use the resources instead for campaigns. He again met vocal resistance from activist members who insisted on the Reform paradigm analysis that the conferences were essential to party democracy, but the committee endorsed his arguments and his decision.[41]

While scaling back organizational support for policy activism, Paul Kirk did not abandon it completely. Instead, he worked to preempt factionalism by staking out a broadly attractive campaign-centered strategy and establishing himself as a national spokesman for a unified Democratic Party. The most visible example was his bitter criticism of the RNC's planned program of challenging Democratic voters in predominantly black precincts in Louisiana, Indiana, and Missouri in 1986. The

Republicans ultimately withdrew the program and settled a DNC-sponsored lawsuit, and Kirk made valuable points for his leadership and for the party in the dispute.[42]

Early in the contest for the 1988 presidential nomination, Kirk followed the example of former Chair Larry O'Brien in proposing a "code of conduct" for the campaign aiming "to discourage negative, polarizing, and party-bashing campaigns and to promote a civil, constructive, and positive debate on policy alternatives."[43] He simultaneously collaborated with RNC Chair Frank Fahrenkopf to set up jointly-sponsored presidential debates, bumping the nonpartisan League of Women Voters from the scene.[44] As the 1988 nominating convention drew near, he urged the contending candidates to unite behind the front-running candidate and a vague, general platform.[45]

Nevertheless, Kirk's clear priorities fit the Accommodationist paradigm: he worked to shift the headquarters away from advancing the Democratic *Party* as the central focus of factional electoral politics, and instead used the party headquarters to support Democratic candidates and support a more *campaign*-centered politics, enabling each candidate and campaign organization to proceed however it liked. With increased revenues and the resources freed up by his earlier moves, Kirk turned his attention to such services. Aside from a small effort to expand the Democratic Training School in collaboration with the Capitol Hill campaign committees, he shifted the focus of virtually all headquarters service activities toward the state-level parties, extending and reworking Manatt's "State Party Works!" program and focusing on the traditional interests of national committee members in state politics.

He began by setting up a system of regional desks and giving each of four regional field coordinators responsibility for integrating services to a specific set of states. He created an Office of Party Outreach to work directly with Democratic elected officials in the state houses, state legislatures, and local governments.[46] And early in 1986 he put national fieldworkers (the "Democratic Party Election Force") to work with the parties in sixteen targeted states with critical gubernatorial or state legislative elections. The Force, initially budgeted at $1.2 million, worked to build and support state party staff organization work in developing fundraising and campaign service capacities.[47] By the summer of 1988, now under the name "Campaign '88," the multimillion-dollar operation was working on fundraising, voter identification, and mobilization programs in the thirty-five most competitive states.[48]

Kirk also launched Project 500, a related program intended to help Democratic state legislative candidates win 500 more seats in swing states before the post-1990 reapportionment, an issue of major concern to many state delegations in the DNC.[49] In combination with the Election Force and an extensive round of DNC-sponsored survey research in the states, Project 500 helped the states develop computerized voter files for voter registration and turnout programs. It also gave the state parties access to the headquarters' new computer facilities and let them tap into the database that the headquarters direct-mail program had developed after bringing the program in-house in 1985.[50]

To fund these campaign-centered initiatives, Kirk began by bolstering the party's large-donor programs, the National Finance Council and the Democratic Business Council.[51] These programs stirred up controversy, especially when the headquarters raised large amounts of soft money for "party building." The Republicans had mastered such fundraising in the 1970s and the Democrats' struggle to catch up was gathering press attention reminiscent of Lyndon Johnson's problems with the "Greatness Fund."[52] Ultimately, the Democrats' large-donor efforts would pay off in grand fashion, raising $20 million in soft money and nearly the same amount in "hard" dollars for DNC-supported state field operations for the Dukakis-Bentsen campaign in 1988.[53]

Kirk's second important financial initiative was to bring the headquarters's direct-mail operation in-house in September of 1985, thus eliminating the dependency and expense of using a private contractor. He saw an increasing reliance on direct-mail receipts as the only way to wean the expanding headquarters from the continuing political liabilities of large donations and soft money, and he directed substantial resources to the effort. Direct mail receipts dropped sharply after the 1984 Reagan landslide, as they had in 1981.[54] But by early 1986, the direct-mail operation was bringing in $600,000 a month, or 75 percent of the organization's operating revenues.[55] Even so, the expanding direct-mail receipts paled in comparison with the headquarters's large-donor fundraising success in 1988.

Kirk's window of opportunity for bringing change to the party headquarters began to close as presidential politics recaptured party activists' attention shortly after the 1986 midterm election. Yet, by the end of the 1985–86 election cycle, Kirk had put his own stamp on the headquarters organization and helped people forget the divisiveness of his decisions to close the caucus offices and end the midterm conference. Those who disliked his treatment of various factions within the party were, nevertheless, more than happy to accept the money and services he generated. The cycle ended with Kirk sharing credit for the successful 1986 campaign, in which the Democrats regained control of the U.S. Senate and held their ground in the state capitals.

Over the next two years, Kirk's star continued to rise. His consensual leadership of the national committee enabled him to serve as an honest broker between Governor Michael Dukakis and the Reverend Jesse Jackson in the tense weeks leading up to the 1988 Democratic National Convention. More important, his efforts resulted in the DNC making a major financial and organizational contribution to the 1988 general election campaign, the first time in twenty years that Democrats came close to matching Republicans organizationally and financially (see figure 6.1, p. 96).[56]

Early in the summer of 1988, when it became clear that Dukakis would win the Democratic presidential nomination, Kirk began developing ties with the Dukakis campaign organization. At the July convention, the DNC and Dukakis fund-raising and campaign organizations were merged. The fundraising operation, run by future DNC Treasurer Robert Farmer, would be an astonishing success, raising $50 million for the Dukakis-Bentsen campaign and funding a major expansion of the "Campaign '88" structure Kirk had already established. This private money, combined with the $46 million contributed by public financing, led former DNC Treasurer Peter G. Kelley to remark, "Money is not going to be an issue this time. The Democratic ticket is going to be able to match the Republicans bullet for bullet."[57] The DNC helped Michael Dukakis and Lloyd Bentsen to stage one of the best organized and financed presidential campaigns ever.

When Dukakis lost the 1988 general election, the contrast with 1980 was striking. Everyone blamed the nominee himself for the loss; nobody pointed to money or DNC problems to explain the outcome. The only complaints came from some state and local activists, who complained that the Dukakis-Bentsen operation had too often been run top-down from Boston, ignoring the knowledge and skills of local campaigners. Yet most agreed that Paul Kirk, and later the joint "Campaign '88," had built a campaign-centered headquarters organization that provided sufficient resources to win. The Democratic ticket had lost the election on the merits, and when the election ended, the DNC headquarters organization remained strong and in the black. As Kirk stepped down in November, he drew almost universal Democratic acclaim.[58]

Consolidation and Success under Ron Brown in 1992

Ron Brown, former DNC deputy chair under Charles Manatt and a participant in the 1988 campaigns of both Jesse Jackson and Michael Dukakis, won the election to succeed Paul Kirk the following February. Brown had nothing but praise for Kirk and entered office pledging to continue Kirk's initiatives at the committee. He promised to build the party headquarters into "a campaign organization."[59] Although he would be distracted in the first year by renewed squabbles over party rules, his campaign-centered actions made good on that promise.[60]

Over the next four years, Brown continued what Manatt and Kirk had begun and demonstrated that the Accommodationist paradigm had become conventional wisdom among Democrats. Brown did not elaborate on the paradigm's analysis of contemporary politics, though he did develop it strategically as he pressed the DNC's campaign-centered program further in three important ways. First, he and DNC Political Director Paul Tully expanded the organization's outreach and coordination to the Capitol Hill campaign committees and, more important, to state parties throughout the country. Tully called the plan "the coordinated campaign." The idea was to have the DNC provide coordination, strategic information and guidance, and financial support, while the state parties became the primary conduit for assistance to Democratic candidates. Components included voter registration, the development of computerized voter lists for direct-mail advertising and fundraising, data and strategic assistance in preparation for post-1990 redistricting, and development of a communications network for Democratic officials throughout the country.[61] Brown hoped the program would assist Democrats during the midterm election in 1990, but Anthony Corrado describes Brown's primary concern as developing "a 'web of relationships' that would serve as an infrastructure designed to mobilize the vote in a presidential race."[62] The program reached thirty states in 1990 and saw nationwide implementation by the summer of 1992.

Brown's second important expansion of already established programs came in finance, where he dramatically increased the committee's use of soft money. The national committees' uses of so-called hard money during presidential campaigns have been strictly regulated since the passage of the Federal Election Campaigns Act (FECA) in 1974: individual contributions to national parties are limited to $20,000 per year, political action committee (PAC) contributions are limited to $15,000 per year, and direct spending by each national party committee on its presidential ticket was limited to $10 million during the 1992 general election campaign.[63] But soft money, contributions to the various participants in Brown's coordinated campaign, remained outside the jurisdiction of the FECA: the party could take unlimited individual and PAC contributions and spend unlimited amounts of money on state "party building" activities. The DNC and the Dukakis campaign had made extensive use of such money during the time leading up to the 1988 national convention. Brown retained Dukakis's Finance Chair Robert Farmer, and Farmer renewed his prior success in raising large amounts of soft money for the coordinated campaign.[64]

The third component of Brown's campaign-centered activity was almost entirely new. Beginning in late 1989, Brown, Tully, and others at the national committee sketched what Brown called "a preliminary strategy for the 1992 general election campaign," which the DNC could implement for whoever won the party's nomination.[65] Tully and his staff conducted polls and focus groups, then consulted Democratic leaders and activists around the country in devising a game plan that could be implemented by the cooperative national network of party organizations and operatives. They went so far as to propose a ranking of states, from most likely to least likely supporters of a Democratic ticket, then plotted state-by-state campaign plans. When the Persian Gulf War delayed the beginning of the Democratic nomination campaign, Tully and Brown used the delay to develop the plan even further and to begin presenting it publicly as a means of "framing" the upcoming election to Democrats' advantage.[66]

Once Arkansas Governor Bill Clinton emerged as the prohibitive favorite for the party's presidential nomination, Brown began to work closely with campaign managers to integrate DNC operations with Clinton's. After a July nominating convention so successful that it drove Ross Perot to drop out of the race—if only temporarily—Brown's three elements fell smoothly into place. Clinton's campaign style and moderate positions meshed well with the state-by-state focus of the coordinated campaign. Contributions of both hard and soft money skyrocketed after the convention, and the unified DNC/Clinton campaign actually raised more money than the incumbent president's campaign in the second half of 1992. The income enabled the DNC nearly to match the RNC in soft money receipts over the full two-year cycle, though the Republican National Committee held the edge in hard money receipts (see figure 6.1, p. 96). This success allowed the DNC to transfer more than $10 million to state and local parties and to run "generic" pro-Democratic advertising across the country.[67] Finally, and most important, Clinton campaign managers James Carville and George Stephanopoulos embraced Paul Tully's targeted game plan for the fall.[68] To Brown, Tully, and the DNC's credit, it worked.

Brown's initiatives had some of the features of a Textbook Party approach to national party development: the effort to draft a national campaign strategy, the collaboration with other national and state-level party organizations, and the fundraising. But critical Textbook Party features were missing, especially a role in nominating party candidates, a focus on programmatic policy, and appointments after the election. Brown prepared the DNC organization to serve whoever was nominated and left the candidate with responsibility for whatever happened after the election. He approached these matters strategically, without any expressed paradigmatic analysis, but his efforts followed Manatt and Kirk's in developing a campaign-centered national party headquarters.

The Transition Complete

In many ways, the development of the Democratic Party's national headquarters from 1981 through 1992 can be viewed as a roughly continuous process. Democrats, frightened at the specter of realignment raised by the 1980 and 1984 landslides, then frustrated by the Bush victory in 1988, wanted a reorientation of their national headquarters organization and its programs away from divisive factional policy brokering and regulation and toward services that could benefit all factions. There was no clear paradigmatic message in that demand, though it had Accommodationist implications. It was simply an expression that the world no longer worked the way Democratic leaders and activists expected, so they wanted something new. In response, Charles Manatt, Paul Kirk, and Ron Brown stepped forward with programmatic proposals for the national committee's headquarters organization. They helped to institutionalize the party, significantly increase the size and capacities of its headquarters, and completely reorient its approach to electoral politics.

Throughout the 1970s the headquarters had been the subject of factional battles within the party, with liberal issue activists winning broad reform and regulations, and regulars demanding autonomy and Textbook Party support for elected officials and state party organizations. The organization's program careened wildly among party governance and reform, service modernization, presidential nomination fights, and disputes between constituency leaders. In the 1980s, Charles Manatt worked to moderate these swings by downplaying reform, giving organizational patronage to the issue activists, then creating arenas and forums for elected party officials and increasing these officials' influence over the headquarters organization. Even as he appeased factional supporters of both the Textbook Party and Reform paradigms, he began to move the organization toward a campaign-centered approach that he hoped would supersede the factional conflict. Paul Kirk developed the Accommodationist paradigm analysis and prescription even further, eliminating patronage and stressing campaign services, and built a party headquarters similar to the Republican National Committee developed by Bill Brock in the 1970s. Ron Brown completed the process and developed operations that helped Bill Clinton win the White House.

Some Democrats resisted these changes, but ultimately the Accommodationist paradigm won. In effect, Democrats both within and outside government agreed in the mid-1980s that they wanted to reconcile—or at least set aside—factional divisions for the sake of party candidates' electoral fortunes. Manatt, Kirk, and Brown's standard argument for such reconciliation was that Democratic factions differed more with Republicans than with each other and that Republicans would retain the presidency as long as Democratic Party elites failed to recognize this fact.

But the Democratic chairs argued further that the best alternative to such intraparty factional warfare was to embrace the campaign-centered politics of money and services for Democratic candidates and campaigns. These newly available DNC resources had no factional content; they enabled Democratic candidates and state parties to campaign however they liked, with whatever policy positions they liked. They could focus on the party or issues or individual candidates, depending on whatever would work with voters in a given election. Clearly, this was not the only available alternative. The Republican National Committee under Ronald Reagan proved, after all, that party organizations can be partisan, ideological, and successful at the same time. But it was an easy alternative for Democrats weary of interminable factional battles and frightened by the growing affluence of their partisan opponents to embrace.

At the core of the Accommodationist paradigm's analysis and prescription, however, is a kind of agnosticism about the value of party as a mediating institution in electoral politics, perhaps driven by the growing indifference of voters toward parties in the 1970s and 1980s. Traditional advocates of strong parties might be troubled by the Democratic headquarters's move to embrace such campaign-centered politics, though most contemporary observers described the program itself as Manatt, Kirk, and Brown's great success.

NOTES

1. Herbert E. Alexander, "Making Sense about Dollars in the 1980 Presidential Campaigns," in *Money and Politics in the United States,* ed. Michael J. Malbin (Washington, D.C.: American Enterprise Institute, 1984). For a more complete discussion of soft money, see Anthony Corrado, "Party Soft Money," in Corrado, Thomas E. Mann, Daniel R. Ortiz, Trevor Potter, and Frank J. Sorauf, *Campaign Finance Reform: A Sourcebook* (Washington, D.C.: Brookings Institution, 1997).

2. On the brief Republican flirtation with national committee regulation of state and local party affairs, see Charles Longley, "Party Nationalization in America," in *Paths to Political Reform,* ed. William Crotty (Lexington, Mass.: Lexington Books, 1980), 175–79.

3. The best survey of this Republican development is John C. Green, ed., *Politics, Professionalism, and Power: Modern Party Organization and the Legacy of Ray C. Bliss* (Lanham, Md.: University Press of America, 1994).

4. Richard Cohen, "The Making of the Congress, 1980—There's a New National Wrinkle This Year," *National Journal,* 5 January 1980, 20–24.

5. See, for example, John F. Bibby, "Party Renewal in America," in *Party Renewal in America,* ed. Gerald M. Pomper (New York: Praeger, 1980); F. Christopher Arterton, "Political Money and Party Strength," in *The Future of American Political Parties,* ed. Joel Fleishman (Harriman, N.Y.: American Assembly, 1982); David Adamany, "Political Parties in the 1980s," in *Money and Politics in the United States,* ed. Michael J. Malbin (Washington, D.C.: American Enterprise Institute, 1984); Cornelius P. Cotter et al., *Party Organizations in American Politics* (New York: Praeger, 1984); Xandra Kayden and Eddie Mahe Jr., *The Party Goes*

On: The Persistence of the Two-Party System in the United States (New York: Basic Books, 1985); and A. James Reichley, "The Rise of National Parties," in *The New Direction in American Politics,* ed. John Chubb and Paul E. Peterson (Washington, D.C.: Brookings Institution, 1985).

6. Cotter et al., *Party Organizations;* Paul S. Herrnson and David Menefee-Libey, "The Dynamics of Party Organizational Development," *Midsouth Political Science Review* 11 (Winter 1990): 3 30.

7. Timothy Clark, "The RNC Prospers, the DNC Struggles As They Face the 1980 Election," *National Journal,* 27 September 1980, 1617–21.

8. Adamany, "Political Parties."

9. Clark, "RNC Prospers, the DNC Struggles."

10. Quoted in Rhodes Cook, "Chorus of Democratic Voices Urges New Policies, Methods," *Congressional Quarterly Weekly Report,* 17 January 1981, 137.

11. For press coverage, see Bill Peterson, "Finger-Pointing Democrats Vent Frustrations at Meeting," *Washington Post,* 10 December 1980, A2.

12. Dom Bonafede, "For the Democratic Party, It's a Time for Rebuilding and Seeking New Ideas," *National Journal,* 21 February 1981, 317–20.

13. Ibid.; Cook, "Chorus of Democratic Voices;" Kathy Sawyer, "Byrd Faults Party Panel on Handling of Election," *Washington Post,* 16 November 1980, A5.

14. Thomas Kuhn notes that such vague transitional figures are common in scientific revolutions. See Kuhn, *The Structure of Scientific Revolutions,* 2d ed. (Chicago: University of Chicago Press, 1970), chap. 8.

15. Manatt described his agenda in his first speech as chair. See transcripts from the meeting of the Democratic National Committee in Washington, D.C., 27 February 1981, DNC Archives. This account also draws on press coverage and interviews with DNC Press Secretary Terry Michael in March 1987 and former DNC Associate Chair William Sweeney in December 1987, both in Washington, D.C.

16. On the development of the commission's proposals, see Rhodes Cook, "New Democratic Rules Panel: A Careful Approach to Change," *Congressional Quarterly Weekly Report,* 26 December 1981, 2563–67; and Michael J. Malbin, "Democratic Rule Makers Want to Bring Party Leaders Back to the Conventions," *National Journal,* 2 January 1982, 24–28. For a summary of the commission's report, see Malbin, "The Democratic Party's Rules Changes," *National Journal,* 23 January 1982, 139, 165. On the DNC's acceptance, see "New Democratic Rules Usher in 550 Uncommitted Delegates," *National Journal,* 3 April 1982, 600.

17. "Dem National Chairman Manatt Plans Council of Top Party Figures," *Washington Post,* 22 April 1981, A1.

18. Quoted in Dom Bonafede, "Democratic Activists, Eager for Combat, Not Willing to Wait 'Til Next Year," *National Journal,* 31 October 1981, 1932–36.

19. See Elizabeth Drew, "A Reporter at Large: The Democratic Party," *New Yorker,* 19 July 1982, 77–94; Dom Bonafede, "Democrats Hope Their Midterm Meeting Will Send a Message of Party Unity," *National Journal,* 19 July 1981, 1098–1100.

20. Dom Bonafede, "Can the DNC Adjust to Being a Minority? Can the RNC Reverse 50 Years of History?" *National Journal,* 5 September 1981, 1586.

21. Federal Elections Commission data on direct contributions to and spending on behalf of congressional candidates for 1982 and 1984.

22. Diane Bryant, ed., *The Democratic National Committee, 1981–1985: Building for the Future* (Washington, D.C.: Democratic National Committee, 1985); "Democratic Party Sponsors First National Training Academy," *Washington Post,* 28 September 1981, 19.

23. Bryant, *Democratic National Committee.*

24. Dom Bonafede, "Strides in Technology Are Changing the Face of Political Campaigning," *National Journal,* 7 April 1984, 660.

25. Bryant, *Democratic National Committee.* See also Dom Bonafede, "Democratic Party Takes Some Strides Down the Long Comeback Trail," *National Journal,* 8 October 1983, 2053–55.

26. The traditional National Finance Council ($5,000 per year), the Business Council ($10,000 for individuals, $15,000 for PACs), the Labor Council (no set fee), the Chief Executives' Council ($5,000 for meetings with Democratic governors), and others are catalogued in the program book for the 1984 Democratic National Convention, *Democrats: Building America's Future* (Washington, D.C.: Democratic National Committee, 1984), 63–66.

27. Xandra Kayden, "The New Professionalism of the Oldest Party," *Public Opinion,* June/July 1985, 43–44; Bonafede, "Can the DNC Adjust." Republicans and independent groups like those of Richard Viguerie and Terry Dolan had reinvested far larger proportions of their income in building their huge lists in the 1970s. See Richard E. Cohen, "Democrats Take a Leaf from GOP Book With Early Campaign Start," *National Journal,* 23 May 1981, 923–25. Evidence of the limits of such fundraising is clear in Tim Hames, "Strengths and Limitations: The Republican National Committee from Bliss to Brock to Barbour," in Green, *Politics, Professionalism, and Power.*

28. Peter Kelley, National Finance Chairman, reports submitted to the Democratic National Committee at its meeting in Washington, D.C., 30 January 1985, DNC Archives.

29. Dom Bonafede, "A Tale of Two Parties," *National Journal,* 24 January 1984, 124.

30. See, for example, Bill Peterson, "Cash Short Dems Cutting Back Staff, Travel," *Washington Post,* 23 July 1982, A2.

31. Diane Grant, "Parties' Schools for Politicians Grooming Troops for Election," *Congressional Quarterly Weekly Report,* 5 May 1984, 1036–37.

32. Interview with former Mondale-Ferraro campaign staff member Michael S. Berman, March 1988, Washington, D.C.

33. These charges resemble the criticism directed toward LBJ's Textbook Party efforts in 1966 (see chapter 5). For an interesting analysis of the "special interest" charge, see Thomas B. Edsall and Mary D. Edsall, *Chain Reaction: The Impact of Race, Rights, and Taxes on American Politics* (New York: Norton, 1991), chap. 10.

34. Manatt did not simply ride off into the sunset. In early 1985 he joined the presidential campaign of Sen. Gary Hart, the presumptive front-runner for the party's 1988 presidential nomination. Before Hart's campaign collapsed in scandal in 1987, Manatt appeared to have been rewarded for his party work with status as a close political adviser to the next Democratic president.

35. Stephen Gettinger, "Democrats Seek a Chairman to Help Redefine the Party," *Congressional Quarterly Weekly Report,* 26 January 1985, 155–56; Ronald Brownstein, "Sanford Entry Tightens DNC Chairman Race," *National Journal,* 19 January 1985, 147, 172.

36. For detail, see transcripts of Kirk's speeches to a meeting of the Democratic National Committee in Washington, D.C., 31 January 1985, DNC Archives.

37. Dom Bonafede, "Saying 'No,'" *National Journal,* 23 February 1988, 441.

38. Transcripts of a meeting of Executive Committee of the Democratic National Committee in Washington, D.C., 17 May 1985, DNC Archives. For a very different interpretation of this episode, see Philip A. Klinkner, *The Losing Parties: Out-Party National Committees, 1956–1993* (New Haven, Conn.: Yale University Press, 1994), 187–88.

39. Ronald Brownstein, "DNC Weighs 'Deregulating' Nomination Rules," *National Journal,* 6 July 1985, 1555, 1574; Rhodes Cook, "Most Democrats Cool to Redoing Party Rules," *Congressional Quarterly Weekly Report,* 24 August 1985, 1687–89.

40. "Kirk Announces $1.2 Million 'Democratic Party Election Force,'" Democratic National Committee press release, 6 March 1986. For commentaries, see Jon Margolis, "Democrats Start to Close Yawning Gap against GOP," *Chicago Tribune,* 6 June 1986; "No Fire in the Democrats," (editorial) *Washington Post National Weekly,* 14 July 1986, 26; and Robin Toner, "Democrats Bring Out New Model," *New York Times,* 24 September 1986, A24.

41. Democratic National Committee press release, 25 June 1985. For press coverage, see Peter Bragdon, "DNC Approves Kirk's Plans to Alter Democrats' Image," *Congressional Quarterly Weekly Report,* 29 June 1985, 1287.

42. E.J. Dionne, "Democrats Sue Republicans on Plan to Challenge Voters," *New York Times,* 8 October 1986, A8; Martin Tolchin, "GOP Agrees to End a Voter Check Program," *New York Times,* 21 October 1986, B20.

43. Quoted in David S. Broder, "Democratic Campaign Pledged," *Washington Post,* 24 November 1986, A10.

44. James R. Dickenson, "2 Parties Say They'll Sponsor Presidential Debates," *Washington Post,* 19 February 1987, A4.

45. James A. Barnes, "The Brokering Game," *National Journal,* 19 March 1988, 724–31; T.R. Reid, "Democrats' Platform is Short, Subtle," *Washington Post,* 28 June 1988, A4.

46. *National Journal,* 20 April 1985, 876.

47. "Kirk Announces $1.2 Million 'Democratic Party Election Force.'" For comment, see David Broder, "Democrat Kirk Deploys His 'Force,'" *Chicago Tribune,* 4 April 1986, 23.

48. "The Force Be With You," *Campaign Hotline,* no. 155, 25 April 1988; Thomas B. Edsall, "Democrats Adopt GOP 'Ground War' Tactics," *Washington Post,* 25 July 1988, A1.

49. "Mapping the Future," *National Journal,* 8 March 1986, 541; Paul Gottlieb, "Democratic 'Summer Camp' for Pols," *National Journal,* 26 July 1986, 1844.

50. Ronald Brownstein, "Party Workers in the Computer Age," *National Journal,* 16 August 1986, 2002–3. On voter registration see Brownstein, "What if Nobody Votes?" *National Journal,* 1 November 1986, 2617.

51. "The Party Circuit," *National Journal,* 2 March 1985, 497. See also Timothy B. Clark, "Democratic Business Council's Top Dog Has One Credo: Money," *National Journal,* 9 March 1985, 545.

52. Thomas B. Edsall, "A Funny Thing Happened to the Party of the Working Class," *Washington Post National Weekly,* 25 August 1986, 13. For a more sensational treatment, see Brooks Jackson, *Honest Graft: Big Money and the American Political Process,* rev. ed. (Washington, D.C.: Farragut, 1990). See chapter 5 for a discussion of the "Greatness Fund."

53. Carol Matlack, "Democrats Love the Money Man," *National Journal, Convention Special,* 23 July 1988, 1913, 1928; and Matlack, "Backdoor Spending," *National Journal,* 8 October 1988, 2516ff.

54. Thomas B. Edsall, "Maybe the Democrats Should Use a Tin Cup," *Washington Post National Weekly Edition,* 3 March 1986, 11.

55. Dom Bonafede, "Kirk at the DNC's Helm," *National Journal,* 22 March 1986, 707.

56. Matlack, "Democrats Love the Money Man"; Matlack, "Backdoor Spending."

57. Quoted in James A. Barnes and Richard E. Cohen, "Unity—Will it Last?" *National Journal,* 30 July 1988, 1960–64.

58. Charles M. Madigan, "Democrats Don't Want Their Leader to Go," *Chicago Tribune,* 21 November 1988, 4.

59. Quoted in David S. Broder, "Ron Brown: Part of the Answer," *Washington Post,* 5 February 1989, D7. See also E.J. Dionne Jr., "First Black Chosen by Democrats to the Head National Committee," *New York Times,* 11 February 1989, 1; Rhodes Cook, "DNC Taps Brown; He Pledges Independence," *Congressional Quarterly Weekly Report,* 11 February 1989, 260.

60. For a survey of the squabble and its resolution, see the sequence of articles by Thomas B. Edsall in the *Washington Post:* "No New Selection Rules, DNC Chairman Vows," 13 April 1989, A22; "Democratic Rules Dispute Simmers," 29 April 1989, A13; "Democrats Avoid Fight on Rules," 18 June 1989, A11.

61. James A. Barnes, "Ron Brown's Fast Start," *National Journal*, 5 May 1989, 1103–7; Robert Kuttner, "Ron Brown's Party Line," *New York Times Magazine*, 3 December 1989.

62. Anthony Corrado, "The Politics of Cohesion: The Role of the National Party Committees in the 1992 Election," in *The State of the Parties: The Changing Role of Contemporary American Parties,* ed. Daniel M. Shea and John C. Green (Lanham, Md.: Rowman & Littlefield, 1994), 67.

63. Frank Sorauf, *Inside Campaign Finance: Myths and Realities* (New Haven, Conn.: Yale University Press, 1992).

64. See, for example, Dan Balz, "Campaign Money Burrows Through a Loophole," *Washington Post National Weekly Edition*, 12–18 February 1990, 15; Charles R. Babcock, "$100,000 Political Donations on the Rise Again," *Washington Post*, 30 September 1991, A1.

65. Brown quoted in Thomas B. Edsall, "Democrats Create 'Geography' for '92," *Washington Post*, 15 June 1991, A4.

66. Thomas B. Edsall and Dan Balz, "DNC Poised to Play Role in Late-Starting Campaign," *Washington Post*, 23 September 1991, A6. See also Corrado, "Politics of Cohesion," 67.

67. Robert Biersack, "Hard Facts and Soft Money: State Party Finance in the 1992 Federal Elections," in Shea and Green, *State of the Parties*. On generic ads, see Associated Press, "Parties' Generic Ads, Paid With Soft Money, Sound Like Nominees'," *International Falls Daily Journal*, 6 October 1992, 12.

68. David Lauter, "Clinton's Strategy of Triage," *Los Angeles Times*, 5 November 1992, A1.

7

The New Politics on Capitol Hill

*Our only interest was in Roll Call One [the party line vote for House
Speaker that opens each Congress]. What happened in the House after
that was somebody else's responsibility.*

— William Sweeney, Executive Director (1977–1981),
Democratic Congressional Campaign Committee

Like the national committees, the parties' Capitol Hill campaign committees went
through dramatic transformations between the 1960s and the 1990s. Their transformation was simultaneously simpler and more complicated. On one hand, continuous
linkage to the House and Senate party caucuses kept their missions more consistent
and narrowly focused. On the other hand, the frequency, number, and diversity of
congressional campaigns required them to develop quickly and improvisationally.
Though the campaign committees usually avoided sharp programmatic shifts, they
gradually but clearly embraced the Accommodationist paradigm.

The Democratic and Republican caucuses in the U.S. House of Representatives
each created campaign committees in the 1860s, predecessors to the current Democratic Congressional Campaign Committee (DCCC) and National Republican Congressional Committee (NRCC).[1] The organizations served a simple purpose: to help
their decentralized parties win elections and take control of the national government.
During the party-centered electoral order of the mid- to late-nineteenth century, this
remained an almost entirely decentralized enterprise, requiring minimal coordination,
and the organizations remained small. Even during the reformed party-centered
order of the 1890s through the 1950s, state and local Democratic and Republican
leaders—and congressional candidates—usually tended to their own local business
with minimal outside help.

The emergence of the campaign-centered electoral order and other develop-ments in the 1950s and 1960s, however, created an unpredictably competitive poli-tics that led some congressional party leaders to seek new initiatives at the national organizations. Each of the organizations—House and Senate, Democratic and Re-publican—followed its own idiosyncratic path. Although the committees' relation-ships with their party caucuses rendered the Reform paradigm irrelevant, each of them experimented with aspects of both the Textbook and Accommodationist par-adigms. By the mid-1980s, however, each of the four had embraced its own variant of campaign-centered politics. Ironically, although they developed services and contributions helpful to congressional campaigns, their activities also fueled the public's cynicism about an insular Washington establishment.

The Old Politics on Capitol Hill

Development of campaign-centered politics in the House of Representatives and the parties' House campaign committees began slowly. On the Democratic side, while political change swirled around the Democratic National Committee and other party activities in the late 1960s, the DCCC remained stuck in something of a time warp, working with campaign strategies and services that had not changed much in twenty years. The committee's chair was Representative Michael Kirwan, a New Dealer from Ohio appointed to the position by Speaker Sam Rayburn (D-Tex.) after the Democrats had lost the House majority in the 1946 midterm election. De-spite complaints from some younger members in the mid-1960s that he was out of touch with modern campaign methods, Kirwan held onto his position by pointing out that the Democrats had lost the House only once during his chairmanship, in the 1952 Eisenhower landslide.[2] In fact, under his leadership the committee had developed a highly successful campaign formula with three elements: a small but reliable funding base; a stable, politically knowledgeable staff; and a consistently useful set of services and contributions to Democratic House candidates and their campaign organizations.

Since 1949 the committee had financed its operations largely on income from annual dinners, jointly sponsored each spring by the DCCC, the Democratic Sena-torial Campaign Committee, and, intermittently, the Democratic National Com-mittee. There is no reliable record of the ticket prices or net income before 1972, but scattered accounts suggest that the dinners consistently raised hundreds of thou-sands of dollars, even in nonelection years.[3] In 1970, Kirwan's final year, the dinner raised about $900,000 and provided nearly $400,000 in DCCC contributions to candidates.[4]

Most of the DCCC's share of this income was spent directly on services and contributions to House candidates, coordinated by a small staff of four to six people. Despite its size, however, the staff was almost certainly the organization's most important asset throughout Kirwan's chairmanship. From 1954 through 1972, Kenneth R. Harding, an attorney with a family history of political campaigning, led the staff. Harding's father, Victor H. (Cap) Harding, had directed the committee from the mid-1930s through 1954 and had a legendary reputation for detailed political knowledge of congressional districts and elections across the country.[5] Shortly after World War II, the senior Harding hired his son and Edmund L. (Ted) Henshaw, protégés who continued Cap Harding's approach for twenty years after his death in 1954. Both maintained a close-knit staff and worked on their inherited agenda.

Their approach was to keep the staff small and offer limited, but continuous, coordinated services to Democratic House members and candidates with whatever money the organization had. Some of the services were simple, as when the committee staff arranged publicity photographs of candidates with the Speaker or other prominent House members, or when they helped newly elected members find housing in Washington. Other, more substantial services drew on the committee's ongoing research. Since the days of Cap Harding, the committee had collected data on district election returns and Republican members' voting records in the House, reaching as far back as the 1920s. Before computers, this data was recorded on cards, then collated and made available to Democratic candidates developing their campaign strategies. Along with this formal data, the staff organization also served as the clearinghouse for whatever informal intelligence information it could gather for members.[6]

The Hardings and Henshaw drew on this pool of formal and informal information and gathered even more when they traveled, talking to state and local party leaders and campaign workers in districts throughout the country. They traveled as widely as money permitted during off-seasons, then targeted their consultations to close elections in marginal districts as November drew near. Based on their knowledge of the districts and Democratic Party organizations, Harding later explained that they tailored their advice to fit the politics of each district rather than trying to enforce a uniform set of national themes or issues:

> It was like Rayburn used to say, and I mean this in the best possible sense, you had to go along to get along. We tried to help the local party and the candidate do what they needed to win in that district.[7]

This particularistic approach was appropriate to the diverse composition of the House Democratic caucus, where members spanned a wide ideological spectrum while remaining united in preserving Democratic control. It also remained valuable during and after the decline of state and local party organizations and was surprisingly congenial to the emergence of the campaign-centered electoral order. By supporting all Democratic candidates and serving the Speaker and the party-in-government, while avoiding Washington-based entanglements with policy and legislation, the campaign committee came to reflect something close to the Accommodationist paradigm's analysis and prescription.

The Hardings and Henshaw worked to teach local party and campaign leaders how to build and run more effective campaigns, showing local people how to be competitive. They based their advice on previous experience in the field, as well as information and intelligence that the DCCC had from Washington. As a result, the approach had both decentralizing and centralizing implications. On one hand, if the DCCC staff did their job well, they could help a district's party or campaign operation become self-sufficient. On the other hand, the Hardings and Henshaw had access to information that people in the district could not obtain, especially before the development of political coverage in the national media. Kenneth Harding noted that local politics was quite parochial when he began working with the committee: "In the early days we were like Columbus coming into some areas, with news of the outside world."[8]

In contrast to these targeted services, much of the committee's money was distributed automatically. During each election cycle, the committee gave all incumbents a flat contribution for use on travel to and from Washington, district political staff, advertising, or whatever they thought their campaign organizations needed. By the 1969–70 election cycle, this allowance reached $1,000 per year for the 244 Democratic House incumbents.[9]

The committee selectively targeted its remaining money to candidates. The staff drew up election profiles for all 435 districts, rating each race A (for sure win), B (close race), or C (sure loss), then presented the list to Kirwan and the Speaker. Based on these profiles and any additional advice from party leaders in the House, the staff would allocate the remaining pool of money to needy Democrats in close races, with first preference going to incumbents up for reelection. Kirwan and the Speaker showed their respect for Harding's political acumen by accepting virtually all of the staff's targeting recommendations. "Kirwan never removed a name from the list. He sometimes added one or two if he had heard something we hadn't."[10]

It is difficult to assess the relative value to candidates of the DCCC's advice and training services versus its cash contributions during the Kirwan era. The cash contributions were not large by current standards, rarely exceeding $2,500 for any single race even in 1970. And it is impossible to assess impacts in individual races, since reporting requirements were lax and committee records from before 1972 have not survived. We know little more than what DCCC staff members recall about the amounts. We know from other sources that the contributions made to Democrats by labor unions (often in cooperation with the DCCC) and to the opposition by Republican campaign committees dwarfed the total amount that the committee spent.[11] And we know from press coverage during the period that many candidates valued the consultation of DCCC staff in close races. Finally, we know that Speakers Sam Rayburn of Texas and John M. McCormack of Massachusetts were satisfied with Kirwan and the Hardings' stewardship of the committee and made no move to change it.

Not everybody was satisfied with the Kirwan/Harding formula, however. As chapters 2 and 3 demonstrate, political campaigns were changing by the late 1960s. Different kinds of Democrats were running for and winning election to the House in unconventional ways. Harding's local party-centered approach meant little to candidates whose campaigns circumvented local party organizations. Freelance political consultants and pollsters, who had first appeared in presidential election politics in the late 1950s, were becoming commonplace in senatorial campaigns and even in some House races by 1970. Television, which Kirwan and Harding tried to play down, was moving to the center of the political universe.[12] Competitive pressures from increasingly well-funded Republican candidates also led some to complain.[13]

Yet the DCCC continued to work from a decades-old formula for several years after Kirwan's death in 1970, even after the retirements of Kenneth Harding and Ted Henshaw. Despite personnel turnover, the staff organization's activities remained largely insulated from turmoil in the committee's leadership and the House Democratic Caucus: over the next seven years and four election cycles, the DCCC worked under no fewer than five chairs, including future House Speaker Thomas P. (Tip) O'Neill of Massachusetts and powerful Ways and Means Committee Chair Wayne Hays of Ohio. In contrast to the swirling institutional environment of the U.S. House of Representatives—the virtual revolution in House structure and procedures, the polarizing politics of civil rights, the Great Society, and Vietnam—the DCCC kept to its routine.

This dynamic stasis poses a paradox: how could such changes in leadership and personnel happen without bringing change to the organization? The answer is that nothing fundamentally challenged the worldview of those who ran the committee. Speakers John McCormack (Mass.) and Carl Albert (Okla.), beneficiaries of the Democrats' perennial House majority, saw no need to change the campaign committee or the services it provided to House candidates. And although DCCC chairs O'Neill and Hays were both ambitious political entrepreneurs with hopes for advancement within the House leadership, they did not need to change the organization in order to receive credit for its help in successful Democratic campaigns. The DCCC expanded and contracted its campaign contributions as money allowed, but the character of the organization and its services remained essentially unchanged.

The DCCC's counterpart, the National Republican Congressional Committee (NRCC), in many ways provides a sharp contrast. Most important, by the late 1960s it faced perennial minority status: though Republicans Dwight Eisenhower and Richard Nixon had won the White House, the party had not come close to majority control of the House of Representatives since 1954. This problem drove two other features that contrasted with the Democrats: the NRCC's evolving strategy and services and its huge cash flow.

The committtee rarely lacked aggressive leadership. Representative Leonard Hall of New York took over the committee in 1947, then established a year-round professional staff and a program so successful that Republicans made him the party's national chair in 1953. A few years later, fellow New Yorker Representative William Miller's success as NRCC chair led Senator Barry Goldwater of Arizona to select Miller as his vice-presidential running mate in 1964. Representative Bob Wilson of California then took over and worked for ten years to keep the committee what he perhaps justifiably called "the most professional political organization in Washington."[14] After the party's devastating 1974 losses in the wake of Watergate, Representative Guy Vander Jagt of Michigan, determined that the organization should lead a Republican resurgence in national campaigns, took over as chair.[15]

Throughout, the NRCC remained a formidable professional organization. It had more than a dozen full-time employees even by the late 1950s, divided about evenly between its Washington-focused public relations wing, its campaign-focused "field service," its finance arm, and its research arm.[16] This scale and organization would grow slowly for nearly twenty years. Like its Democratic counterpart, the committee's first service obligation in the 1950s and 1960s was to Republican members of Congress, and the NRCC offered research and briefings on issues and voting records as well as help with public relations–style press releases and photographs. Unlike the Democrats, the NRCC also had the money to expand these services to include television and radio recording equipment for campaign use. As the Republicans continually failed to gain control of the House, however, the committee could not justify retaining the tried and true formulas that Cap Harding had used. They began to develop more extensive and varied campaign-related services appropriate to the changing world around them. By the early 1970s, in collaboration with the Republican National Committee (RNC) and the National Republican Senatorial Committee (NRSC), the NRCC began to train both candidates and campaign managers in the strategy and tactics of the new politics. Though the committee continued to help incumbents in close races, it also began to shift the focus of its services to challengers and open-seat candidates to gain the seats necessary for a majority.[17]

Even without full reports on party finances for the period, it is clear that the NRCC had a dramatic financial advantage throughout the 1950s and 1960s. In the 1960 election, for example, Herbert Alexander reported that the NRCC outspent the DCCC more than ten to one, $2.23 million to $210,700.[18] The NRCC sustained that advantage well into the 1970s by simultaneously building two fundraising bases. One was made up of small individual donors, who contributed the lion's share of the committee's budget by subscribing to the committee's weekly newsletter or responding to direct-mail appeals (the latter were computerized by the late 1960s). The second fundraising source was large donors, whose money was channeled through the Congressional Boosters Club, established as a joint operation by the NRCC and NRSC in 1965. The NRCC kept the two sources nominally separate, but the Boosters shared offices and coordinated its contributions with the NRCC. While the majority of the NRCC's small-donor money was spent on services and campaign contributions to incumbents, the Boosters Club money was targeted exclusively to challengers and open-seat candidates.[19]

Despite these contrasts, the National Republican Congressional Committee's overall orientation remained similar to that of its Democratic counterpart. The committee remained attentive to the diverse local influences that shaped each House campaign, but these services remained party focused and served the party's House caucus. Though Republican services and assistance were provided largely in Washington, their purpose remained empowering the Republican Party in Congress.

Accommodating Campaign-Centered Politics

A series of political events in the early and mid-1970s shocked the national parties and their congressional campaign committees out of their relative stability.[20] One was the emergence of "stagflation"—simultaneous high unemployment and high inflation—provoked by the guns-and-butter policies of presidents Lyndon Johnson and Richard Nixon and deepened by the oil crises of 1973 and 1978. As first Nixon and then Presidents Gerald Ford and Jimmy Carter struggled unsuccessfully to develop effective economic policy responses, presidential and congressional elections became more unpredictable. Candidates who tapped into public anger about stagflation could compete even against formerly entrenched incumbents, or in districts and states where their party affiliation would otherwise have doomed them.

The second destabilizing event was the wide-ranging Watergate crisis, which began as an investigation of simple political espionage in a Washington hotel suite. As the congressional investigation revealed White House corruption and illegal campaign finance practices during Nixon's 1972 campaign, "Watergate" ultimately became the focus of growing public discontent with American politics in general. The voting public became more fickle, willing to split tickets or stay home on election day, which further increased the unpredictability of national elections.

The third destabilizing event was the passage of the Federal Election Campaign Act (FECA) in 1971 and substantial post-Watergate expansions of the act in 1974 and 1976.[21] This law required public financing of presidential general elections and limited both contributions to and expenditures by national candidates and parties. FECA also required full disclosure of contributions and expenditures and created the Federal Election Commission to monitor enforcement. Though the 1976 *Buckley* v. *Valeo* decision by the U.S. Supreme Court struck down FECA limits on campaign expenditures by candidates, individuals, and interest groups, the new law dramatically changed the rules of American elections. Most important—and unexpected—the law changed the electoral role of interest groups through its provisions allowing a wider variety of political action committees, or PACs. Organized interests, particularly conservative activists and corporations, quickly established their own PACs as new financial and ideological forces in electoral politics. In contrast to the years before the FECA, when the largely pro-Democratic and pro-incumbent labor union PACs had dominated the world of independent campaign finance, by the late 1970s corporate and conservative PACs steered a greater share of campaign money toward both incumbent and challenging Republicans.[22] Their participation sharply increased the amount of money in national campaigns and, in turn, improved Republican competitiveness in House races across the country.

These dramatic events—particularly the disastrous post-Watergate elections of 1974 in which Republicans lost forty-four House seats—combined with the emergence of campaign-centered politics to provoke a period of extraordinary growth and development at the National Republican Congressional Committee. Under Representative Guy Vander Jagt's leadership and influenced by Tennessee Senator Bill Brock's aggressive revitalization of the Republican National Committee, the committee dramatically improved its fundraising, simultaneously expanding and diversifying the services it provided to candidates.[23] From the late 1970s through the 1980s, the NRCC internalized the norms of campaign-centered politics and emerged as one of the most affluent and powerful political organizations in Washington.

The committee's financial performance was astonishing as it raised unprecedented amounts of money from small and large donors alike (see fig. 7.1, p. 127).

The NRCC's direct-mail operation was the principal engine of growth, with its computerized lists and mailings drawing in first millions and then by the early 1980s, tens of millions of dollars.[24] Millions of dollars of contributions channeled through such large-donor vehicles as the Republican Congressional Leadership Council, a successor to the Republican Boosters, supplemented these small-donor funds. The committee received little money from the newly formed conservative and corporate political action committees; instead it encouraged the PACs to contribute directly to like-minded congressional candidates.[25] The flow of money increased most dramatically after Republicans won control of the White House and the U.S. Senate in the 1980 election, and the U.S. House of Representatives stood as the last bastion of Democratic control of the federal government.[26]

This explosion of political money enabled the NRCC to expand both its financial contributions and its services to virtually all Republican congressional candidates. The financial growth is perhaps best conveyed visually. Figure 7.2 (p. 128) shows that committee increased its contributions to campaigns from just over $1 million in 1974 to nearly $9 million in 1984. Figure 7.3 (p. 129) and 7.4 (p. 130) together show that this enabled the committee to sharply increase its *share* of Republican House campaign spending even as total spending on congressional campaigns was increasing, dramatically expanding the committee's influence in individual campaigns nationwide. Though the NRCC continued to steer a substantial proportion of its contributions to incumbents, figure 7.5 (p. 131), which combines NRCC with RNC spending, shows that open-seat candidates and especially challengers also received increasing amounts of money. As memories of Watergate faded and Republicans regained their competitiveness in the late 1970s and early 1980s, these contributions enabled Republicans to genuinely contest control of the House. The NRCC proved incapable of sustaining such fundraising and spending levels, but they established an enormous competitive advantage during the mid-1980s.

The NRCC also enhanced candidate competiveness with a growing array of services and strategic support. Figure 7.5 (p. 131) shows that, as the NRCC's contributions to individual candidates began to reach FECA limits, the committee began to shift toward spending *on behalf of* candidates. That is, the committee purchased services and media time *for* candidates and guided candidates toward what the committee judged to be promising strategies and expert campaign professionals. The Federal Election Commission data for such spending is unfortunately missing for the 1980 election cycle, but the trend of growth from 1978 to 1982 is clear and striking, and dwarfs the comparable Democratic assistance shown in figure 7.6 (p. 132).

The Republican committee expanded its services as well, and by 1982 its more than 120 full-time employees increasingly engaged in recruiting quality candidates,

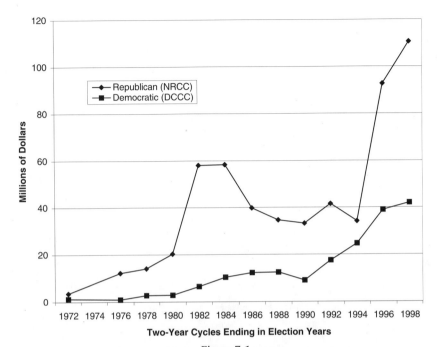

Figure 7.1
Campaign Committee Receipts, 1972–92
(Notes: [a] 1975 data missing; [b] 1992 data includes soft money)
Sources: Herbert Alexander, *Financing the 1972 Election* (Lexington, Mass.:
Lexington Books, 1976); Campaign Finance Monitoring Project, *1972 Federal
Campaign Finance,* vol. 3, *Interest Groups and Political Parties* (Washington, D.C.:
Common Cause, 1974); Campaign Finance Monitoring Project, *1974 Congressional
Campaign Finances,* vol. 5, *Interest Groups and Political Parties* (Washington, D.C.:
Common Cause, 1976); Campaign Finance Monitoring Project, *1976 Federal
Campaign Finances,* vol. 1, *Interest Groups and Political Party Contributions to
Congressional Candidates* (Washington, D.C.: Common Cause, 1977); Federal
Election Commission reports 1978–1982.

training both candidates and party workers, supplying research and issue information to office seekers, and providing polling and technical media assistance.[27]
Though Vander Jagt and the committee insisted that they supported all of the
party's candidates in keeping with the committee's embrace of the Accommodationist paradigm, the NRCC program particularly aided the emergence of the party's
newly confident conservative wing. In 1978 and 1980, conservative Republicans
blamed the Democrats for stagflation and proposed a remedy called Kemp-Roth (its
sponsors were Rep. Jack Kemp of New York and Sen. William Roth of Delaware), a

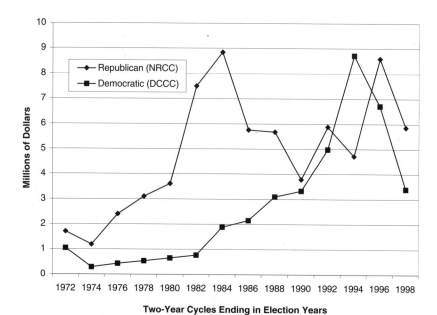

Figure 7.2
Campaign Committee Contributions to General Election Candidates, 1972-92
(Note: Includes in-kind contributions and expenditures in support of candidates)
Sources: See fig. 7.1.

33-percent cut in income tax rates to stimulate the economy and end the recession. In the midst of Proposition 13 politics and a "Sagebrush Rebellion" in the Rocky Mountain West, the party's congressional candidates endorsed the plan and they had Democrats on the run.

Though Democrats had won control of the White House and both houses of Congress, they were anything but comfortable in the majority. Despite the advantages of solid in-party status, the years from 1976 to 1980 proved very difficult for the party-in-government. President Jimmy Carter's honeymoon with Congress ended quickly as he blundered repeatedly in his handling of legislation and policy. Congressional Democrats, for their own part, seemed incapable of pulling together and using their control of the government to pass substantial legislation, and many senior members announced their retirements in frustration.

With these factors and the growing influence of conservative PACs forming an increasingly hostile and unpredictable political environment, the Democratic Congressional Campaign Committee began to complete its movement toward the Accommodationist paradigm. Partially driving this development was the new

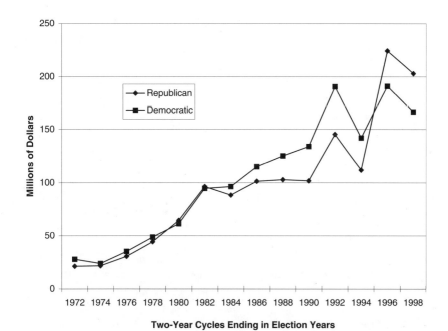

Figure 7.3
Spending by General Election Candidates for House, 1972–96
(Note: Includes party in-kind contributions in candidate spending)
Sources: See fig. 7.1.

Speaker of the House, Tip O'Neill, who had chaired the DCCC in 1972 and had a broader view of the organization's role than the retiring Speaker Carl Albert. O'Neill and his majority leader, Representative Jim Wright (Tex.), faced the continuing factional challenge of Representative Phillip Burton (Calif.) and his allies (Wright defeated Burton in the majority leader election by a single vote), and viewed the campaign committee as one means of building support within the caucus even as it helped to sustain the Democratic majority. O'Neill quickly found a leader for the DCCC willing to pursue just such an agenda: Representative James Corman of California.

Corman wanted to improve fundraising, disperse control over the organization among his colleagues, and generally make the DCCC more effective in providing services to Democratic candidates, but he had no detailed analysis or plans to achieve these goals. For those details, he relied upon the DCCC's new twenty-five-year-old executive director, William Sweeney, who had been with the committee since 1974

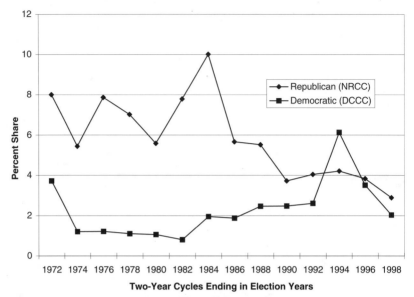

Figure 7.4
House Campaign Committee Contributions as a Share of General Election
Candidates' Campaign Expenditures, 1972–96
(Note: Includes party in-kind expenditures)
Sources: See fig. 7.1.

and had worked his way up to Research Director and also director of the 1976 Democratic Congressional Dinner. In his three years with the committee, Sweeney had earned the respect of Albert and O'Neill, and he had learned the needs of House campaign organizations. He had also developed his own analysis of the campaign-centered electoral order, and a strategy he would pursue with the organization if he got the chance to run it. Sweeney wanted to make the DCCC into a free-standing, campaign-oriented political organization working for the election of House Democrats.[28]

He faced a daunting task: there were 435 races to attend to immediately in 1978, and historical precedent was less than encouraging. Every president since Franklin Roosevelt had lost House seats in midterm elections. Yet Sweeney had a clear view of the organization's relationship to the Speaker and the House Democratic Caucus and saw the committee as a single-purpose service organization dedicated to maximizing the number of Democrats in the House: "Our only interest was in Roll Call One [the party-line vote for House Speaker that opens each Congress]. What happened in the House after that was somebody else's responsibility."[29]

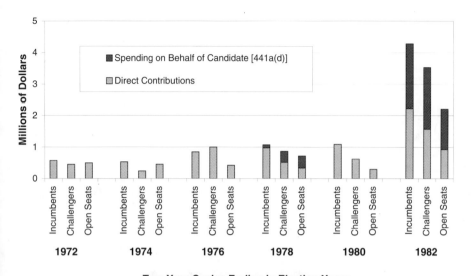

Figure 7.5
Republican National Party Contributions to House Candidates, 1972–82
(Note: 1980 441a(d) data unreported by FEC)
Sources: See fig. 7.1.

Sweeney understood the new politics as well and offered a three-part prescription for the DCCC's success in that environment. First, it had to reestablish itself as a permanent organization with a professional staff. Second, it needed to expand its financial base through more systematic fundraising and direct mail. Finally, it had to serve Democratic candidates by following the lesson Sweeney had learned from Edmund Henshaw, the DCCC director when he started there in 1974: target resources and services carefully to those Democratic candidates who can benefit most.

Sweeney quickly set to work. Though short on staff, he benefited from a move to new offices across the hall from the Democratic Senatorial Campaign Committee (DSCC), with whom the DCCC could join forces and work on tasks they had in common, such as fundraising and political intelligence and strategy making. They already had cooperated on the annual Democratic Congressional Dinner, and Sweeney worked well with DSCC Executive Director William Wester. In October 1977 they established a new Democratic House and Senate Council as a large-donor fundraising and campaign services organization.[30]

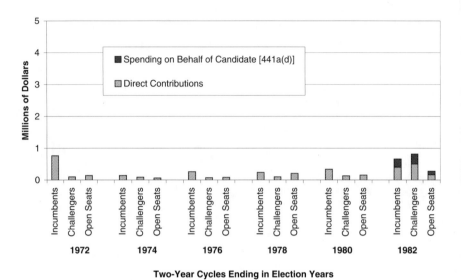

Figure 7.6
Democratic National Party Contributions to House Candidates, 1972–82
(Note: 1980 441a(d) data unreported by FEC)
Sources: See fig. 7.1.

Lee Kling, the outgoing DNC treasurer, and Charles Manatt, a friend of Sweeney's who would later become Democratic national chair, headed the council. Starting with only two staffers, the council grew dramatically through the 1978 and 1980 election cycles. It raised more than a $1 million during the period, about one-fourth from PACs and the remainder in $1,000-plus donations from individuals. This may have seemed small change by Republican standards, but for the Democratic committees it was a major funding source. Although the council transferred less than $20,000 directly to the two campaign committees, it spent the remainder of its funds helping both committees staff and equip a professionalized political operation in their joint offices.[31] The council came to serve as an organizational bridge between the campaign committees, not only raising money but also helping Democratic House and Senate candidates raise money for themselves. It provided training and consultation for candidates setting up fundraising events, made lists of labor and business PAC representatives available to them, and even hired temporary staff for campaign mailings and phone banks.[32] It supplemented the services provided by each of the campaign committees and enabled a broad pattern of cooperation among Democratic congressional candidates across the country.

Another ad hoc tool for cooperation between the Democrats' House and Senate campaign committees was the Democratic Congressional Dinner Committee. That committee had started out as a volunteer operation, staffing DCCC Chair Michael Kirwan's annual St. Patrick's Day fundraising dinner for the committee in the 1950s and 1960s. By 1979, the dinner committee's staff had become stabilized enough to take on other tasks. In June of that year, the staff set up an operation they called Democratic Campaign Services (DCS), a fundraising tool for Democratic House and Senate candidates. In contrast to the House and Senate Council, which was oriented exclusively toward large donors, DCS offered Democratic candidates assistance for all kinds of fundraising. A letter mailed to Democratic senators and representatives in January 1981 lists twenty-six Senate and ninety-five House candidates DCS had served in 1977–78 and notes that DCS helped them raise more than $4.5 million during that election cycle.[33]

In a time of limited resources and staff for the campaign committees, the council and DCS enabled the DCCC and DSCC to cooperate and build economies of scale, allowing the committees to extend their work serving their party's candidates and the party-in-government. The work of these supplemental organizations also helped Sweeney focus on the DCCC's financial base and services. He wanted to create a direct-mail operation, but lacking the large initial investment necessary to build one quickly, Sweeney established a small pay-as-you-go seed program. As that program matured, the committee's finances depended on the annual dinner, which raised more than a million dollars for the first time in 1977, as well as individual fundraising events around the country. The results were encouraging for the committee, which had increased its income from less than $800,000 in 1975–76 to almost $3 million in each of the 1977–78 and 1979–80 cycles. The increases were dwarfed by the successes of the NRCC, but they enabled the DCCC to expand its professional staff gradually and increase the committee's contributions to Democratic House campaigns.

The third major task on Sweeney's agenda was to establish a program of carefully targeted DCCC contributions and services to Democratic congressional candidates. Sweeney and his staff gathered political intelligence from every available source—including the Democratic House leadership, Corman, and the DCCC's executive committee—in evaluating races and making recommendations. But, when it came to money, the executive committee was initially skeptical of narrow targeting. As Democratic members of the House of Representatives, several on the committee argued that the DCCC should continue its practice of giving a flat base contribution to all Democratic incumbents, arguing that the DCCC should serve the interests of the House Democratic Caucus rather than nonincumbent candidates who were not yet members of the caucus.

On the face of it, this dispute over DCCC resources seems rather mundane: members of Congress wanted the money spent on their own campaigns, while members of the DCCC staff wanted to spend it as they saw fit. The implications of the dispute, however, ran deeper. Members of the DCCC's executive committee— what V.O. Key would have called the "party-in-government"—argued from the perspective of the Textbook Party paradigm, which views the party-in-government as the sole focus and master of party organization. If party leaders want to target the money ineffectively, so be it, as long as the party-in-government has its say. Sweeney and Corman, in contrast, argued from the perspective of the Accommodationist paradigm. The commanding purpose of party organizations such as the DCCC, they argued, should be to work as effectively and influentially as possible in the world of campaign-centered politics. Such work required that the decisions of the committee be based on the disinterested professionalism of campaign operatives rather than the immediate expressed interests of party officeholders.

The two paradigms did not directly conflict; they simply led the executive committee and Sweeney to see the world differently. Ultimately, the officeholders and the professionals found common ground not in worldview but in strategy. The representatives wanted to retain (and maximize) majority control of the House and were thus willing to support an Accommodationist strategy of services to any Democratic candidates in competitive races. As long as Speaker O'Neill and DCCC Chair Corman (legitimate leaders of the party-in-government) backed the professionals' targeting strategy, the executive committee would go along. According to Sweeney, they "accepted ninety-five percent of what Marta [David, the DCCC's political director] and I recommended by the time we were finished."[34] The argument over paradigms was set aside for another day.

As a result, the targeting patterns of 1978 were dramatically different from those of 1974 and 1976: 25 percent fewer candidates received DCCC money (so that competitive candidates could each get larger contributions). Figure 7.6 (p. 132) shows also that the overall focus of contributions shifted from incumbents and toward candidates for open seats. (That chart, drawn on the same scale as figure 7.5 [p. 131], also shows how Democratic resources continued to falter in comparison with Republican Party organization money.) Incumbents drew increased attention again in 1980 when Reagan and the Republican ticket sharply challenged Democratic House members. The committee, nevertheless, kept to its new targeting standards.

The committee also increased its nonfinancial contributions to congressional candidates during the 1978 and 1980 cycles. These began in much the same vein as the help Harding and Henshaw had provided Democratic candidates in the late 1960s and early 1970s: bits of information and strategic advice to various campaigns, with occasional field trips and focused intervention into particularly critical races. Gradually, such assistance became more systematic and institutionalized. In cooperation with its Senate counterpart, the committee ran three-day training sessions for candidates and their campaign staffs in seven cities around the country, reaching more than 100 House candidates and their aides. The committee also commissioned forty-two polls for twenty-seven candidates in close races during 1980, and developed detailed voter targeting analyses for thirty-two candidates. In all, the DCCC spent about $35,000 on these "coordinated" expenditures for House candidates in 1980. This was a new enterprise for the Democratic organization, which started far behind its Republican counterpart. The National Republican Congressional Committee had more than a million dollars in coordinated spending in 1980 alone.[35] Despite these advances, the impact of DCCC money and services on Democratic House races in 1978 and 1980 remained fairly limited. The committee provided formal services to fewer than 50 of the 435 House candidates in 1980. And it contributed just over $537,000 to Democratic candidates in 1978, when total spending by House Democrats was more than $46 million (see figs. 7.2 and 7.3, pp. 128 and 129). Figure 7.4 (p. 130) shows that the DCCC contributed just over 1 percent of all campaign spending, compared with the NRCC's more than 6 percent share at $2.7 out of $28.4 million. In 1980 the shares were about the same: the DCCC contributed just under $649,000 of Democrats' total $57.3 million, while the NRCC contributed just over $3.2 million of Republicans' total $59.8 million.

Sweeney's efforts were more important in setting the DCCC on a path of long-term growth and disinterested professionalism within the Accommodationist paradigm. He had established a permanent organization with a small but professional staff, many of whom remained with the committee after 1980. He had laid the foundation for a direct-mail fundraising program that would ultimately become the committee's primary financial source, and he had professionalized the process of targeting and delivering contributions and services to Democratic House candidates. Sweeney's ideas for specific initiatives came from his earlier education by Edward Henshaw, his observations of the Republican opposition, and from his own experience with House campaigns. His work came to be respected in Democratic circles, and his stamp on the organization's long-term agenda was clearly visible in the DCCC's development through the 1980s. As Sweeney put it in 1987, "Corman and I left Coelho with an embryo that grew into the committee you see now."[36]

Joining the Washington Establishment

Though Ronald Reagan's presidential victory and the new Republican Senate majority commanded most headlines in 1980, the election was a disaster for the House

Democrats. Republican congressional candidates and the NRCC had joined with Reagan and the Republican National Committee in campaigning on the national slogan "Vote Republican. For a Change," capitalizing on voter frustration. Twenty-seven Democratic incumbents lost, and Republicans won ten of the eleven contested open seats. The Republicans scored a net gain of thirty-three seats, more than half the nominal margin of Democratic control. When the new Congress convened in January, conservative "boll weevil" Democrats routinely crossed the aisle with impunity, giving the Republicans effective legislative control over budget and tax issues. With another similar landslide in 1982 or 1984, Republicans could win an outright majority in the House and control the full Congress for the first time since 1954.

Speaker Tip O'Neill and the House Democratic leadership made it absolutely clear that they expected party organizations to help congressional Democrats fend off further losses.[37] In the face of these demands, however, the DCCC had been cast adrift. Its chair, Representative Corman, had lost his own House seat by 750 votes in the Reagan landslide. And shortly after the election, DCCC Executive Director William Sweeney, who had guided the organization's modest development over four years, left to become deputy to incoming DNC Chair Charles Manatt. No one remained to lead the organization in developing a response to the Republican threat that Democrats were expecting in 1982.

The only members showing interest in the job were junior: Representatives Floyd Fithian of Indiana, Tom Harkin of Iowa, and Tony Coelho of California. Of the three, Coelho was the most junior (he had been elected in 1978, while Fithian and Harkin entered the House in 1974), but paradoxically he had the longest experience in Congress. He had worked as an aide to Representative B.F. Sisk from 1965 until he succeeded the retiring Sisk in 1978. An ambitious man with career aspirations in the House, Coelho had spent much of his first term improving his already friendly relationships with senior Democrats in the chamber, and when the DCCC position came open in 1981, he asked O'Neill for the appointment. Noting Coelho's proven fundraising skills and knowledge of the House, O'Neill gave him the job.[38]

Coelho entered the chairmanship of the DCCC with the same energy that Representative Lyndon Johnson of Texas had devoted to the organization forty years earlier.[39] He set aside his minimal responsibilities as a junior member of the House Agriculture Committee and worked on his new job virtually full time. His first move was to appoint as executive director Martin Franks, an experienced professional who had worked on the staff of the DSCC and as research director for the 1980 Carter-Mondale Committee. But, as Franks later noted, Coelho "had a grand strategy for getting the job, but no grand strategy for what he was going to do with the committee once he became chair."[40] Working collaboratively with Franks, Coelho spent his first few months as chair developing an organizational agenda.

They worked initially on what Franks called a two-track strategy: first, "buying time" for the organization with "brave talk and lots of public relations work" to keep morale up and make the DCCC appear to be a major actor in congressional elections even though it had little money; and second, building the base for a permanent, strong organization providing party services to House candidates.

Even if he had done nothing else, Coelho's program of "brave talk" was a major success for the organization. He took over the DCCC at a time when Ronald Reagan looked invincible both personally and politically (and even physically, after surviving an assassination attempt in April 1981). Most Democratic House members were afraid to challenge the president for fear of weakening support in their own districts. Coelho, coming from what was then a safe Democratic district in central California, decided that the DCCC could serve as a platform for partisan attacks on the president's policy initiatives. Armed with the files that Martin Franks brought with him from the Carter-Mondale campaign, the DCCC began the counteroffensive by publishing "The Yellow Book," which catalogued Reagan's 1980 campaign promises and would provide the grounding for future "oppo" or opposition research.[41] The organization also started up a "Congressional News Service" that distributed clippings and biting commentary on Republican activities and policies to the Washington press corps.

Coelho continued the effort by pressing successfully for a broadcast "Democratic response" to Reagan's 1982 State of the Union message. Later in the 1981–82 cycle, he took the lead in articulating and hammering away at "the fairness issue," which emphasized the regressiveness of the Republican economic program in the midst of the 1982 recession. "It's Not Fair—It's Republican," was the theme of DCCC television ads during the fall campaign.[42] He and Franks continued to maintain the organization's combative partisan visibility throughout his chairmanship, a dramatic contrast to his predecessors' "inside" approach to the job. Their efforts drew strong support from the House Democratic caucus and particularly from O'Neill, who appreciated the support as he fought to maintain his control of the House under attacks from the conservative coalition.

The second, institutional track of Coelho's initial strategy was to build a permanent, professionalized party service organization. With low expectations from his colleagues, Coelho was initially free to build the DCCC from the ground up. But that was to prove more difficult than "brave talk" because it required far more resources, and Democratic House members expected the organization to provide services even as it gathered those resources. Coelho likened the process to building a house and living in it at the same time. Instead of following Manatt's model of pursuing several programmatic ideas at once, Coelho drew on the ideas of the transitional task force to work on a "project" basis, with one major initiative per campaign cycle. Even as he tried to provide immediate support to his colleagues, he devoted more attention to these projects, investing a substantial portion of the DCCC's resources into long-term development rather than immediate services.

Coelho's 1981–82 project addressed the DCCC's most pressing need: money. Without it, he could not provide the contributions Democratic congressional candidates needed for their campaigns. Like DNC Chair Manatt, Coelho saw direct mail as a safe, stable source of future money for the party organization. But, also like Manatt, Coelho recognized that it would take years to build a large list of consistent donors. So he looked for faster producing sources of cash in large donations from unions, PACs, business leaders, and others. Contributions from these sources at the annual Democratic Congressional Dinner still provided the lion's share of the operating budget, and Coelho wanted more opportunities to get their money. He established a "Speaker's Club," which promised $5,000 individual donors and $15,000 PAC contributors regular opportunities to meet with the Democratic House leadership.[43] And, through such vehicles as the National Democratic Caucus, a group of businessmen and moderate House members, he also began directly and aggressively to approach large political contributors, including traditionally Republican donors. Arguing that the Republican Party was unlikely to win a majority in the House, he told these contributors to "hedge their bets" by maintaining contact with and giving money to Democrats.[44]

He used the money drawn from these large-donor appeals to finance both the DCCC's new campaign activities and its nascent direct-mail program. Because of Sweeney's earlier efforts, the DCCC was the only one of the three Democratic organizations able to run most of its own direct-mail program in-house in 1981–82. This allowed greater DCCC control of the program, but led to a slow start (only 40,000 donors by January 1982, compared with 1.3 million for the National Republican Congressional Committee).[45] The committee sent out more than 1.5 million pieces of mail in 1981–82, and Coelho plowed the $3 million that this raised—more than half of the organization's $6 million income—back into the program.

This reinvestment strategy initially enraged some Democratic House candidates, who wanted the money to be paid out immediately in contributions. Again, the issue at hand was DCCC autonomy: would the committee work within the Textbook Party paradigm and remain constantly accountable to the party-in-government? Or would it work within the Accommodationist paradigm, supporting party candidates but working as an autonomous professional organization, seeking a niche from which it could wield maximum influence in campaigns? Again, partisans of the Accommodationist paradigm won the day, with Speaker O'Neill's support; the DCCC would spend the money as it thought best.

Coelho's approach to direct mail paid off eventually. Like Corman and Sweeney in the 1970s, Coelho and Franks resisted the temptation to simply pay out the cash and instead invested in developing the DCCC's institutional capacity to provide services. The strategy enabled the direct-mail program to grow, and by 1986 it provided $250,000 monthly, almost half of the committee's expanded income.

But the money was not an end in itself. At the same time Coelho, Franks, and their growing political staff worked to develop a campaign-centered program of contributions and direct services for Democratic House candidates. They were open about the source of their ideas and their views of what constituted skilled campaign professionalism. As Franks told an interviewer late in 1981, "I'm trying to do the best damn job of copying the Republicans that I can."[46]

The committee made its general issue research and strategic support available to all Democrats, serving as a national intelligence center and "gossip clearing-house" for campaigns. But, because of the committee's limited resources, Coelho and Franks tried to target the rest of its services more narrowly. They took the risk of initially targeting only 80 selected House candidates (less than 20 percent of the House's 435 seats) for financial support in 1981–82.[47] The strategy pressed DCCC autonomy too far, however, and proved politically untenable in the House Democratic caucus: members were nervous about the Republican challenge and the junior Coelho did not have enough clout to enforce austerity. The members questioned the judgment of the campaign professionals. In consultation with O'Neill and the DCCC's supervisory committee, Coelho and Franks eventually developed a much broader roster that targeted even more candidates than Corman and Sweeney had supported in 1980.

The committee had only modest resources to offer such a large number of Democratic House candidates. In fact, the median direct contribution to the 219 targeted candidates was only about $2,570, less than the DCCC median contribution in 1980. But the committee in 1981–82 began two campaign-centered initiatives that increased the impact that even these modest contributions would have on candidates' campaigns. First, targeted candidates did not receive money until they agreed to cooperate with the committee's efforts at quality control. As Martin Franks later said,

> We want to know intimately about the details of a campaign. We won't give money until a campaign has demonstrated that it is well-run. We use the carrot and stick to assure there is good polling, sufficient fund raising, a budget we can review and a strategy. There is no monopoly on how to run a good campaign . . . but we want to make sure that campaigns are progressing and to see who can make the best use of our money.[48]

So, in providing financial support, the DCCC further established its niche as an expert—meaning disinterested and professional—national partner in the targeted campaigns. Some candidates resisted this intrusion, but most acquiesced in order to get the money.

The second important funding initiative was "coordinated expenditure" or "441a(d) money," named after the provision in the Federal Election Campaign Act that allows for it. When party committees support candidates by offering in-kind services or paying bills for services bought by candidates for their campaigns, instead of directly giving cash, they must report the value of this support as a coordinated expenditure to each recipient campaign. The Republican Party committees had mastered this approach in 1978 as a way of supporting campaigns after they had made the maximum allowable direct contributions.[49] For the first time, the DCCC made about a quarter of its contributions in 1981–82 in the form of coordinated expenditures rather than direct contributions.

When these contributions are taken into account, as they are in figures 7.5 (p. 131) and 7.6 (p. 132), a somewhat different pattern emerges. The DCCC concentrated its efforts on the small number of Democratic candidates for open seats in 1982, and the committee made nearly half its contributions to those candidates in coordinated expenditures. Because open-seat candidates usually have far less experience in running for national office, Coelho and Franks used 441a(d) money to intervene and improve the quality of their campaigns. Even with these funds, however, figure 7.4 (p. 130) demonstrates that the committee was still not a major financial force in the 1982 midterm election. While the NRCC was providing almost 8 percent of the $95 million spent by Republican House candidates, the DCCC's share of the $89 million Democratic House candidates spent was less than 1 percent.

The DCCC developed an array of services in 1981–82 in addition to this financial support for targeted candidates. As Reagan's popularity faltered in the face of a growing national recession, the committee actively recruited candidates for marginal and open seats.[50] The committee also continued and expanded its campaign training program in cooperation with the DNC's headquarters organization. Coelho set up "candidate forums," in which Democrats could meet with a number of PAC representatives and solicit direct contributions.[51] The committee also provided polling support and extensive strategic advice to a few dozen candidates during the cycle. For some novice candidates, committee staff served as a referral service, offering rosters of experienced political professionals who could serve as consultants to Democratic campaigns.

In developing these services, Coelho and Franks achieved a remarkable amount of organizational development in just two years, though they met some resistance along the way. House Democrats who preferred more of a Textbook Party approach to the organization's work continued to challenge Coelho's chairmanship and his initiatives. Many members of the House Democratic caucus objected to limiting DCCC financial contributions to targeted competitive races, rather than allocating money to the entire caucus or targeting it to the most loyal Democrats. Several senior Democrats raised hell over being left off the list in 1982, though their criticism faded when the party picked up twenty-six seats in November.[52]

The second set of challenges to Coelho came from some liberal Democrats and "good government" activists, who objected to his wide-open campaigning and fundraising methods. They called his candidate forums with PACs "cattle shows," and argued that the party should not build its organizations with such "tainted" funds.[53] Coelho challenged the criticisms head on, arguing that PACs had a legitimate role in campaign finance, and insisting that he would continue to solicit their contributions. Embracing the Accommodationist view, he insisted that the DCCC's central mission should be helping Democrats to win elections, not creating litmus tests.

By the time the 1983–84 election cycle got under way, the DCCC had emerged as a more serious player in national campaigns. In just two years, it had grown from a low-profile, nine-person operation to a multimillion-dollar, thirty-person professional organization entrusted with helping Democratic House candidates resist Ronald Reagan's coattails in his reelection campaign. Between the continued large-donor fundraising and the direct-mail revenues, the DCCC would have more than $10 million to use for that purpose (up from $2.8 million in 1980 and $6.5 million in 1982). But, unlike in 1982, expectations were high; Coelho had convinced Democratic House members that they should expect great things from him.

Coelho's "project" for the cycle was institutionalization. Working closely with Charles Manatt at the DNC, he began a series of moves to make the DCCC organization a permanent fixture in Washington. With an array of loans and a major grant from millionaire activist Pamela Harriman, the two committees opened a media center on Capitol Hill, for use by Democratic House candidates. The center provided production facilities for television and radio ads for more than 150 candidates in 1984, at a fraction of retail costs.[54] Coelho also pushed successfully for a permanent Democratic headquarters building on Capitol Hill. The idea had been floating around the party at least since Robert Strauss chaired the Democratic National Committee, but this time the DNC and the Senate Campaign Committee accepted the proposal and the three committees finally broke ground.

The DCCC again expanded the number of Democratic House candidates targeted for contributions in 1983–84, but it also had twice the resources available for such contributions. Fearing that Reagan's looming reelection landslide would lead to broad losses by Democratic House members, incumbents drew a disproportionate share of the organization's resources. But with a larger and more experienced in-house political division, the organization spent more than half of all contributions in the form of coordinated expenditures (see fig. 7.7, p. 142). The division worked closely with individual campaigns, advising them on campaign issues and providing research support on opposition candidates.

Even as Coelho and the Democrats expanded their finances and operations, the Republican developments described earlier continued to dwarf their efforts.[55] In this context, Coelho became much more aggressive in recruiting PAC support for Democratic candidates, telling business PACs (as he later recounted):

> You people are determined to get rid of the Democratic Party. The records show it. I just want you to know we are going to be in the majority of the House for many, many years and I don't think it makes good business sense for you to try to destroy us.[56]

The committee also initiated a monthly newsletter to PACs keeping them up to date on the dynamics of particular races. He also continued bringing together groups of PAC representatives and Democratic candidates, acting as matchmaker between particular interest groups and candidates they might find congenial.

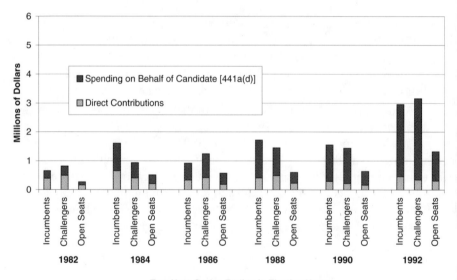

Figure 7.7
Democratic National Party Contributions to House Candidates, 1982–92
Source: Federal Election Commission reports.

With Coelho's heightened public profile, these relationships drew increasing attention and criticism, as some complained that Coelho was using the organization to advance his personal career in the House. Democrats' strong showing in the fall—losing only seventeen seats in the face of Reagan's landslide reelection—silenced many of the critics, since Democrats no longer feared that Republican control of the White House threatened their control of the House of Representatives. That electoral success also created a constituency that changed the dynamic of the debate over the relative merits of a Textbook Party versus an Accommodationist DCCC: the growing number of new members he had helped elect and marginal incumbents who owed their reelection to the committee's support. After a brief rehearsal of the two sides of the debate, Speaker O'Neill and the Democratic caucus endorsed Coelho's program.[57]

Innovations became more incremental during the 1985–86 election cycle, as the DCCC settled into a routine. After moving the committee and the media center into the new headquarters building south of the Capitol, Coelho's project for the cycle was "computerization," getting the organization's records and data and research and communications together into a manageable system that could communicate quickly with Democratic House candidates. The change was expensive and helped the committee deliver services more efficiently, but it did not compare to the revolution Coelho and Franks had brought to the organization in the previous four years. They were consolidating the operation for the long term.

Growth in the organization's revenues slowed down in the off-year cycle, but still enabled the staff to expand from forty to ninety as the cycle went on. It also enabled the committee to expand its contributions to candidates to over $2 million, with the lion's share going to challengers and open-seat candidates. The organization supported fifty-one open-seat candidates, more than ever before, and contributed an average of more than $11,000 to each of their campaigns. Even with these contributions, the committee had enough resources left to develop general support for the Democratic House campaign and services available to every Democratic House candidate.

The real innovation for the DCCC in 1985–86 blended Textbook Party and Accommodationist purposes, as the committee engaged in broader strategic activities Coelho thought would improve election fortunes for all Democratic House candidates. When the National Republican Congressional Committee unveiled plans for a national advertising campaign attacking congressional Democrats in early 1985, Coelho retaliated immediately.[58] He publicly notified President Reagan that the attack would undermine bipartisan consideration of his defense proposals, particularly the controversial MX "Peacekeeper" missile. Reagan eventually instructed the NRCC to cancel the ads.[59] The gambit cost the DCCC virtually no money, but it made reelection easier for several conservative Democratic House incumbents. It also showed the growing capability of professionals at the DCCC party organization

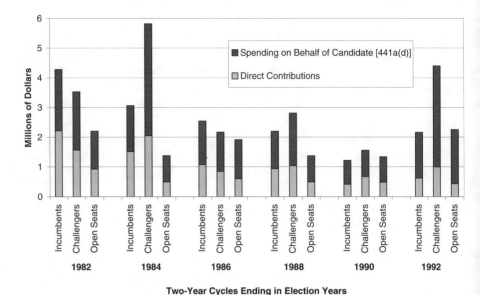

Figure 7.8
Republican National Party Contributions to House Candidates, 1982-92
Source: Federal Election Commission reports.

to collaborate with the House Democratic party-in-government without endangering their own autonomy.

The DCCC also supported the new Democratic national chair, Paul Kirk, as he launched his Election Force and Project 500 programs for state Democratic parties and solicited Coelho's collaboration with the DNC's efforts. (See chapter 6 for detail.) Coelho joined in wholeheartedly, setting up joint training programs and cooperative political strategies in the states.[60] Even though Kirk's program would not serve them directly, members of the House Democratic caucus had a strong interest in it: if the DNC succeeded in winning 500 more state legislative seats in the targeted states, it increased the chances of favorable reapportionment of their own districts after the 1990 census.

By the time the 1986 national election was over, and Democrats had increased their already solid majority in the House by six seats, the Democratic Congressional Campaign Committee had developed into an active and influential participant in national electoral politics, a fixture in the Washington establishment. It had helped Democratic House candidates rebuff the Republican challenge that had seemed overwhelming in Ronald Reagan's landslide elections. In more institutional terms, its new permanent headquarters on Capitol Hill housed a professional staff that had grown from nine to ninety in six years, with a two-year budget that had grown from less than $3 million in 1979–80 to more than $12 million. Its Republican counterpart, the National Congressional Campaign Committee, still outspent the DCCC almost 5 to 1; however, contributions to the Republican committee plummeted in 1986 after years of explosive growth, and Republicans appeared likely to remain in the minority for years to come (see fig. 7.1, p. 127) Some claimed that the House Democrats' stubborn control of the House—along with the party's 1986 success in regaining majority control of the U.S. Senate—had finally broken the confidence of Republican contributors and activists. Coelho and the DCCC were cited by many congressional Democrats as central to their party's success in preserving its House majority.

Coelho had helped complete the transition begun by Corman and Sweeney nearly a decade before, embracing the Accommodationist paradigm and professional, campaign-centered politics, and building a broad supportive coalition of support within the House. A *New York Times* reporter wrote that "he is widely credited with transforming a dormant organization into a sophisticated, computer-oriented center for fundraising and strategic planning."[61] That assessment overlooked the work of Bill Sweeney that Coelho built on, but it became the conventional wisdom. Some critics remained, but when Tip O'Neill retired in December, and Representative Jim Wright moved into the Speaker's chair, the Democratic caucus rewarded Coelho by electing him House Democratic Whip.[62]

The Bloom Comes Off the Rose

The period after 1986 began as one of continuity and consolidation for House Democrats. Representative Beryl Anthony of Arkansas, a moderate Democrat and former DCCC deputy chair comfortable with the big-money and ideologically neutral work of Coelho, easily won election to succeed Coelho as chair. The only real controversy was whether a single member would be allowed to take control of such a powerful and successful organization. Anthony quelled those fears by establishing four regional DCCC chairs and promising to collaborate with them as he continued his predecessor's fundraising and service work.[63] With control of the House apparently secure, donations to the DCCC leveled off somewhat in 1988, but the committee continued to expand its direct and in-kind contributions to Democratic House candidates. The future looked almost dull, and Representative Anthony looked forward to a secure and successful term. His biggest problem seemed to be finding ways to spend greater amounts of DCCC money on highly competitive races.[64]

Republicans at the NRCC entered a period of reorientation and slow rebuilding after the 1986 election. The committee's fundraising had fallen off badly, and the committee encountered increasing difficulty recruiting strong candidates as House Republicans became tainted as a "permanent minority." As Ronald Reagan's presidency waned, Republicans increasingly disagreed about the wisdom of the NRCC's frequent advice to join together as a Textbook Party and "nationalize" individual House races into referenda on the party's conservative agenda. Though Representative Guy Vander Jagt remained as chair, he responded to the criticism by hiring Accommodationist political consultant Ed Rollins as the committee's executive director. Rollins trimmed national office staff services, and shifted more of the committee's money into contributions and spending on campaigns. When the party fared no better in 1988 and 1990 and the debate continued, he quit in disgust.[65]

This relative continuity and consolidation masked deeper problems, however. Internally, the competitive tension that had fed both the DCCC and the NRCC's growth and development throughout the 1980s was lost, and in 1988 the organizations were eclipsed by the first open presidential election (one in which an incumbent was not running) since 1968. The DCCC's professional staff found it more and more difficult to influence the definition of House campaigns, and thus became strategically less useful to Democratic candidates. Though the Democrats easily retained control of the House in 1988—gaining five seats even as George Bush won the White House—some Democratic members grew uneasy as well.

More important, the campaign committees' success provoked a backlash. As both Democratic and Republican House incumbents raised and spent increasing amounts of money and won reelection at increasing rates, the public expressed growing disgust with big-money professional politics, and began to complain that permanent incumbency made House members unresponsive and unaccountable to voters. The public was perhaps not surprised when Democratic majorities in the House and the Senate established staunch opposition to the lame-duck President Reagan in 1987 and 1988, but when Democrats expressed open disdain for newly elected Republican President George Bush's legislative agenda in 1989, journalists and scholars began to fret publicly about "divided government."[66]

These problems burst open early in 1989, as Representative Beryl Anthony began his second term as DCCC chair. Republican Whip Newt Gingrich of Georgia, who had gained public attention in 1988 by accusing House Democrats of arrogance and ethical lapses, began a full-scale assault on the Democratic leadership early in 1989. In response to Gingrich's accusations, the House Ethics Committee launched probes of Speaker Jim Wright for money laundering on a book deal and Democratic Whip Tony Coelho for shady investments on junk bonds.[67] The charges ultimately led to Coelho and Wright's resignations, and contributions to the DCCC faltered. As the conventional wisdom about Coelho soured, Anthony revealed that he had inherited nearly a million dollars in debt upon taking the DCCC chair in 1987 and that the debt had grown to almost $1.8 million. He promised that the DCCC would help to run an effective Democratic campaign in the fall, and then announced that he would leave the committee's chair after the coming election.[68]

Things would only get worse for Anthony. Though he kept to his word in sustaining the DCCC in 1990, even helping Democrats gain ten seats, he left the committee nearly $3 million in debt.[69] He returned home to Arkansas the following year to discover that he faced a strong challenge for renomination to his own House seat. Foreshadowing what would become a familiar theme in 1994, his race had become a small referendum on the Washington establishment, and Anthony was doomed: he lost a primary runoff in June of 1992 and left the House. In a strikingly similar primary two months later, Anthony's Republican counterpart Representative Guy Vander Jagt of Michigan, longtime chair of the National Republican Congressional Committee, lost his own nomination.[70]

Things would get worse for the House Democrats as well. A scandal broke out early in 1991 over the House's internal bank and members' common practice of writing overdraft checks.[71] A similar scandal arose concerning the House post office and allegations of drug dealing on Capitol Hill. The public was outraged, and "career politician" became a damning epithet.[72] Partisan differences over the Gulf War further poisoned relations in the chamber, and members left in droves. Some did so voluntarily, as sixty-six members—a post–World War II record—simply retired. Others did so under duress, as a record nineteen incumbents lost primary battles. More than two dozen more lost their races in the fall, and more than one quarter of the House membership turned over to newcomers in November 1992.[73]

Despite this public outrage, the DCCC and NRCC worked through the 1992 cycle almost unscathed. When Representative Vic Fazio of California took over as DSCC chair in 1991, no one doubted that he would embrace the Accommodationist paradigm and carry on what Bill Sweeney and Tony Coelho had begun. Similarly, few Republicans expected that Representative Bill Paxon would dramatically change the NRCC's operations when he took over in 1992. In the midst of the House exodus, financial contributions to candidates and both committees increased dramatically (see figs. 7.1 and 7.3, pp. 127 and 129]). The committees collaborated effectively with their respective national committees throughout the 1992 cycle.[74] When the election was over, Democrats had lost ten seats in the House and entered 1993 as partners in the first unified Democrat-controlled government since 1980.

Ironically, the 1992 election confirmed that the Democratic Congressional Campaign Committee's transition was complete, as the NRCC's had been ten years earlier. The DCCC's leaders had followed their Republican counterparts in embracing the Accommodationist paradigm and had gradually convinced Democrats in the House that the DCCC could play an influential role in national elections just as the NRCC did. The committees and their professional staffs had become full-fledged partners in the Washington establishment, for better and for worse. And though they could not insulate themselves entirely from the turbulent politics of the party-in-government, they had gained a large degree of autonomy and stability. The public clearly disliked the professionalized system of representation, deliberation, and choice the committees served, but the system worked, and both Democrats and Republicans in Congress intended to keep it.

NOTES

1. Hugh Bone, *Party Committees and National Politics* (Seattle: University of Washington Press, 1958), chap. 5.

2. Neal Gregory, "New Shriver Group Bolsters Democrats' Congressional Campaigns," *National Journal*, 12 September 1970, 1993.

3. Herbert Alexander, *Financing the 1960 Election* (Princeton, N.J.: Citizens' Research Foundation, 1962), 80–81; and Alexander, *Financing the 1964 Election*, (Princeton, N.J.: Citizens' Research Foundation, 1966), 114–15.

4. Gregory, "New Shriver Group," 1994.

5. Bone, *Party Committees and National Politics*, 141.

6. Kenneth Harding, telephone interview by author, June 1988, and Edmund Henshaw's wife, Barbara, telephone interview by author, May 1988.

7. Harding, interview.

8. Harding, interview.

9. William Chapman, "Democrats Advance Fund Aid," *Washington Post*, 18 September 1969; and Andrew J. Glass, "Low Cost TV and Radio Facilities Prove Popular in Election Year," *National Journal*, 11 July 1970, 1484.

10. Harding, interview.

11. See, for example, Alexander, *Financing the 1960 Election*, chaps. 5–7.

12. For contemporary discussions of the rise of this new politics in congressional races, see Dwight Jensen et al., "Professional Managers, Consultants Play Major Roles in 1970 Political Races," *National Journal*, 26 September 1970, 2077–87; and Robert Agranoff, "The New Style of Campaigning: The Decline of Party and the Rise of Candidate-Centered Technology," reprinted in *Parties and Elections in an Anti-Party Age*, ed. Jeff Fishel (Bloomington: Indiana University Press, 1978, 230–40.

13. Rep. Lionel Van Deerlin, the only Democrat serving in Congress from San Diego in 1969, went as far as to read a brochure of the NRCC's services into the *Congressional Record*. He opened his readings by explaining "Mr. Speaker, in the manner of a hungry waif pressing his nose against the delicatessen window, I herewith submit the [Republican] campaign committee's bill of fare for the Record." *Congressional Record*, 26 February 1969, 4522.

14. Quoted in Andrew J. Glass, "National Republican Congressional Committee," in *Political Brokers: Money, Organizations, Power and People*, ed. Judith G. Smith (New York: Liveright, 1972), 172.

15. Paul S. Herrnson and David Menefee-Libey, "The Dynamics of Party Organizational Development," *Midsouth Political Science Journal* 11 (Winter 1990): 13–14.

16. Bone, *Party Committees and National Politics*, chap. 5.

17. Glass, "National Republican Congressional Committee," 178–79.

18. Alexander, *Financing the 1960 Election*, 32–33.

19. Glass, "National Republican Congressional Committee," 176–83.

20. The following account draws from Godfrey Hodgson, *America in Our Time: From World War II to Nixon* (New York: Random House, 1976); and Peter N. Carroll, *It Seemed Like Nothing Happened: America in the 1970s* (New Brunswick, N.J.: Rutgers University Press, 1990).

21. Frank J. Sorauf, *Money in American Elections* (Glenview, Ill.: Scott Foresman, 1988), chap. 2.

22. Richard E. Cohen, "Congressional Democrats Beware—Here Come the Corporate PACs," *National Journal*, 9 August 1980, 1304–11. On the development of PACs in the 1970s, see Michael J. Malbin, ed., *Money and Politics in the United States* (Chatham, N.J.: Chatham House, 1984); the special issue on political action committees, *Arizona Law Review* 22, no.2 (1980); and Larry Sabato, *PAC Power: Inside the World of Political Action Committees* (New York: Norton, 1984).

23. On the influence of Sen. Bill Brock (Tenn.) as Republican national chairman, see David Adamany, "Political Parties in the 1980s," in Malbin, *Money and Politics*; Herrnson and Menefee-Libey, "Dynamics of Party Organizational Development"; and Philip Klinkner, "A Comparison of Out-Party Leaders: Ray Bliss and Bill Brock," in *Politics, Professionalism, and Power: Modern Party Organization and the Legacy of Ray C. Bliss*, ed. John C. Green (Lanham, Md.: University Press of America, 1994).

24. Steven Stockmeyer, "Commentaries," in *Parties, Interest Groups, and Campaign Finance Laws*, ed. Michael J. Malbin (Washington, D.C.: American Enterprise Institute, 1980), 309–14.

25. Richard E. Cohen, "Running Scared in Congress—The Parties Go Head-to-Head Over Money," *National Journal*, 8 April 1978, 557–61; Timothy B. Clark, "The RNC Prospers, the DNC Struggles as They Face the 1980 Elections," *National Journal*, 27 September 1980, 1617–21; Adamany, "Political Parties in the 1980s."

26. Jack W. Germond and Jules Witcover, "GOP Puts 'Venture Capital' into House Races," *National Journal*, 20 July 1985, 1697.

27. Adamany, "Political Parties in the 1980s"; Paul S. Herrnson, *Party Campaigning in the 1980s* (Cambridge, Mass.: Harvard University Press, 1988); Herrnson and Menefee-Libey, "Dynamics of Party Organizational Development."

28. "I have to tell you," Corman said in an interview with the author. "All of the initiatives were Sweeney's. If I am to take any credit, it would be that I was smart enough to see a talented person and let him do the job." This account is based largely on separate interviews with Rep. James Corman and William Sweeney in Washington, D.C., June and August 1987.

29. Sweeney, interview.

30. Democratic House and Senate Council memorandum, "Democratic House and Senate Council: Past Present and Future," undated (1981?), DCCC Archives.

31. *FEC Reports on Financial Activity, 1977–1978, Final Reports on Party and Non-Party Political Committees,* vol. 1, *Summary Tables* (Washington, D.C.: Federal Election Commission, April 1980), 35–40; and *FEC Reports on Financial Activity, 1979–1980, Final Reports on Party and Non-Party Political Committees,* vol.1, *Summary Tables* (Washington, D.C.: Federal Election Commission, January 1982), 1–6.

32. Internal memoranda of the Democratic House and Senate Council, DCCC Archives.

33. "Democratic Campaign Services," unsigned letter on Democratic Congressional Dinner Committee letterhead, January 1981, DCCC Archives.

34. Sweeney, interview.

35. Adamany, "Political Parties in the 1980s."

36. Sweeney, interview.

37. O'Neill complained to the DNC that "our opposition is at the cutting edge of a technological revolution taking place in American politics that has given Republican candidates a definite advantage over our Democrats who seek public office." Transcript of the meeting of the Democratic National Committee, 26 February 1981, Washington, D.C., DNC Archives.

38. Interviews with Martin Franks, April 1987, Washington, D.C. See also Gregg Easterbrook, "The Business of Politics," *Atlantic Monthly,* October 1986, 33–35.

39. For LBJ's use of the committee as a conduit for Texas oil money in the 1940 election, see Robert Caro, *The Years of Lyndon Johnson: The Path to Power* (New York: Knopf, 1982), chaps. 31–33.

40. Franks, interview.

41. DCCC press release, 19 May 1981, DCCC Archives. The book proved so popular that Franks updated and republished it for each of the next three election cycles.

42. For press coverage, see Richard E. Cohen, "The Best Offense," *National Journal*, 22 March 1986, 738.

43. Richard E. Cohen, "Democrats Take a Leaf from GOP Book with Early Campaign Financing Start," *National Journal*, 23 May 1981, 920–25.

44. On the National Democratic Caucus, see *National Journal*, 23 July 1983, 1612; and 30 July 1983, 1564. For Coelho's "hedge your bets" pitch, see Richard E. Cohen, "The Object is Control," *National Journal*, 29 October 1983, 2262.

45. Coelho report to a meeting of the Democratic Congressional'Campaign Committee, 15 September 1981, Washington, D.C., DCCC Archives.

46. Dom Bonafede, "The One Bright Spot for the Democrats: The House Elections in 1982," *National Journal*, 31 October 1981, 1935.

47. Notes from a meeting of the Democratic Congressional Campaign Committee, 15 September 1981, Washington, D.C., DCCC Archives.

48. Quoted in Richard E. Cohen, "Party Help," *National Journal*, 16 August 1986, 2001.

49. There are limits on 441a(d) contributions as well, but they are much higher than for direct contributions. For discussion from that period, see Malbin, *Money and Politics*.

50. Richard E. Cohen, "You Say You Want to Run For Congress? Step Right Up, 1982 May Be Your Year," *National Journal*, 3 October 1981, 1752–56. Adam Clymer, "Those Who Recruit Candidates Say that Parties are Running About Even," *New York Times*, 8 March 1982, B4.

51. Rob Gurwitt, "Democratic Campaign Panel: New Strategy and New Friends," *Congressional Quarterly Weekly Report*, 2 July 1983, 1347.

52. Easterbrook, "Business of Politics," 32; Gurwitt, "Democratic Campaign Panel," 1346.

53. The "cattle show" complaint is quoted in Gurwitt, "Democratic Campaign Panel," 1347.

54. Coelho to Democratic House colleagues, 20 June 1983, DCCC Archives. See also Dom Bonafede, "Strides in Technology Are Changing the Face of Political Campaigning," *National Journal*, 7 April 1984, 657–61; and Easterbrook, "Business of Politics," 32.

55. For example, with a nearly $60 million budget, the NRCC actively recruited strong candidates and then "maxed out"— contributed the maximum allowed under law—to all competitive Republican candidates during the 1984 election cycle. See Jack W. Germond and Jules Witcover, "GOP Puts 'Venture Capital' into House Races," *National Journal*, 20 July 1985, 1697.

56. Quoted in Thomas B. Edsall, "If You've Got the Dime, Coelho's Got the Ear," *Washington Post National Weekly*, 23 December 1985, 14.

57. "One Step Ahead," *National Journal*, 23 February 1985, 407; "Democratic Reorganization," *National Journal*, 29 June 1985, 1542.

58. Dan Balz, "GOP Plans Early Blitz of Democratic Lawmakers," *Washington Post*, 28 February 1985.

59. Carl Leubsdorf, "Reagan Tells Republicans to Drop Plans for Ads Targeting Democrats," *Dallas Morning News*, 26 March 1985.

60. DCCC press release, 18 June 1986, DCCC Archives.

61. Linda Greenhouse, "Anthony L. Coelho," *New York Times*, 9 December 1986, B17.

62. The strongest objections came from members who worried about conflicts of interest between the predominantly liberal party delegation and its campaign committee if the latter raised its money from large, conservative donors. Their arguments were publicized by Robert Kuttner, "Ass Backward: A Bestiary of Democratic Money Men," *New Republic*, 22 April 1985, 18–23; David Broder, "Less than the Sum of Its Parts," *Chicago Tribune*, 9 June 1986, 13; and Easterbrook, "Business of Politics," 37. On Coelho's election as Whip, see Jacqueline Calmes, "Coelho Harvests the Fruits of His Labors in the Vineyard of House Democratic Politics," *Congressional Quarterly Weekly Report*, 13 December 1986, 3068–69.

63. "Arkansas Rep. Anthony Succeeds Coelho as Chief Democratic Fund-Raiser," *Washington Post*, 30 January 1987, A4; "Rep. Anthony Names Regional Chairmen for DCCC," *Congressional Quarterly Weekly Report*, 31 January 1987, 214–15.

64. Bob Benenson, "Once a Key Force in Elections, House is Now Just a Sideshow," *Congressional Quarterly Weekly Report*, 3 October 1987, 2379–82. On the emergence of soft money spending as a way of circumventing FECA limits, see "'Soft' Money is Closing the Gap for Democrats," *National Journal*, 9 July 1988, 1821.

65. William F. Connelly Jr. and John J. Pitney Jr., *Congress' Permanent Minority? Republicans in the U.S. House* (Lanham, Md.: Rowman & Littlefield, 1994), 34–36.

66. For discussion, see David Menefee-Libey, "Divided Government as Scapegoat," and other essays in a symposium on "Divided Government and the Politics of Constitutional Reform," in *PS: Political Science and Politics* 24 (December 1991): 634–57.

67. Richard E. Cohen, "Congressional Focus: 'Ethical Mess,'" *National Journal*, 11 July 1987, 1806; Connelly and Pitney, *Congress' Permanent Minority?*

68. Dan Balz and Maralee Schwartz, "DCCC Chief Blames Coelho for Debt, Won't Run Again," *Washington Post*, 21 June 1989, A8; Tom Kenworthy, "Democrats' Debt Tied to Hill's Image," *Washington Post*, 22 June 1989, A6.

69. James A. Barnes, "Four for the Money," *National Journal*, 16 March 1991, 636–40.

70. Associated Press, "Democrat Loses Arkansas Runoff," *New York Times*, 10 June 1992, A20; Associated Press, "'Ferocious Tide' Ends the Career of Vander Jagt," *New York Times*, 6 August 1992, A20.

71. Adam Clymer, "The House Bank: Trying to Halt a Scandal," *New York Times*, 17 April 1992, A1.

72. Adam Clymer, "After Election Day, a Revolution with a Mixed Message for Congress," *New York Times*, 28 September 1992, A10.

73. Marjorie Randon Hershey, "The Congressional Elections," in *The Election of 1992*, ed. Gerald M. Pomper (Chatham, N.J.: Chatham House, 1993).

74. Paul S. Herrnson, *Congressional Elections: Campaigning at Home and in Washington* (Washington, D.C: CQ Press, 1995), chap. 4.

8

Campaigns and Parties in the Senate

An important difference between Republican and Democratic Party leaders is that Democrats are relatively undisturbed by—and often seem to thrive on—the ad hocness of politics. Republicans embrace order; they try to impress it on the anarchy of politics. Democrats resist order or accept it only as a last resort.

—Cornelius Cotter and Bernard Hennessy, 1964

Like their counterparts in the House of Representatives, Democratic and Republican Party leaders in the Senate have shepherded their campaign committees through dramatic transformations since World War II. As in the House, close linkages to their respective party caucuses have kept the Senate committees focused on the simple goal of majority status and control of the chamber. Each committee's practical mission is to help incumbents win reelection and to help challengers and open-seat candidates in whatever way they can. After the campaign-centered electoral order unfolded in the 1950s and 1960s, Senate Democrats and Republicans gradually embraced the Accommodationist paradigm.

Despite these similarities, the Senate committees differ from their House counterparts in several ways. They are younger, for one thing: the Democratic Senatorial Campaign Committee (DSCC) was created shortly after popular election of senators was amended into the Constitution in 1913, and the Republicans responded by creating the National Republican Senatorial Committee (NRSC).[1] Senate campaigns also work on a different scale: senators represent entire states and thus must appeal to larger and more diverse constituencies. As a result, Senate candidates more quickly recognized the emergence of the campaign-centered electoral order, and both Democratic and Republican Senate leaders pressed the campaign committees to adapt and professionalize. Such adaptation was easier than for the House because Senate elections are fewer and less frequent.

Robert Kennedy's 1964 campaign for a U.S. Senate seat from New York offers a familiar illustration of what Senate campaign committees have worked with. Kennedy, a carpetbagger challenging popular Republican incumbent Senator Kenneth Keating, found that the Kennedy name and a traditional local party–based campaign would not be enough to win. He turned to what aide and historian Arthur Schlesinger called "the Madison Avenue magicians" to mount a mid-October advertising blitz that would put him over the top.[2] Kennedy's national prominence may have been unusual, but his campaign typified the new politics in many ways. The candidate had essentially nominated himself and hired professionals to plan, finance, and coordinate his campaign. He welcomed the help of local party organizations and partisan groups but relied on polls for information on how he was doing with important constituencies. Though he ran as a partisan Democrat, Kennedy showed little interest in the concerns of city and county party leaders across New York.

In working with such campaigns, the DSCC and the NRSC entered the new politics era as small, informal organizations. According to Hugh Bone's early research on party committees, the DSCC, for example, has been a year-round operation only since 1952, when the Republicans briefly won majority control of the Senate. There are few detailed records of either committee prior to 1968, but available accounts suggest that they were viewed as generally adequate organizations with well-established traditions offering modest services to a large proportion of campaigns.[3] By 1967, however, leaders on the Democratic side saw signs of danger and began to press for further organizational development and adaptation to campaign-centered politics. Party leaders running the DSCC quickly embraced the Accommodationist paradigm, but it would take nearly twenty years for them to develop the organization's professional and financial capacity to strongly affect Senate campaigns. The NRSC developed somewhat earlier, but not nearly at the pace of its counterpart in the U.S. House.

Adapting to the Campaign-Centered Electoral Order

The 1966 midterm election, which had proven disastrous for President Lyndon Johnson and Democrats in the House, had a much smaller immediate impact in the Senate, where the Democrats lost only three seats. Still, Senate Majority Leader Mike Mansfield (D-Mont.) watched as President Johnson's popularity declined, and Democrats worried about more serious challenges from a Richard Nixon–led ticket in 1968. The DNC's 1966 "Greatness Fund" controversy lingered and threatened to bring greater scrutiny of both parties' financial and campaign practices, which David Broder charitably described as "informal."[4] Mansfield decided in early 1967 to initiate changes in the campaign committee as one way of improving the party's prospects. He sought an analysis and prescription that could insulate his fellow Democrats from the unpredictability that came with campaign-centered politics. He appointed Senator Edmund Muskie of Maine to chair the committee and start the ball rolling. (Unlike their House counterparts, the chairmanships of the DSCC and the NRSC traditionally rotate every two years.[5])

Muskie hired Nordy Hoffman, longtime legislative director for the United Steelworkers of America, as DSCC executive director at the end of 1967. Muskie gave Hoffman the general task of formalizing and modernizing the committee's operations and services.[6] Hoffman, in turn, drew on decades of experience in Washington and developed a strategy appropriate both to the campaign-centered electoral order and the idiosyncrasies of the Senate. For the next nine years, Hoffman managed the committee's staff organization out of a three-room suite in the Old Senate Office Building, putting his own stamp on the committee's work to the point that by 1970 a *National Journal* reporter described the DSCC as "essentially Hoffman's one-man operation."[7]

In his first few months as executive director, Nordy Hoffman established a formula that he followed throughout his tenure. In the only Textbook Party aspect of this formula, he maintained frequent contact with the Senate party leadership, responded to their direction, and coordinated his advice to coincide with the caucus's legislative activities. The rest of his work embodied the Accommodationist paradigm: a formalized professional staff organization; a small, mostly young staff; and particularized services appropriate to the changing needs of Democratic Senate campaigns.

Hoffman was virtually alone when he took over the organization in 1968, bringing only his personal secretary with him from the steelworkers's union. In staffing the committee, he quickly established a practice of hiring what he called "a bunch of young kids": ambitious and energetic men and women in their twenties with college or legal education, some of whom were still in school in the Washington area.[8] Although he kept the staff small (never more than six), these young people gave Hoffman two advantages over a larger or more experienced operation. They worked with the energy of youth and, because they had no long-standing prejudices about how the DSCC should work, they helped him adapt the organization to the dramatic changes occurring in Senate campaign politics during the late 1960s and 1970s. In keeping with the campaign-centered order's newly emerging patterns of campaign professionalism, they learned their trade as generic national partisans rather than as state or local party operatives. Campaign-centered politics and the Accommodationist paradigm were all these "kids" had ever known.

Hoffman immediately set them to work providing year-round services to incumbent senators up for reelection, in much the same way Harding and Henshaw did at the House campaign committee. Services to campaigns included early campaign visits and fundraising help from popular senators not up for reelection, a $10,000 political allowance for all incumbent candidates, and assistance with radio and television production.[9] At the beginning there was little difference between DSCC and DCCC services to Democratic campaigns: both focused on political intelligence, advice and field training for candidates, with special attention to incumbents. Most of these practices were apparently continuations of DSCC services from long before Hoffman arrived, and they continued to draw strong support from Mansfield and the Senate leadership. Hoffman's primary initial contribution was in professionalizing their delivery.

By the 1970 election cycle, however, Hoffman stepped beyond his initial formula and gradually changed the committee's services to candidates.[10] In response to the increasing number of senatorial candidates hiring independent political consultants to coordinate their campaigns, Hoffman started a biennial "dog and pony show" in Washington early in the election cycle. He and his staff gathered Democratic consultants to put on a kind of trade fair and invited the party's senators to "see how things were done now, to see how things had changed since the last time they ran," and to assess the advantages of hiring one or another of the exhibitors. Hoffman knew that, unlike members of the House, who run every two years and must remain consistently attentive to the changing world of campaigns and elections, most senators he served had not campaigned in nearly five years and did not understand how different that world had become.

In contrast to the DCCC under O'Neill and Harding—who resisted collaboration with the emerging consulting profession they feared would undermine the party's electoral role—Hoffman initiated this show with the explicit approval of Majority Leader Mansfield and the new DSCC chair, Senator Daniel Inouye of Hawaii. He also commissioned consultants to conduct several broad polls for the DSCC to help target and tailor the committee's efforts.[11] In effect, Hoffman recognized, understood, and accepted the new electoral order. In developing his own version of the Accommodationist paradigm, he acknowledged that campaigns, rather than parties, were the central focus of the new electoral order. He thus directed the committee's attention outward, toward campaigns, more than inward, toward the whims of the party caucus. Hoffman insisted that party organizations could carve out an important niche as skilled and influential professionals in this new electoral order, and he worked to that end.

Hoffman also responded in part to competitive pressures. Though the National Republican Senatorial Committee remained a fairly small operation working in the shadow of the NRCC, its weakness was little comfort to the DSCC in 1970. President Richard Nixon thought Republicans had an opportunity to win control of the Senate that year, and he had worked to recruit strong candidates and steer contributions to their campaigns.[12] Nixon had proven an effective campaigner for Republican congressional candidates in 1966, a banner year for the party, and Democrats across the country were worried. A surge of contributions to Democratic candidates reinforced the support and services provided by Hoffman and the DSCC, however, and the party limited Republican gains to only two Senate seats in the fall.

Buoyed again in 1972 by the explosion of fundraising led by Robert Strauss's National Committee for the Reelection of a Democratic Congress, Hoffman pressed for even greater committee attention to candidates challenging Republican incumbents and running for open seats. Presenting his case to Majority Leader Mansfield and Senator Ernest Hollings, the new DSCC chair, he reminded them that Republicans elected in the Republican boom of 1966 held nineteen of the thirty-three seats being contested that year. Hoffman convinced Mansfield and Hollings that challengers deserved a greater share of the committee's resources than in the past, then capitalized on their agreement by offering more professional innovation. He commissioned pollster Peter Hart to do several state benchmark surveys that could guide candidate training or recruitment.[13]

Hoffman's views clearly shaped the committee's financial decisions in 1972. Although contributions continued to be heavily weighted toward incumbents—for example, it gave $64,000 to Senator Walter Mondale's landslide reelection effort in Minnesota compared with just over $30,000 to upstart Joseph Biden in his close Delaware race against incumbent Senator J. Caleb Boggs—the committee did more generously fund several challengers and open-seat candidates.[14] Those candidates raised far greater sums from other sources, but the targeted DSCC funds did contribute to their success. Surprisingly, in the midst of Nixon's landslide win over McGovern, the Democrats picked up a net gain of two seats in the Senate election.

In 1974 Hoffman pressed for further expansion of the DSCC's professional autonomy from the Democratic caucus, advocating targeted contributions without any regard to incumbency. Some senators resisted the move, arguing, as Hoffman later put it, that "our first job was to help the incumbents get reelected, that was why we had the committee in the first place. Their other claim was that it was the incumbents who raised the committee's money, and they deserved their fair share."[15] Both claims were valid, and they were particularly powerful because they were advanced by members of the Democratic caucus that Majority Leader Mansfield relied on to maintain his leadership of the Senate. But Mansfield and the

DSCC's new chair, Senator Lloyd Bentsen of Texas, parried the complaints, telling members that the committee's job was not simply to provide money and services to members' campaigns regardless of need. The committee's job was to use its limited resources to help insure Democratic control of the Senate, and giving those resources to campaigns that didn't need them was a waste.

Similar arguments had erupted at the DCCC under Bill Sweeney, with similar implications. The points raised neatly summarize the conflict inherent in the campaign committee's mission as it serves the party-in-government. On one hand, the individual members of the party-in-government want support for their own campaigns to assure their own reelection, and they collectively create a strong mandate for Textbook Party responsiveness to incumbents. Such views offer a pure expression of the Textbook Party paradigm, which views the party-in-government as the sole focus and master of party organization. On the other hand, those same members recognize that their collective power is much greater when their party maximizes (or regains) majority control of the body, so they will have incentives to support an Accommodationist strategy of allocating services to viable party candidates in (potentially or actually) close races, incumbent or not incumbent, regardless of their views on policy and regardless of their relationships with caucus members. In effect, Bentsen made the case for turning from the Textbook Party paradigm to the Accommodationist paradigm, arguing that disinterested professionals could more efficiently target the committee's money.

He reminded members that he had benefited from DSCC contributions in his first successful race in 1970 and strongly pressed the point. Besides, he and Mansfield argued, the Watergate scandal was growing and most incumbents were going to have an easy time of it. Some Democrats even talked publicly about the possibility of gaining six seats and having a "veto proof" majority of sixty-seven senators.[16] Most of the complaints died down and the targeting went forward. For the first time on record, the committee's average contribution to each open-seat candidate outstripped its average contribution to each incumbent (though the committee's *overall* spending remained slanted toward incumbents).

Some targeting controversies remained, however. The most difficult came when incumbent Democrats were challenged for nomination. The usual practice was to make contributions to incumbents before the nomination process was complete, and challengers complained about the unfairness of a national party committee that gave money to a candidate before the party's nomination was decided at the state level. In 1974, for example, Senator Howard Metzenbaum—running for a full term after his appointment to the Senate in 1973—was challenged in the Ohio primary by fellow Democrat John Glenn. The DSCC gave $5,000 to Metzenbaum before he lost to Glenn in the primary, then made the same contribution to Glenn afterwards.[17] Such cases demonstrate that the transition from the Textbook Party to the Accommodationist paradigm remained controversial and incomplete. Some preferred the DSCC to be a creature of the Democratic Senate caucus rather than a neutral resource for all Democratic Senate campaigns.

Faced with a 1974 committee budget only a third of what it had been in 1972, and without a serious competitive challenge from Republicans, Hoffman improvised to maximize the effect of the reduced resources. He collaborated with Henshaw's DCCC and the Democratic National Committee's midterm campaign effort, set up by DNC chair Robert Strauss and headed by Georgia Governor Jimmy Carter and his aide, Hamilton Jordan.[18] Carter and Jordan helped the DSCC train campaign staffs in Washington and also went out into the field to work directly on campaigns. Additionally, Hoffman brought in independent political consultant Michael S. Berman to help him with training and campaigns' organizational problems. Finally, Hoffman sent his professional staff to work from regional field bases in the Midwest, Southeast, and Far West, renting office space in several airports and flying out to nearby campaigns.[19] When the campaign was over, the DSCC had contributed to a net gain of three Democratic seats in the Senate.

By 1976 Mansfield and Hoffman were satisfied, and Hoffman introduced no further changes in the DSCC operation. With the help of Senator J. Bennett Johnston of Louisiana, the new DSCC chair, he guided the organization through the final Democratic campaign under Mansfield's leadership. The turbulent campaign, with its anti-Washington rhetoric and deceptive outcome—the net party change was nil, even though eight senators retired and fourteen of the thirty-three contested seats changed party—was overshadowed by Jimmy Carter's surprising triumph in the presidential race. The full sweep of the campaign and election escaped the attention of many political observers, but it offered hints of the upheavals to come later in the decade, after Hoffman's departure in 1977.

In the span of five election cycles over ten years, Hoffman had shepherded the DSCC's transition into the campaign-centered era and established a niche for the organization in Senate elections. He had broadened the committee's professional campaign services and adapted those services to the new politics by drawing on the technologies and skills of pollsters and political consultants. And he had helped cajole Democratic senators into embracing the Accommodationist paradigm, which meant accepting professional norms for targeting the committee's limited funds, focusing more on candidates in close races regardless of whether they were incumbents. Hoffman's only failing, one which would come back to trouble the organization, was in not establishing a faster pace of growth in the committee's fundraising and organizational capacity. Even as senators spent increasing amounts of money on their campaigns, much of it raised from political action committees, the DSCC continued to work from a submillion-dollar budget (see figs. 8.1 and 8.2, pp. 161–62). While Hoffman shepherded in changes in the content and orientation of party services, he failed to help the committee grow consistently in the scale of resources it marshaled for these service activities.

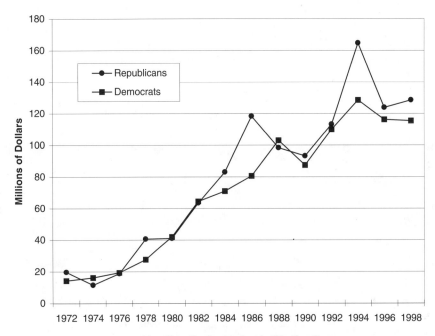

Figure 8.1
Spending by General Election Candidates for the U.S. Senate, 1972–96
(Note: Includes party in-kind contributions and party independent expenditures for
and against candidates in candidate spending)
Sources: Herbert Alexander, *Financing the 1972 Election* (Lexington, Mass.: Lexington
Books, 1976) and Campaign Finance Monitoring Project, *1972 Federal Campaign
Finance,* vol. 3, *Interest Groups and Political Parties* (Washington, D.C.: Common
Cause, 1974); for 1974: Campaign Finance Monitoring Project, *1974 Congressional
Campaign Finances,* vol. 5, *Interest Groups and Political Parties* (Washington, D.C.:
Common Cause, 1976); for 1976: Campaign Finance Monitoring Project, *1976
Federal Campaign Finances,* vol. 5, *Interest Groups and Political Party Contributions to
Congressional Candidates* (Washington, D.C.: Common Cause, 1977); and for 1978
and after: Federal Election Commission reports.

Republican Challenge and Democratic Drift

The DSCC's Republican counterpart, meanwhile, began to shake out of its Watergate-induced lethargy. Spurred by Ronald Reagan's surprisingly strong campaign for the party's presidential nomination in 1976 and funded by emerging corporate and ideological political action committees, Republicans and conservatives began in 1977 to focus again on winning back control of the U.S. Senate. Senator Bill Brock of Tennessee, a former chair of the NRSC, won the chairmanship of the Republican National Committee early that year, promising to revitalize the party's organizations in preparation for the 1978 election. With the RNC's help, new NRSC chair

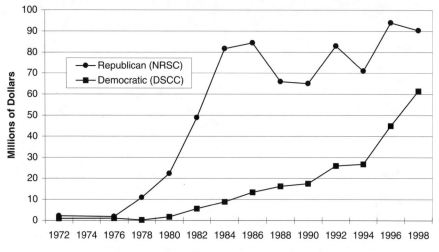

Figure 8.2
Senate Campaign Committee Receipts, 1972–96
(Notes: [a] data for 1974 missing; [b] includes soft money beginning in 1992)
Sources: See fig. 8.1.

Senator Robert Packwood of Oregon initiated a direct-mail program for the committee that raised more than $10 million through the 1977–78 election cycle, and more than $20 million as Senator Packwood stayed with the committee in 1979–80[20] (see fig. 8.3, p. 164). Those funds, along with support from emerging PACs, enabled the committee to dramatically expand its activities to include recruiting candidates, training them, helping them with polls, research, strategy, and consultants, and directly contributing cash to their campaigns. Under Senator Packwood's leadership, the Republican organization helped recruit a very strong set of challengers against Democratic incumbents and for open seats, including several veteran congressmen.[21] In a remarkably short time, the NRSC had emerged as a major participant in Senate elections, and figure 8.4 shows that it also emerged as a major source of funding of Republican candidates.

As the committee's fundraising continued to grow in 1980, the NRSC quickly ran up against the relatively low direct contribution limits established in the Federal Election Campaign Act. A competitive Senate campaign might cost hundreds of thousands of dollars, but FECA limits allowed party committees to contribute only $17,500 directly to such a campaign. On the other hand, FECA provision 441a(d) allowed party committees to make "coordinated expenditures" *on behalf of* a candidate, purchasing polls, broadcast time, or other contract services that might help the campaign. These 441a(d) limits are much more lenient—and subject to a sliding scale based on the size of a candidate's homestate electorate—allowing committees to spend more than half a million dollars on a Senate campaign in a large state such as California, New York, or Texas. As long as the funds are spent by the committee rather than directly by that candidate, the money can be used for a wide range of campaign expenses. With far more than $17,500 to spend on each race in 1980, the NRSC made the largest portion of its contributions to 441a(d) money, and it continued to seek other legal channels for the cash that poured in as the decade went on.[22]

One such channel was the soft or nonfederal money discussed in chapter 6, which party organizations could transfer to their state and local party affiliates without facing regulation under the Federal Election Campaign Act. NRSC worked closely with those affiliates to improvise a multimillion-dollar system of "agency agreements" in 1980.[23] "Independent expenditures" offered another channel, through which the party could purchase advertising time or use other vehicles to attack its opponents. Along with the Republican National Committee and the National Republican Congressional Committee, the NRSC helped develop and coordinate a powerful nationwide conservative challenge to the Democratic Party. According to Gary Jacobson, the NRSC channeled more than $1.2 million into such expenditures attacking Democratic Senate candidates in 1979–80 and more than $3 million in 1981–82. Millions more were spent by the National Conservative Political Action Committee (NCPAC) and conservative and corporate PACs, attacking prominent liberal Democrats including Senators George McGovern (S.D.), John Culver (Iowa), Birch Bayh (Ind.), Warren Magnuson (Wash.), and Gaylord Nelson (Wisc.), all of whom were unseated.[24]

Such PACs proved powerful allies during this period. As noted in chapter 7, thousands of these organizations had been formed in the few years since the Federal Election Campaign Act passed, and 1978 was the first time many of them exerted a coordinated influence in a congressional campaign.[25] These organizations, by tradition cautiously bipartisan in their contributions to campaigns (in sharp contrast to the openly pro-Democratic labor PACs), changed their strategy late in the 1978 cycle to strongly support the Republican Party. In the last months of the campaign, with the strong encouragement of the NRSC, corporate PACs directed almost three-quarters of their Senate contributions to Republicans. The late surge, which continued after the election ended, ultimately lifted the Republican share of corporate PAC contributions to 66 percent over the entire cycle, where it remained for three succeeding election cycles.[26]

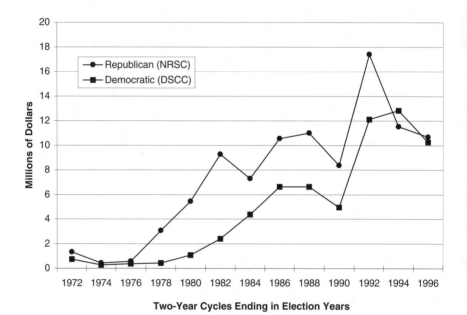

Figure 8.3
Senate Campaign Committee Contributions to General Election Candidates, 1972–96
(Note: Includes in-kind contributions and expenditures in support of candidates)
Sources: See fig 8.1.

In the four short years between 1976 and 1980, the NRSC had moved from the periphery to the center, transformed into a wealthy, versatile, and influential participant in the campaign-centered electoral order. Emerging from the shadow of the NRCC, the Senate campaign committee achieved what its House Republican counterpart never had: majority status. Virtually all observers agreed that the NRSC had been a major factor in Republicans gaining three seats in 1978, then twelve more in 1980, as the party won a solid majority in the U.S. Senate. As its receipts grew to nearly $50 million in 1982 and beyond $80 million in 1984, the NRSC continued to develop its Accommodationist program of contributions and services.

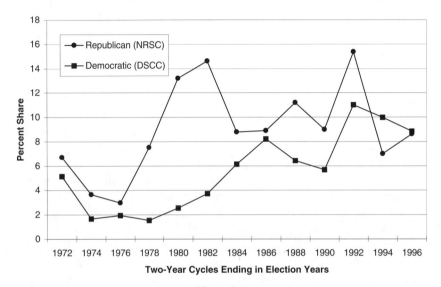

Figure 8.4
Senate Campaign Committee Contributions as a Share of General Election Candidates'
Campaign Expenditures, 1972–96
(Note: Includes party in-kind expenditures, party independent expenditures for and against candidates)
Sources: See fig. 8.1.

Despite this challenge, the Democratic Senatorial Campaign Committee drifted through the late 1970s and early 1980s. After Senator Mike Mansfield's retirement and the election of Robert Byrd as Senate majority leader in 1977, then Hoffman's subsequent departure as DSCC executive director, the committee's service development stalled as its leadership emulated Byrd's more cautious style. Byrd, a politically and institutionally conservative Senate insider from West Virginia, showed little interest in electoral politics or the reworking of the DSCC's role in campaigns. As a Democratic political operative from the period later recalled bitterly,

> Robert Byrd's understanding of politics is limited to the Senate floor. He didn't
> see the broader changes going on in campaign politics in the 1960s and 1970s,
> didn't understand the use of television, didn't see what people were doing to win

Senate seats, didn't see the changes in the kinds of people who were entering the Senate. The man was an island. He had no earthly idea of what was going on.[27]

Byrd preferred that the DSCC provide nonintrusive services and money to his colleagues, and little more. He wished to prevent the creation of an autonomous professional DSCC that might intrude into his colleagues' campaigns. If anything, he acted as though he wished to turn the committee back toward a more Textbook Party approach, placing the committee at the service of the Senate Democratic caucus.

At first, Byrd's lack of interest seemed justified. After a brief scare in 1970 and 1972, the Democratic majority in the Senate remained large, and Byrd saw no immediate threat from the Republicans. Members of the Senate Democratic caucus, with only modest help from the DSCC, maintained their individual ability to build successful campaigns for nomination and election. Republican Senate candidates, in contrast, had only come close to matching Democrats' fundraising for the first time in 1976, and even with the help of the National Republican Senatorial Committee, they couldn't consistently outspend Democratic campaigns (see fig. 8.1, p. 161). Byrd's colleagues did not press him to make any bold new moves with the organization through 1978 and well into the 1980 election cycle, and Byrd was happy to turn his attention elsewhere.

But Byrd and other Senate Democrats badly misjudged deeper changes in national politics. By mid-1978, it became clear that Democrats and the DSCC risked being overwhelmed by more powerful forces in the campaign. As DSCC Executive Director William Wester later noted, "The Republicans had a much stronger organization. We weren't blind, we could see that. We wanted to respond to it, but we just didn't have that kind of money."[28] In the face of this challenge, Wester and his successors struggled to retain the advances made under Nordy Hoffman. Through both the 1978 and 1980 election cycles, they collaborated with William Sweeney at the DCCC, sharing ideas and campaign strategies as well as office space. Both organizations benefited from the creation and growth of the Democratic House and Senate Council described in chapter 7. They also continued to jointly sponsor the annual Democratic Congressional Dinner, sharing the money it produced.

The contrasts between the two organizations nevertheless grew quite striking during this collaborative period. DSCC chair Senator Wendell Ford (Ky.) and his executive directors remained more ambivalent about discarding the Textbook Party paradigm than Senate Republicans or Sweeney, who had worked hard to build the DCCC within the Accommodationist paradigm. The clearest illustration of the DSCC's ambivalence can be found in the committee's allocation of campaign contributions on the basis of clout rather than disinterested professionalism. In 1978 only four Democratic Senate candidates—all challengers—were completely passed over, despite the certainty or hopelessness of several incumbent races. On the other hand, the committee contributed to two incumbents even though they faced serious primary challengers. Further, the variance in DSCC contributions between high-priority and low-priority races did not begin to approach that of DCCC targeting in the same election cycle.

The targeting controversy continued in 1980, as the committee struggled to marshal its limited resources in response to the growing Republican challenge. New Executive Director Tom Baker recalled arguments about targeting contributions as the committee passed over several incumbents in easy races:

> You can't imagine the trauma these decisions caused with the incumbents. It was like pulling teeth with some of them. They looked at the organization as their baby, they looked at the money as theirs.[29]

Though the controversy faded when Byrd quietly endorsed the decisions, it revealed many Democratic senators' resistance to any degree of DSCC autonomy.

As the committee's fundraising grew in 1980, the DSCC increasingly spent funds on 441a(d) or "coordinated expenditures" on behalf of targeted Democratic candidates. In the 1980 election, the DSCC did not begin to approach the legal limits on 441a(d) spending, but it did spend nearly $600,000 on behalf of campaigns.[30] The committee spent funds on behalf of Democratic candidates to pay for polls, opposition research, and professional campaign consultation. Such coordinated spending had been mastered by the Republican campaign committees only two years earlier, and the DSCC learned about it and fairly quickly put it to good use as a tool to further emphasize their targeting choices. Yet the way the DSCC handled coordinated expenditures in 1980 offers further evidence of Byrd and Ford's view of the organization. That is, they wanted the committee's contributions to Democratic Senate campaigns to grow, but they had little interest in seeing the party organization itself develop into a strong and autonomous professional operation over the long term. So, instead of developing a stable, expert professional staff to provide the services, the committee paid the money out for whatever the candidates wanted.

As Baker later described it, "We let them call the shots and we picked up the bills." In the short run, this was clearly a cost-effective strategy that the candidates preferred: "I think we reflected what the senators wanted. They wanted the money, whether it was the $17,500 [the FECA limit for direct contribution] or the 441(a)d."[31] But over the long term it slowed the party organization's halting transition toward influence in Senate elections. Its leaders had embraced the explanation of the political world offered by the Accommodationist paradigm, but they balked at its strategy of building autonomous campaign-centered professionalism at the party organizations even as they lost control of the Senate.

The DSCC did provide some limited services to Democratic Senate candidates and their campaigns as well in 1978 and 1980. Wester and the small DSCC staff continued Hoffman's practice of consulting directly with campaigns in the field, though Wester spent almost all of those efforts on challengers and open-seat candidates. He later explained this was partly because such candidates generally lacked incumbents' expertise, but also because incumbents did not want him to interfere with their established campaign practices.[32] In the 1980 cycle, the DSCC and the DCCC jointly sponsored a series of training sessions for Democratic campaign staffs in several cities around the country. The DSCC also made use of the campaign experiences of 1978 Democratic Senate candidates to train incumbents up for reelection in 1980. It was a low-cost service, but the DSCC action was genuinely helpful; the group continued to meet informally throughout the cycle.[33]

As the DSCC developed these financial and professional service contributions, some things did not look so bad. Many Democrats interpreted the turbulent 1978 election, during which the Republicans had presented a formidable challenge, as a wash, because they lost a net of three seats, despite the drag of a weak incumbent president on the Democratic ticket. Still, the aggregate figures concealed some very disturbing events for the Democrats. Five of their incumbents had been defeated in 1978 (compared with only two Republican incumbents), and Democrats had won only seven of the thirteen open seats contested. In all, thirteen seats changed parties, and Republicans won all the close races. The election foreshadowed the end of the Democratic Senate majority only two years later.

The external challenges that the DSCC and Democratic Senate candidates faced were growing. Individual candidates and campaigns continued to raise the lion's share of Democratic money, and the strong financial performances of some individual incumbents did not help the party competitively.[34] As noted earlier, figure 8.4 (p. 165) shows that a much larger share of Republican spending was controlled by the national party organizations, and they used it strategically to the party's collective advantage. By pooling such a large share of the party's resources, the NRSC targeted Republican money more professionally and efficiently among candidates in close races.[35] And while the DSCC allowed Democratic senators to call the shots, the National Republican Senatorial Committee played an increasingly autonomous role in recruiting, training, and financing powerful challengers to Democratic incumbents. As a result, only ten of the nineteen incumbent Democrats running for reelection won in 1980, and the party kept only two of the five open seats formerly held by Democrats. NRSC targeting helped Republican candidates win ten of the twelve Senate races decided by less than 4 points and helped turn an extremely close national election into a landslide in 1980.

Shaken, many Democratic senators up for reelection in 1982 scrambled to get their campaigns in order as gleeful Republicans talked of realignment and long-term majority status. Yet, in contrast with ambitious initiatives at the Democratic National Committee under Charles Manatt and at the Democratic Congressional

Campaign Committee under Representative Tony Coelho, the Democratic Senatorial Campaign Committee continued to stumble through most of the 1982 election cycle.

Senate Democratic Leader Robert Byrd criticized the failures of the Democratic National Committee immediately after the election.[36] Other Democratic senators joined in that criticism and also asked for future assistance from their own campaign committee; however, Byrd quickly lost interest in improving the DSCC. Apparently comforted by arguments that the landslide had been broad but shallow, Byrd refused to view the election as evidence of a trend that required an organized response. Democrats had lost the Senate, after all, because they happened to lose several close races simultaneously. Further, the party's 1980 incumbents had been elected or reelected in the post-Watergate backlash of 1974 and were less prepared for a serious challenge. Democratic members up for reelection in 1982 were on firmer ground, more likely to be able to protect themselves. Byrd coaxed a reluctant Senator Wendell Ford to serve an unprecedented third term as DSCC chair, then turned his attention elsewhere.

Byrd also took comfort from the work of Senate Democratic Whip Alan Cranston (Calif.), who in 1981 formed the Democratic Leadership Circle as a financial adjunct to the DSCC, copying the National Republican Senatorial Committee's large-donor fundraising.[37] The Leadership Circle brought in hundreds of thousands of dollars through the fall and winter, but the small DSCC staff organization continued to flounder well into 1982. Democratic senators and political activists became seriously concerned that the DSCC would lose the whole cycle and miss an opportunity to help Senate candidates in what was emerging as a promising year for Democrats. Only in late spring, six months before the election, did the committee establish a hasty program of contributions and professional services. Luckily for Senate Democrats, the 1982 election turned out to be a wash: each party lost one incumbent, and there was no net change in the composition of the Senate.

Despite Republican organizational growth and electoral success, six years of near stagnation at the DSCC had apparently convinced Democratic candidates that they could practice campaign-centered politics quite effectively without professionalized party organization help. Even when party leaders and activists embraced the *worldview* of the Accommodationist paradigm, they could ignore its *prescription* and ignore the party organization, often with impunity.

The Democratic Counterattack

Ultimately, however, Democratic Party leaders and activists decided that professionalized party organizations might be a good idea. Immediately after the 1982 election, several Democratic senators made it clear that they were no longer satisfied with Senator Robert Byrd's individualistic electoral norms, and that they would advocate a stronger and more professional DSCC role. They set the tone for the DSCC's next four years at a December 1982 candidates' retreat, during which incumbents facing reelection in 1984 listened to 1982 candidates talk about the just-finished campaign. Winners and losers told the senators and their aides about the National Conservative Political Action Committee (NCPAC) and other New Right groups, about media tactics, direct mail and other fundraising devices, and about how campaigns had changed since they last ran for office.

Several participating senators immediately approached Senator Lloyd Bentsen, who had just won a difficult reelection campaign in Texas and asked him to serve again as DSCC chair. Bentsen had chaired the committee in 1973–74 and helped elect many of the members who had lost in 1980. More important, as an ambitious and respected senior member with strong political and fundraising skills, he believed strongly in developing the DSCC as a professional organization.[38] Bentsen accepted their invitation on the condition that they agree to focus first on establishing the organization's professional credibility among Democratic senators, campaign operatives, and electoral activists. Before the DSCC could provide resources and services to Democratic campaigns for the next general election, he argued, the party organization needed to build a professional staff and put on an effective campaign to gain resources and respect.

The first target of their campaign was the party-in-government. As incoming Executive Director Brian Atwood later noted, Bentsen recognized that "he had to convince [Democratic] senators that they had some stake in the organization" in order to get their short-term help raising funds and providing services, and their long-term help institutionalizing those activities.[39] Bentsen himself worked to "sell" the organization to his fellow members of the Senate Democratic caucus, and he assigned Atwood to sell it to their administrative assistants and campaign directors. Members of the DSCC staff worked to raise the organization's profile among activists and financial contributors.

The DSCC's funding base continued to grow after the election, but it depended heavily on PACs and large contributions to the Leadership Circle. Bentsen did quite a bit of fundraising himself, urging—as DCCC Chair Coelho did—that PACs and other donors "hedge their bets" by giving to Democrats.[40] He also pressed his fellow members of the Senate Democratic caucus to help with such fundraising. When some of them expressed reluctance to raise money for the committee, preferring to raise it for their own campaigns, Bentsen convinced them that they all shared an interest in a strong DSCC. If they ran into trouble with their own campaigns, he assured them, the committee would help when the time came. "Some of the members that went along with him were shocked later in the cycle when we actually gave them money," Atwood later noted.

But, following the lead of Coelho at the DCCC, Bentsen and Atwood also moved to diversify the DSCC's fundraising base with direct mail. Floyd Fithian, the committee's new finance director (a former U.S. representative and Senate candidate), proved the key to that effort. Bentsen was uncomfortable with the ideologically liberal mail appeals that had proven most effective for Democratic candidates and organizations. A centrist who recognized the ideological diversity of his Democratic Senate colleagues and valued his own business support, Bentsen did not want the DSCC to be labeled as a liberal funding source. The remedy was to have Fithian send out partisan but nonideological letters under his own signature, stating, in effect, "Democratic Senate candidates need money to compete with their well-financed Republican opponents. I know, because I was an under-funded candidate in a winnable race in 1982, and I lost to a well-funded Republican. Send the DSCC money so this doesn't happen again." Variations on this theme raised hundreds of thousands of dollars for the committee in 1983 and 1984. Fithian sent out ideological letters as well under his own signature, and by the end of the cycle direct mail provided nearly a third of the committee's income.[41]

With this improved financial base, the committee gradually expanded its direct contributions and coordinated spending; its share of all spending on Democratic Senate campaigns candidates grew from 3.9 percent to 6.1 percent. Though the committee's spending continued to be dwarfed by its Republican counterpart, the DSCC's influence grew much as the NRSC's had: as Bentsen and his professional staff worked to target contributions carefully, the DSCC became the single largest donor to most competitive Democratic Senate candidates. To begin with, he made $1,500 preprimary contributions to all Democratic candidates in four states where incumbent Republican senators seemed vulnerable, and the signal these contributions conveyed drew strong candidates and further Democratic donations to those races.[42] Next, he served notice that sure winners and sure losers would not receive any money from the committee. Several of the ten candidates whom Bentsen ultimately shut out complained strongly—five were shoo-in incumbents, the other five were hopeless challengers—but Bentsen had the stature to make the decisions of his professional staff stick.

Facing the Federal Election Campaign Act's $17,500 limit on direct contributions to candidates, Bentsen and Atwood also found that they were spending a growing share of the committee's money on 441a(d), or coordinated, expenditures. This form of contribution had the unexpected benefit of enabling the committee to work more effectively with Senate campaigns, particularly those of candidates inexperienced with the new politics. Like the DSCC under Coelho and Franks during this period, DSCC Political Director Audrey Sheppard used the lure of coordinated expenditures to exercise "quality control" over Democratic campaigns that fall. Sheppard and the committee's professional staff advised candidates on strategy and tactics as well as their choices in media advisers and pollsters. Such intrusions brought some resistance—especially from professional campaign consultants who challenged the committee's growing encroachment on their professional turf—but Bentsen consistently supported it.[43]

With its increased income, the DSCC provided more substantial professional services to Democratic Senate candidates. The organization's staff, which grew to about a dozen, worked on candidate recruitment in several states and served as an intelligence and strategy clearinghouse for all Senate campaigns. The committee also copied the Republican practice of purchasing "blocks" of polling research from Washington-based consulting firms, providing benchmark polls for several candidates in the early stages of their campaigns. Such research, purchased wholesale by the committee, enhanced candidates' strategies as well as their credibility with fundraisers.[44] Under Bentsen the committee did not even attempt to build the broad service menu of Coelho's DCCC or the Republican campaign committees, but it did become more involved in the day-to-day operations of many Senate campaigns.

The 1984 Senate election returns were largely a wash for Democrats, but there were some bright spots. In part because of the DSCC's contributions, Democrats defeated two incumbent Republicans and won three of the four open seats contested. Republicans defeated only one Democratic incumbent. The Republicans still controlled the Senate, but their margin of control had been reduced to 53–47. Despite these unspectacular results, Bentsen and the DSCC had made substantial progress establishing their professional niche in national politics. Bentsen had solidified and diversified the organization's fundraising; improved and expanded its staff; and raised its profile in the Senate Democratic caucus, in Senate elections, and among Democratic campaigns.

Additionally, Lloyd Bentsen reestablished the traditional rotation of the DSCC's chairmanship, stepping down in favor of freshman Senator George Mitchell of Maine in December of 1984. Mitchell, a national party activist who had campaigned for Democratic national chair in 1972, built on and developed Bentsen's initiatives in much the same way that Paul Kirk built on and developed the work of Charles Manatt at the headquarters organization. He retained most of Bentsen's lead staff people and continued Bentsen's development of both fundraising and professional campaign services. Most important, he consolidated and extended the DSCC's role in Senate elections.

The 1986 election shaped up as a very difficult one from the outset. Control of the Senate was clearly at stake in the election: as the high turnover "class of

1980" (and 1974) came around on its six-year cycle, Republicans held twenty-two of the thirty-four seats. Observers predicted more than a dozen close races as President Ronald Reagan's popularity inevitably waned during his second term. With the large number of nonincumbent Democratic candidates, demands for DSCC support were especially high, and committee resources were short.[45] Figure 8.3 (p. 164) shows that the committee had dramatically closed the gap in contributions to campaigns under Bentsen, but figure 8.1 (p. 161) shows that the DSCC's financial resources were still dwarfed by those of its Republican counterpart.

Without the need to spend time convincing anyone of the DSCC's legitimate importance, Mitchell was able to focus on the basics. In finance, he directed the organization to continue seeking both large contributions and direct-mail support. The organization aggressively worked on both labor and business PACs, challenging the Republican biases of the latter.[46] The direct-mail program continued to lag, providing only a third of the committee's funds, but strong efforts doubled the list of donors during the cycle and tripled the cash income of the program. As a result, the DSCC's budget remained more dependent on PACs and large events than any other national party organization, Democratic or Republican.[47]

Mitchell largely followed Bentsen's formula in targeting contributions. Like Bentsen, he paid out nearly half of all DSCC spending in direct contributions and coordinated expenditures for Democratic Senate campaigns. Because the committee had more money to work with, it did not completely shut out any candidate. But it did give only "token" contributions of $17,500 or less to six shoo-in incumbents and four hopeless challengers. Because far more Republican than Democratic seats were open in 1986, the lion's share of the committee's contributions again went to challengers and open-seat candidates. Overall, figure 8.4 (p. 165) shows that the DSCC's financial role in Senate elections continued to grow: the committee contributed more than 8 percent of all Democratic candidate spending for the cycle.

Mitchell and the committee took advantage of a major opportunity presented by the DSCC's established legitimacy: they began the cycle by greatly expanding recruitment efforts. Mitchell was often unsuccessful in luring those whom the committee targeted as the strongest potential challengers to Republican incumbents, but he recruited several who would ultimately win, including Terry Sanford in North Carolina and Representative Richard Shelby in Alabama. Perhaps unexpectedly, the flurry of recruitment activity in 1985 worked more broadly to signal the organization's intentions to play a significant role in the election.[48]

The committee continued to work closely with such challengers throughout the cycle, providing them with a variety of professional services. Each candidate received advice on hiring Washington-based polling and media consultants, regular briefings on their opponents' activities, and information on national political issues and party strategies. And, perhaps most important for challengers, the DSCC was the single largest financial contributor to most of their campaigns.

All of this work paid off on election day in 1986, when Democrats turned the 1980 result on its head. Winning virtually every close race, Democrats unseated nine Republican incumbents and won five of the seven open seats at stake. They gained a net of eight seats, and finished the election with a ten-seat majority in the Senate.

After a season of squabbles over resources, disputed targeting decisions, and ideological differences within the party, the 1986 election result provoked widespread praise for Senator George Mitchell and the Democratic Senatorial Campaign Committee. Mitchell's work at the DSCC was compared favorably with Representative Tony Coelho's at the DCCC, and both organizations drew recognition as important professional partners in congressional campaigns. Proof of the importance senators attributed to the DSCC came less than two years later, when they rewarded Mitchell by electing him Senate majority leader. The Accommodationist paradigm and the strategic program of professional party organization participation in campaign-centered politics were no longer disputed in the United States Senate.

Consolidation and the Beginnings of Doubt

Like the party campaign committees in the U.S. House of Representatives, the DSCC and NRSC had by 1987 become part of the "Washington Establishment," highly visible players filling a valued niche in national politics. Democratic and Republican senators alike essentially agreed on the tasks the organizations should perform: recruit candidates, raise money and contribute it strategically to competitive campaigns, provide professionalized strategic and informational support to campaigns, and extol the virtues of their party everywhere.

The committees were certainly not invulnerable. Though the NRSC's leaders expressed confidence early in the 1985–86 cycle, as the election drew near they saw the Republicans' majority status slipping away as the campaign committee's receipts stagnated.[49] Thomas Griscom, the committee's executive director for the cycle, tried to deflect criticism even as he moved on to another job. "The fallacy of this committee is that we are looked at as the driving force for all Republican campaigns," he was quoted as saying. But he complained that incumbent candidates themselves controlled many of the losing campaigns, taking the committee's money while ignoring the committee's advice and assistance.[50] His complaints angered Republicans around the country and brought about a reassessment of the committee's role and work. The subsequent debate covered familiar Textbook versus

Accommodationist ground: should the committee have mounted a programmatic conservative Republican campaign, or should it have simply provided money and expert support to candidates?[51]

Though Senator Rudy Boschwitz of Minnesota trimmed the committee's staff when he took over as NRSC chair and evaluated the organization in 1987, he did not deviate from the Accommodationist paradigm in any fundamental way. He acknowledged that the committee had made some mistakes but insisted that it should continue to follow the program his predecessors had begun to develop ten years earlier.[52] Figures 8.1 and 8.2 (pp. 161–62) show that the committee's fundraising— and overall Republican Senate candidate fundraising—faltered in the aftermath of 1986, but NRSC fundraising eventually recovered and the committee remained a fixture in Senate elections through the 1980s and into the 1990s.

Things looked rosier at the DSCC. Given Democrats' success in 1986, the principal tasks remaining for Mitchell's successors in the DSCC chair were consolidation and expansion of the organization. The first to follow Mitchell, freshman Senator John Kerry of Massachusetts, proved the point. Kerry took the DSCC chair only two years after winning his own Senate seat, having refused PAC contributions to his own campaigns. He faced immediate questions about whether he could raise money effectively for other Democrats in order to "build on the 1986 success of his predecessor, George J. Mitchell of Maine."[53] Those doubts faded after the DSCC staged its first successful fundraising dinner of the cycle, and further when it became clear that the NRSC faced its own problems recruiting candidates and raising money for 1988.

Kerry shepherded a continuation of the DSCC's steady financial growth and continued the practice of targeting funds toward competitive Democratic challengers during the 1987–88 election cycle. The committee's central innovation during the cycle came in professional and financial collaboration with the Democratic National Committee and its efforts to fund the Dukakis-Bentsen presidential ticket. The DSCC now had enough money to bump up consistently against federal contribution limits in competitive states, and the DNC was prohibited from spending private money on behalf of the Democrats' general-election ticket. The two committees collaborated on an alternative way of helping their campaigns in competitive states: channeling private contributions to state parties as soft money, contributions for voter registration and other party activities not directly connected to federal candidates' campaigns and thus not subject to federal regulations.[54] Though Michael Dukakis lost to George Bush in November, he avoided a Reagan-style landslide, and Democrats easily held the Senate.

By the time Senator John Breaux of Louisiana took over the DSCC from Kerry in 1989, however, American attitudes toward Congress and electoral politics had clearly begun to sour. Though the Senate escaped scandals like those in the House of Representatives, Breaux and the committee worked in a difficult setting. Financial contributions to both parties' candidates and Capitol Hill campaign committees faltered. More importantly, Breaux and his colleagues faced substantial difficulty recruiting strong candidates for open seats and mounting challenges against Republican incumbents. Those who did run were often unconventional politicians—businesspeople, or activists openly antagonistic toward the Washington establishment—which made the work of party committees even more difficult.[55] Though Senate Democrats continued to hold their majority—congressional incumbents of both parties won at record rates in both 1988 and 1990—the DSCC ended the 1990 cycle more than a million dollars in debt.[56]

After Breaux stepped down, DSCC chair Senator Chuck Robb and his staff faced an even more hostile setting. Though Harris Wofford of Pennsylvania gained Democrats a seat in a November 1991 special election, the Gulf War erupted in December and spurred Republican hopes (and fundraising). Four of twenty-one Democratic incumbents facing reelection in 1992 announced their retirements, and one—Alan Dixon of Illinois—lost his primary to unknown State Senator Carol Mosely Braun. Recruitment proved even more difficult than in 1990, though a substantial number of strong women candidates emerged.[57] None of these developments, however, provoked doubts among Senate Democrats about what the DSCC should be doing. Democratic candidates pressed Robb simply to raise the money, provide the expected professional services, and collaborate effectively with the Clinton-Gore ticket in the fall.[58]

Robb did his job as expected and the Democrats again held their ground. With Bill Clinton winning the White House, Democrats had won control of the national government for the first time since Ronald Reagan and the Republicans came to power in 1980. In their euphoria, Democrats could not have imagined in November 1992 how short-lived their unified government would be. Public doubt about the entire system of professionalized campaign politics was turning into an open hostility that would soon sweep them from power. Though Republicans would benefit in the short term, they would soon find the public equally impatient and hostile.

NOTES

1. Hugh Bone, *Party Committees and National Politics* (Seattle: University of Washington Press, 1958), 127–28.

2. Arthur M. Schlesinger Jr., *Robert Kennedy and His Times* (New York: Random House, 1968), 729.

3. Bone, *Party Committees*, chap. 5; Cornelius P. Cotter and Bernard Hennessy, *Politics without Power: The National Party Committees* (New York: Atherton, 1964), chap. 9.

4. David S. Broder, *The Party's Over: The Failure of Politics in America* (New York: Harper and Row, 1971), 58–64.

5. Also by tradition, the chair is given to a senator not up for reelection during that two-year cycle.

6. Frank N. "Nordy" Hoffman, interview by author, Washington, D.C., June 1987.

7. Neal Gregory, "Democratic Senators' Campaign Unit," *National Journal,* 12 September 1970, 1995.

8. Hoffman, interview.

9. Neal Gregory, "Democrats Fight to Retain Control of Senate against GOP Challenge," *National Journal*, 18 April 1970, 845–47. See also Andrew J. Glass, "Prime Republican Goal: Control of the Senate in 1970," *National Journal*, 26 September 1970, 2108–9.

10. Hoffman, interview.

11. Gregory, "Democrats Fight."

12. Neal Gregory, "Republicans Gamble House Seats in Campaign to Capture Senate," *National Journal*, 28 March 1970, 689–90; Gregory, "Democrats Fight"; Glass, "Prime Republican Goal."

13. Hoffman, interview.

14. The Campaign Finance Monitoring Project, *1972 Federal Campaign Finances: Interest Groups and Political Parties,* vol. 3 (Washington, D.C.: Common Cause, 1974), 117.

15. Hoffman, interview.

16. Michael J. Malbin, "Veto-Proof Congress Emerges as Major 1974 Election Issue," *National Journal*, 1 June 1974, 809–16.

17. Ibid.

18. Hoffman, interview.

19. Martin Franks, interview by author, Washington, D.C., April 1987; and Michael S. Berman, interview by author, Washington, D.C., March 1988.

20. Richard E. Cohen, "Running Scared in Congress—The Parties Go Head-to-Head over Money," *National Journal*, 8 April 1978, 558; Timothy B. Clark, "The RNC Prospers, the DNC Struggles As They Face the 1980 Elections," *National Journal*, 27 September 1980, 1617–21; and David Adamany, "Political Parties in the 1980s," in *Money and Politics in the United States,* ed. Michael J. Malbin (Washington, D.C.: American Enterprise Institute, 1984), 78–85.

21. On NRSC recruiting and services, see Richard Cohen, "Are the Senate's Liberal Democrats Becoming an Endangered Species?" *National Journal*, 14 July 1979, 1152–55. See also Paul S. Herrnson and David Menefee-Libey, "The Dynamics of Party Organizational Development," *Midsouth Political Science Journal* 11 (Winter 1990): 3–30; Adamany, "Political Parties in the 1980s"; and John F. Bibby, "Party Renewal in the National Republican Party," in *Party Renewal in America,* ed. Gerald M. Pomper (New York: Praeger, 1980).

22. Gary C. Jacobson, "Money in the 1980 and 1982 Congressional Elections," in Malbin, *Money and Politics*, 45–51.

23. On the committee's "agency agreements" with state Republican Party organizations, see Larry Light, "Republican Groups Dominate in Party Campaign Spending," *Congressional Quarterly Weekly Report*, 1 November 1980, 3234–36.

24. Jacobson, "Money in the 1980 and 1982 Congressional Elections," 51–55.

25. For a fuller account from the period, see Larry J. Sabato, *PAC Power: Inside the World of Political Action Committees* (New York: Norton, 1985). For an interesting case study of conservative PACs' national campaigns, see Thomas J. McIntyre and John C. Obert, *The Fear Brokers* (New York: Pilgrim Press, 1979). Democrat McIntyre had lost his reelection to the Senate from New Hampshire in 1978.

26. Maxwell Glen, "At the Wire, Corporate PACs Come through for the GOP," *National Journal*, 3 February 1979, 174–77; Maxwell Glen, "The PACs are Back, Richer and Wiser, to Finance the 1980 Elections," *National Journal*, 24 November 1979, 1982–84; and Richard E. Cohen, "Congressional Democrats Beware—Here Come the Corporate PACs," *National Journal*, 9 August 1980, 1304–11.

27. Interview by author, Washington, D.C., December 1987.

28. William Wester, telephone interview by author, 27 August 1987. See also Warden Moxley, "GOP Has a Lot at Stake in '78 Senate Elections," *Congressional Quarterly Weekly Report*, 17 December 1977, 2609–14; and Richard E. Cohen, "Open Seats—Where the Action Is in This Year's Congressional Races," *National Journal*, 7 October 1978, 1588–93.

29. Tom Baker, interview by author, Washington, D.C., December 1987.

30. Federal Election Commission reports.

31. Baker, interview.

32. Wester, interview.

33. Baker, interview. For a full discussion of this group, see chapter 8 of Marjorie Randon Hershey, *Running For Office: The Political Education of Campaigners* (Chatham, N.J.: Chatham House, 1984).

34. Democratic front-runners' failure to share their wealth drew criticism from observers during the campaign, one of whom was quoted as saying, "The Democratic incumbents were

a bunch of prima donnas who did not want to join others to help themselves. The Democrats don't know what's going on." See Light, "Republican Groups Dominate," 3234.

35. Gary Jacobson and Samuel Kernell, "Party Organizations and the Efficient Distribution of Congressional Campaign Resources," paper presented at the Weingart-Caltech Conference on the Institutional Context of Elections, California Institute of Technology, February 1984.

36. Kathy Sawyer, "Byrd Faults Party Panel on Handling of Election," *Washington Post*, 16 November 1980, A5.

37. The Circle charged wealthy donors $15,000 a head for membership and promised to pay the money out in contributions to Democratic Senate campaigns. Richard E. Cohen, "Democrats Take a Leaf from GOP Book with Early Campaign Financing Start," *National Journal*, 23 May 1981, 922–23.

38. Leon Billings, former DSCC executive director, interview by author, Washington, D.C., June 1987.

39. Brian Atwood, interview by author, Washington, D.C., March 1987.

40. See Richard E. Cohen, "The Object is Control," *National Journal*, 29 October 1983, 2261–62.

41. Atwood, interview.

42. Atwood, interview; FECA reports.

43. Audrey Sheppard, interview by author, Washington, D.C., September 1987.

44. For example, 1983 DSCC polls signaled to Sen. Carl Levin that he needed to start his campaign early against a well-financed challenge from former astronaut Jack Lousma in Michigan. Levin fought back hard and eventually won by a wide margin. Atwood, interview.

45. For press coverage of the problem, see Thomas B. Edsall, "Democrats Lack Cash to 'Max Out,'" *Washington Post*, 30 September 1986, A6; Richard L. Berke, "3 Funds for Republicans Lead Democrats $5 to $1," *New York Times*, 24 October 1986, B8; and Paul Taylor, "David Johnson: Helping Senate Candidates Share Democrats' 'Half a Pie,'" *Washington Post*, 27 October 1986, A13.

46. Maxwell Glen, "Wooing Business Money," *National Journal*, 16 August 1986, 2009.

47. Thomas Byrne Edsall, "A Funny Thing Happened to the Party of the Working Class," *Washington Post National Weekly Edition*, 25 August 1986, 13.

48. See, for example, Richard E. Cohen, "Lonely Business," *National Journal*, 16 November 1985, 2626; and Paul Taylor, "The Democrats Can Recapture the Senate—If Anybody Will Run," *Washington Post National Weekly Edition*, 20 January 1986, 13–14.

49. Richard E. Cohen, "[NRSC Chair Sen. John] Heinz Sees Republican Senate Gains in 1986," *National Journal*, 16 February 1986, 382; "Pity the Poor GOP," *National Journal*, 5 July 1986,

1643; and Thomas B. Edsall, "When in Doubt, Spend," *Washington Post National Weekly Edition*, 14 July 1986, 13.

50. Richard E. Cohen, "GOP Senate Losers Said to Deserve It," *National Journal*, 20 December 1986, 3086–87.

51. See, for example, Sidney Blumenthal, "This Year, the Republicans Are a Party in Search of a Theme," *Washington Post National Weekly Edition*, 31 March 1986, 12; Associated Press, "GOP Staff Given Bonus after Loss of the Senate," *Washington Post*, 2 January 1987, A14; and Rowland Evans and Robert Novak, "Dunning the GOP," *Washington Post*, 7 January 1987, A21.

52. Ronald D. Elving, "GOP Faces Tough Odds in Bid to Regain Senate," *Congressional Quarterly Weekly Report*, 3 October 1987, 2371–77.

53. Ibid., 2371.

54. Carol Matlack, "Backdoor Spending," *National Journal*, 8 October 1988, 2516–19; and Richard E. Cohen, "Running with the Hill," *National Journal*, 24 September 1988, 2403–5.

55. See, for example, George Skelton, "Running From, Not For, Office," *Los Angeles Times*, 23 July 1990, A1.

56. James A. Barnes, "Keeping the Senate in Democratic Hands," *National Journal*, 5 January 1991, 32.

57. Helen Dewar, "A Time for Incumbents to Tremble," *Washington Post*, 5 April 1992, A20.

58. James A. Barnes, "Four for the Money," *National Journal*, 16 March 1991, 636–40.

9

The New Conventional Wisdom, Fraying at Its Edges

The FECA rests on the premise of campaigns centered on candidates and largely controlled by them. In 1996, however, the door was opened for major parts of the campaign to go forward without the participation of the candidates and without any statutory limits.... Although the constitutional expansions did not benefit the parties exclusively, they augmented their role in the campaigns far more than that of any other participant.

—Frank Sorauf, 1998

After the campaign-centered electoral order emerged in presidential and congressional politics during the 1950s, it took nearly two decades for the new politics to permeate most American elections. This new order—with its distinct patterns of representation, deliberation, and choice—presented difficult challenges to party activists and leaders, as well as to candidates. They first had to develop an analysis which made sense of the new order, a new paradigm that could explain how and why the new politics worked. To complete their analysis, they had to develop strategic responses to this order that would allow them to compete effectively in elections. Previous chapters show that by 1992 most Democratic and Republican leaders and activists had arrived at an analysis and response that satisfied their competitive needs.

This chapter opens with a capsule description of their dominant response to the campaign-centered electoral order: the Accommodationist paradigm as a new conventional wisdom about the role of parties and party organizations in American elections. Then it briefly surveys the role of Democratic and Republican Party organizations in national elections since 1992. Two especially important influences on their continued development deserve attention: the major parties' surprisingly close competition for control of Congress and the explosion of political money spurred by the partial collapse of federal campaign finance regulations in 1996. Next, it considers the resilience of the campaign-centered order as its central features remain even in the face of ongoing political turmoil. Finally, this chapter looks forward and asks a broader question: what are the implications of campaign-centered politics for representative democracy in America?

The New Conventional Wisdom

I have argued in this book that both Republicans and Democrats came to understand and adapt to campaign-centered politics by the mid-1980s. Though campaigns, candidate strategies, election issues, campaign finance, and media participation continue to evolve, party organizations and candidates have settled into clear patterns of thinking and action. In the language of this book, they have developed a workable paradigmatic analysis of the world around them, as well as a workable strategic response. More colloquially, activists and leaders within each party have figured out the new politics and constructed their own ways of working with it.

Thomas Kuhn argued that such paradigms, once developed and accepted, tend to become conventional wisdom. They shape future thinking until some new crisis casts doubt on their adequacy in explaining and engaging the world.[1] This is precisely the case with political parties: widespread acceptance of the Accommodationist paradigm has led to a new conventional wisdom about the role of party organizations in contemporary elections.

Consider the parties' national committees. Of course, the national committee of the party holding the White House—the in-party—plays a different role from that of the out-party, but both engage in a remarkably consistent set of activities. To begin with, both continue their century-old Textbook Party role of coordinating the logistics of the presidential nominating process and the quadrennial party conventions. Afterward, both also join forces with the campaign organization of their party's presidential nominee to stage the general election campaign.

Perhaps more important, both spend the three years between presidential election campaigns working to support and develop professional party organization and activity at all levels of American government. They help raise money for and provide whatever support they can for state and local party leaders and activists, helping to build an increasingly Accommodationist party infrastructure across the country. They may continue such activities partly in deference to the state and local party activists who still dominate the parties' national committee memberships, who themselves often struggle with the vagaries of campaign-centered politics.[2] But they also developed this "party building" work in response to regulations under the Federal Election Campaign Act (FECA) which—though they limit the money a national committee can spend in support of candidates for the presidency or for Congress—place no limits on the money those committees spend helping state and local parties do the same thing.[3]

The Democratic and Republican national committees have developed an impressive and expensive array of professional services to candidates, supporters and state parties, and they have come to organize them in a standard way, as reflected in figure 9.1. They have large *political* divisions with campaign management, polling, and strategic consultants on staff who can develop an array of possible issues and themes for legislative and electoral battles. These political divisions also often coordinate their own field operations, staging voter registration, contact, mobilization, and turnout programs. The national committees have large *research* staffs and operations that gather strategic information on major policy issues, as well as on opposition officeholders, candidates, and campaigns. They have *communications* offices that distribute this information both to party leaders and activists across the country and to strategic media outlets. Both parties house their own media production facilities, which enable party leaders and activists to record and broadcast live and taped productions for television, radio, and the Internet. To support all this, both national committees have large *finance* operations to raise money in large and small donations in a variety of ways from individuals, interest groups, and political action committees.

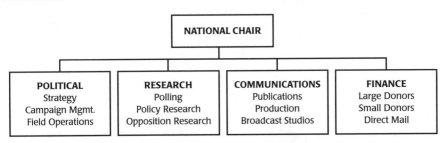

Figure 9.1
Party National Committee Organization

The in-party's national committee must balance all of these activities with the additional responsibility of acting as a political arm of the White House, which leaves party leaders and activists more willing to consider Textbook Party initiatives. Different presidents have handled their party's national committees in different ways, but all have shared common practices. All have used the national committee as a shell organization for the president's "permanent campaign." Major portions of Bill Clinton's 1992 and 1996 campaign staffs, for example, simply moved to the DNC after the election and continued their operations: polling, issue development, research, public outreach, coalition liaison, fundraising, and so on. Clinton merely followed the examples of Ronald Reagan and George Bush, and the winner of the 2000 presidential election can be expected to do the same. Such activities siphon resources from— and often create conflicts with—the national committees' other responsibilities, but few party leaders and activists challenge them effectively.[4]

The House and Senate party campaign committees have had similarly well-established roles since at least the mid-1980s. Like the in-party's national committee, the Capitol Hill campaign committees must remain attentive to the demands of party officeholders and the party-in-government. For the most part, however, that attention is now limited to the simple imperative of gaining or protecting majority control of the chamber, which means attention to legislative issues but not day-to-day legislator oversight of the committee. This is especially true on the Republican side, where senators and representatives seem somewhat more willing to defer to the judgment of professionals on the campaign committee staffs (with some notable exceptions). But it has been increasingly true on the Democratic side since the party's leaders accepted the Accommodationist paradigm in the mid-1980s.

The Capitol Hill campaign committees have similar structures and perform many of the same activities and provide many of the same services as the national committees, though for a much narrower constituency. They have their own *political* divisions that provide strategic consultation, polling, and issue development for congressional candidates. To a lesser degree, they often have the capacity to conduct their own voter-related field operations. They also have extensive *research* and *communications* divisions, *media centers,* and *finance* divisions much like the national committees.

These Capitol Hill campaign committees differ substantially from the parties' national committees in three areas, however. First, they devote substantial resources in off-years to identifying and recruiting candidates to run for open seats and to challenge opposition incumbents (in addition to helping party nominees in special congressional elections).[5] Second, as noted in chapters 7 and 8, the committee staffs often perform a sort of quality-control function for candidates and campaigns. They investigate whether a candidate's campaign organization meets current standards of professionalism and attempt to intervene when necessary (though candidates often notoriously resist such intervention). Third, and most dramatic, they contribute money to—and spend money on behalf of—those Senate and

House campaigns in ways that the Federal Election Campaign Act prohibits in presidential campaigns.

There are, of course, important differences between the House and the Senate as well. Because each general election brings 435 House contests and only 33 or 34 Senate contests, the House (or "Congressional") campaign committees of both parties provide a more generic set of professional services to candidates than do the Senate campaign committees. The smaller number of Senate campaigns also means that the senatorial campaign committees more quickly run into FECA limits on direct contributions to candidates, and they thus provide a greater share of their contributions in-kind, under section 441a(d) of the act.

Despite these differences, however, there remains broad agreement across the parties about the Accommodationist paradigm and the strategic role of the national party committees. In a nutshell, virtually everyone agrees that a Capitol Hill campaign committee's mission is to help its party's candidates stage professional and competitive campaigns and thus to win majority control of the Congress.

It is important to note that there is no functional imperative to embrace this Accommodationist paradigm or its strategic prescription. These are established and conventional patterns of party organization activity, but party leaders and activists can think and do otherwise. Indeed, a sizable minority of officeholders continues to press for Textbook Party initiatives. Though few of them embrace that paradigm's original conclusion that a party-centered strategy can transform the campaign-centered nature of American politics, they do argue forcefully that parties should actively organize to shape their constituent coalitions, offer coherent national platforms, recruit only those candidates who support the platforms, and actively support the platform once party candidates gain office. This view is honored more often in the breach than in the observance, and Accommodationist pragmatism usually carries the day. But if any party leaders or activists can develop a more compelling analysis of the campaign-centered electoral order that enables them to pursue a more successful strategy in winning elections, they remain free to do so.

Still, if the analysis presented in this book is accurate, this new conventional wisdom enables us to form hypotheses—predictions—about what party organizations will do in future elections. If the parties did indeed settle on predominantly Accommodationist politics by the late 1980s, then a look at more recent elections will reveal that the party organizations have continued to perform that consistent set of party roles and professional functions. Even a cursory look reveals a great deal of continuity, despite some profound changes in the political environment of recent elections.

The Tumultuous Elections of 1994, 1996, and 1998

The elections of 1990 and 1992 established the 1990s as a period of political tumult, change, and uncertainty. Long-standing patterns of two-party politics and of a Republican "lock" on presidential elections fell in 1992 as Ross Perot entered the presidential race and Bill Clinton won the White House. The change and uncertainty continued in 1994 as Republicans won complete control of Congress for the first time in forty years, and Perot established a Reform Party infrastructure throughout the country. By the time the dust had settled on the 1994 election, it was clear that the competitive balance of partisan politics in the United States had changed dramatically.[6] Though Democratic House candidates drew 2 million fewer votes than in the previous midterm election in 1990, the number of voters supporting Republican House candidates had increased by more than 5.5 million.[7] It now seemed especially ironic that some commentators had only three years earlier asked in a book whether elections even mattered, expressing their dismay at stagnant patterns of party control.[8]

The 1996 and 1998 elections proved that the see-saw results of 1992 and 1994 would continue. After spending early 1995 pleading that he was "still relevant" to national policymaking, the following year a resilient Bill Clinton easily won reelection to the White House over Republican Bob Dole and a receding Ross Perot. Perhaps more surprisingly, Democrats in 1996 were able to recruit strong candidates and capitalize quickly on public discontent with Speaker of the House Newt Gingrich (R-Ga.) and Republican partisanship. They surged to popularity in public opinion polls and very nearly won back control of the House of Representatives, narrowing the Republican margin in the House to only twenty-one seats.[9] The 1998 election narrowed the margin to only twelve seats in the House, though Republicans retained clear control of the Senate. Both elections demonstrated that this new and closely divided electoral environment means that party control of the national government—and of a growing number of state governments—depends on the success of each party in turning out its voters on election day.[10]

This closely divided electorate also means that party organization activities at all levels can play an increasingly important role in elections. As the amount of money in politics grows, these organizations continue to expand their role beyond candidate recruitment, campaign strategy, and fundraising. More and more of each organization's work—and the work of their allies—involves activities that seek to mobilize supporters, discourage opposition voters, and convert the undecided. Such activities include public opinion polling and focus groups, extensive efforts to gain media coverage of party views, and grassroots programs of voter registration, identification, and GOTV (get-out-the-vote). Election results in 1998 demonstrated the power of such efforts. One Republican observer acknowledged that "Democrats beat Republicans on the ground . . . . [T]he increase in turnout among two key Democratic base groups was staggering—African-Americans and union households."[11]

The other important electoral development of the late 1990s came in campaign finance, as federal courts struck down important provisions of the Federal Election Campaign Act's restrictions on party soft money and independent expenditures, and the amount of money flowing into campaigns grew beyond all expectations.[12] Since the initial passage of the FECA in 1971, Congress and the Federal Election Commission had struggled to maintain limits and regulations over money spent in federal election campaigns. The act initially limited virtually all aspects of campaign finance: how much individuals and organizations could contribute to party organizations and campaigns, how much party organizations could contribute to and spend on campaigns, and (briefly) how much candidates themselves could spend on campaigns. The U.S. Supreme Court quickly struck down limits on candidate spending in the 1976 *Buckley* v. *Valeo* decision, ruling that such limits violated First Amendment protections of free expression.[13] The rest of the law's provisions remained in place, however, and strongly shaped political practices of the 1970s and 1980s.

As the party committees' fundraising effectiveness grew and as political action committees (PACs) formed in the 1970s and began pouring money into party coffers, both Republican and Democratic committees developed ways of circumventing the FECA limits. Their first important innovation was "agency agreements," through which the national party organizations could transfer unlimited funds to their state and local affiliates for "party building" and other campaign-related activities. By the end of the 1980s, both parties' organizations also routinely transferred cash to various other kinds of supportive "independent" organizations.[14] Though the "agency" and "independent" funds were initially raised by the national parties, they were not subject to the "hard" fundraising restrictions of the FECA and were thus dubbed "soft" money.

The FEC could not control such spending, but it did succeed in publicizing its existence beginning in the 1992 election cycle, during which national party organizations were first required to report on their "nonfederal" accounts. The reporting had little effect, however, as the parties raised ever-greater amounts and looked for new ways of circumventing FECA limits. By 1996 they had found two new methods. One was "issue ads" that advanced the party point of view but did not specifically mention any election contest. The other was "independent expenditures" that party organizations could transfer to political organizations that would then spend the money to support or oppose Senate and House candidates. Discussion later in this chapter shows that both parties steered tens of millions of dollars into these devices in 1996 and 1998, with substantial effect.

All of these developments whittled away at the FECA's regulatory regime, but a Supreme Court decision in 1996 took an ax to the law. In *Colorado Republican Federal Campaign Committee* v. *Federal Election Commission*, the Supreme Court "ruled that party committees had the same right to make independent expenditures as other committees" as long as the expenditure was not done in collaboration with a candidate's campaign.[15] In effect, the Court extended the reach of the *Buckley* doctrine and ruled that FEC limits violated party committees' First Amendment rights to speak freely in advancing their political views.[16] The Court reaffirmed this free-speech argument in November 1998, when it rejected appeals in *City of Cincinnati* v. *Kruse* (98–454). Plaintiffs in that suit wanted to reinstate a 1995 city ordinance that placed limits on campaign spending by city council candidates and had pressed the suit specifically to give the Supreme Court a chance to reconsider its prior rulings.[17] These decisions created ample opportunities for the national party committees to raise and spend political money and, though they still had to obey hard-money limits on direct contributions to federal campaigns, the committees responded quickly.

Spurred by the *Colorado* decision, a bipartisan group of congressional reformers pressed for campaign finance reform legislation. Senators John McCain (R-Ariz.) and Russell Feingold (D-Wisc.) drafted legislation that would sharply limit "soft" money donations and place strict limits on "issue ads," but it was killed by filibusters in October 1997 and February 1998. Opponents led by NRSC Chair Mitch McConnell (R-Ky.) argued that the bills would trample on free political expression, and further that the effort was pointless, since the *Buckley* and *Colorado* cases indicated that the Supreme Court would strike down the legislation.[18] Nevertheless, the following summer Representatives Christopher Shays (R-Conn.) and Martin Meehan (D-Mass.) proposed similar legislation in the House, where it won narrow passage and renewed hopes that senators would accede to the public's demands for reform. Led again by McConnell, a Republican minority in the Senate sustained a filibuster in September, however, and the reformers abandoned their efforts.[19] Despite public anger and frustration over the rapid growth of unregulated campaign spending, the system seemed unlikely to change.

Throughout these legal and legislative maneuvers most party leaders and activists maintained their conventional adherence to the established Accommodationist paradigm. Others, led especially by Gingrich and his cadre of House Republican insurgents, started a somewhat ill-fated revival of the Textbook Party paradigm. A brief survey of organizational activity in each party, and in each kind of party organization, demonstrates the range of possibilities.

The Republican National Committee

Losing the White House for the first time in twelve years in 1992 did little to change Republicans' views about the campaign-centered electoral order or about their strategy for accommodating it. Republican leaders and activists gathered shortly after that election and chose as chair Haley Barbour, a former Reagan White House political director and RNC member from Mississippi.[20] Party scholar Philip Klinkner observed that Barbour, once elected, "made it clear that he intended to follow the same organizational path chosen by his Republican out-party successors," Ray Bliss and Bill Brock.[21] He continued the RNC's conventional organization with its political, research, communications and finance divisions and moved to establish himself as a unifying national spokesman for Republican causes in preparation for the 1996 presidential campaign.[22]

Though he stayed clearly within the Accommodationist paradigm, Barbour nevertheless pressed for tactical innovation at the party headquarters. The quick end to President Clinton's postinaugural honeymoon drove a mild fundraising boom at the organization (see fig. 9.2, p. 190), which enabled Barbour to move on several initiatives at once. In a gesture reminiscent of Textbook Party actions of the 1950s and 1960s, he used soft money to create a National Policy Forum where Republican activists could gather and consider the party's legislative program. The forum revealed policy splits within the party, however, and after a brief controversy over whether this nominally independent organization complied with FECA limits, Barbour shut it down.[23] More important, Barbour moved the committee toward more effective use of quickly changing communications technology, establishing a "GOP-TV" network broadcasting on more than 160 cable stations in forty-two states, as well as a World Wide Web information and strategy clearinghouse site on the Internet.[24] The RNC also worked closely with state parties and congressional Republicans during the 1994 midterm elections, providing a full array of professional services as well as tens of millions of soft dollars to support their efforts.[25]

Once the 1995–96 election cycle got under way, Barbour quickly shifted the organization to focus on preparation for the 1996 convention and general election campaign. He drew widespread praise among Republicans, especially in using RNC money to sustain Kansas Senator Robert Dole's presidential campaign during the late spring and early summer, after Dole had reached FECA spending limits but could not yet draw on public funds for his general election campaign. Between March and the Republican National Convention in August, Barbour spent $20 million on a television "issue advertising" campaign focusing on Dole and the party's major themes for the fall election: welfare reform, congressional reform, and Medicare.[26] Though they provoked regulatory challenges, the ads remained legal because they never explicitly mentioned Dole or the November election. After August, though Dole's lackluster fall campaign never seriously threatened Clinton's reelection chances, Barbour drew wide praise for providing a strong RNC infrastructure and supporting Republicans at all levels across the country through the November elections.[27]

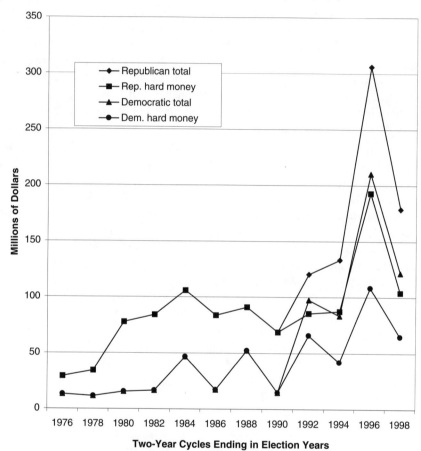

Figure 9.2
Party National Committee Receipts, 1976-98
Source: Federal Election Commission reports.

Barbour's most important innovations, however, were financial. He dramatically expanded the RNC's soft-money fundraising and then carefully channeled millions of dollars of RNC money to sympathetic interest groups who "pushed for voter registration or backed party positions in advertisements or direct mail campaigns."[28] For example, during the last two months of the 1996 campaign the RNC gave more than $4.5 million to Americans for Tax Reform, a conservative group headed by Newt Gingrich ally Grover Norquist. During October, the committee also transferred hundreds of thousands of dollars to the National Right to Life Committee, the American Defense Institute, and other groups. The strategy drew howls of protest from Democrats, but it complied with the letter of the FECA (or what remained of it). Perhaps ominously for the RNC, however, an increasing share of the committee's growth in fundraising was coming in soft money: 29 percent in 1992, 35 percent in 1994, 37 percent in 1996, and 42 percent in 1998.

Barbour, labeled by one reporter "perhaps the most successful RNC chairman since Ray C. Bliss rebuilt the party after the electoral disaster of 1964," stepped down as chair shortly after the 1996 election. After a brief factional skirmish, RNC members replaced him with Jim Nicholson, a fellow RNC member and Denver businessman.[29] Nicholson proved to be a more cautious chair than Barbour, but he worked successfully on three tasks. First, he presided over the committee's continued fundraising success, avoiding the scandal and notoriety that plagued the Democratic National Committee during the same period. Second, he pressed for further deregulation of campaign finance, rallying House and Senate Republicans against the McCain-Feingold and Shays-Meehan bills in 1998 and pressing the FEC to further deregulate issue advertising and soft money. Finally, he took the traditional out-party chair's role as a national policy and political spokesperson for the party, rallying the party faithful and attacking the opposition. Factional skirmishes occasionally deflected him: he spent several weeks of early 1998 fighting an effort by antiabortion Republicans to withhold party money from candidates who refused to take a strong pro-life stand.[30] Most of the time, however, he spoke for all Republicans in denouncing Bill Clinton and supporting the party's off-year candidates in congressional and state elections.

The House Republicans

The Republican Capitol Hill campaign committees had been no less creative during the election cycles since 1992. Perhaps the most striking development came in a Textbook Party initiative by Republicans in the House of Representatives. Embittered by decades of entrenched Democratic control of the House, a cadre of conservative Republican leaders organized by Representative Newt Gingrich had worked since 1980 to lay the groundwork for a programmatic campaign for majority status. They had systematically recruited and trained Republican House candidates in districts across the country and developed a complex system of "independent" foundations and political action committees to finance their campaigns. The most important of these committees was GOPAC, the conduit for millions of dollars in soft money later challenged by Democrats, the FEC, and the Internal Revenue Service.[31] Though congressional investigations led the House to reprimand and fine Gingrich in January of 1997, the results of this network of organizations remained in place.

The work of these conservatives culminated in 1994 with a powerful merging of Textbook Party and Accommodationist efforts. One component of those efforts was the Contract with America, a sweeping platform of conservative initiatives to reform and reorient American national government. Written by Gingrich, Representative Dick Armey (Tex.), and others, the Contract offered a programmatic challenge to Clinton and the Democrats, and hundreds of Republican House candidates gathered in September 1994 to endorse it on the steps of the Capitol in Washington.[32] It was a purely Textbook Party initiative, contesting the election on a coherent platform and committing members to vote for the program should they win office, and it ultimately led to increased expressions of public support for Congress as an institution.

The second and third components of the 1994 Republican surge blended Textbook Party with Accommodationist strategies once again. Gingrich enlisted Republican colleagues to help recruit dozens of high-quality challengers and open-seat candidates for the 1994 election. To the greatest extent possible, they recruited candidates who endorsed the Contract's legislative program, but they also focused on conventional professional measures of candidate quality and sophistication.[33] Finally, as NRCC revenues dipped somewhat (see fig. 9.3, p. 193), Gingrich recruited more than 130 of his House Republican colleagues to personally raise more than $5 million on behalf of newly recruited Republican challengers who were locked in tight races. As with the RNC, however, a growing proportion of these revenues came in soft money that had to be channeled through state and local Republican parties and independent organizations.

Throughout, Gingrich worked closely with the National Republican Congressional Committee and its chair, Representative Bill Paxon of New York. The committee's professional staff integrated the Gingrich Contract initiative with support from Barbour's RNC and the more conventional work of the NRCC, including fundraising, research and communications, campaign management consultation, and other professional services.[34] In this instance, Textbook Party and Accommodationist strategies meshed almost perfectly. With full support from House Republicans, the committee steered a record level of contributions, services, and other expenditures toward Republican challengers. These efforts were guided in part by dramatically expanded public opinion research based on NRCC-funded polling and focus groups conducted by Republican pollsters including Gingrich ally Frank Luntz.[35] In the end, all of the party's incumbents won reelection and scores of challengers and open-seat candidates swept Democrats aside, as Republicans won majority control of the House for the first time since 1954.

For the 1996 election cycle, Representative Paxon retained most of his top staff and the NRCC simply carried on, the only difference being that they were working to *retain* control of the House. Details of the committee's work were different—they now had a far larger number of incumbents to attend to, for example, and the committee drew a larger share of PAC contributions than before—but the essential strategy of the organization changed very little.[36] They remained in close

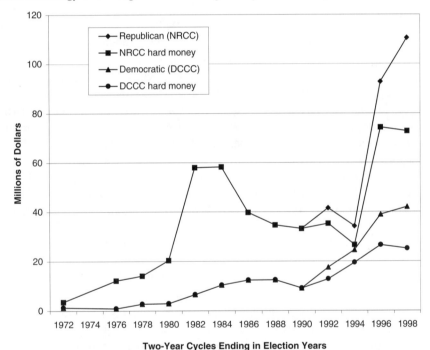

Figure 9.3
House Party Committee Receipts 1972-98
Source: Federal Election Commission reports.

contact with the House Republican leadership and continued to work to blend Textbook Party commitments with Accommodationist professionalism.

Majority status and incumbency brought a surge of hard- and soft-money contributions throughout the cycle, and it turned out that the NRCC would need the funds. Emboldened by their 1994 victory and the political success of the Contract with America, Gingrich, Senate Majority Leader Trent Lott (R-Miss.), and the congressional Republicans challenged President Clinton head-on in late 1995.[37] They sent him an omnibus collection of appropriations bills containing provisions he opposed, combined with the budgetary legislation necessary to fund the federal government. Clinton called the Republicans' bluff and vetoed the legislation, and the stalemate produced two partial shutdowns of the federal government in late 1995. The public soured on the Republicans' confrontational tactics, and support for Democratic congressional candidates surged. It took every penny the Republicans could raise to give the party's candidates a chance to repair their image during the following summer and fall, but they ultimately pulled it out.[38] They ended the election (and subsequent run-offs) with only seven fewer seats and a 228–207 majority.

As members of the 1994 Republican freshman class won reelection and began to gain seniority, Gingrich's and the NRCC's unprecedented paradigmatic blend began to show further signs of strain. The House Ethics Committee spent 1995 and 1996 investigating charges that Gingrich had commingled hundreds of thousands of dollars from tax-exempt foundations, political action committees, his personal campaign fund, and his congressional office funds in clear violation of law and FEC regulations. Shortly after the 1996 election, Gingrich admitted submitting false financial statements to the committee, and he won reelection as Speaker by only eleven votes before being reprimanded by the House.[39] When budget talks in the House began to unravel under Gingrich the following summer, a group of his lieutenants (including former NRCC Chair Bill Paxon) decided that they'd had enough of his erratic and confrontational leadership. Though Gingrich loyalists discovered and blocked a July 1997 "coup," the Speaker never recovered his full authority. Gingrich remained as Speaker through the 1998 election, then abruptly resigned after Democrats narrowed the Republican majority to 223–212.[40]

The work of the NRCC during the 1997–98 election cycle was strongly shaped by this turmoil and the growing national polarization over Independent Counsel Kenneth Starr and congressional Republicans' efforts to impeach and remove President Clinton from office. As Paxon moved up the party ranks, Representative John Linder (R-Ga.) took over as NRCC chair and worked to expand the Republicans' majority in the House. Linder, a close ally of Gingrich's, was successful at the conventional business of candidate recruitment and fundraising. His most important contribution to the NRCC was to increase the organization's focus on mobilizing and turning out Republican voters on election day.[41] With the support of Gingrich and House Majority Leader Dick Armey (R-Tex.), Linder proposed to allocate $37 million to "Operation Breakout," a national campaign of televised "issue ads" from Labor Day to election day touting the accomplishments of the Republican Congress and laying out the party's issue agenda for the future.[42]

The release of Independent Counsel Kenneth Starr's report on the Lewinsky affair in September disrupted their plans, however, and in the final week of the campaign Gingrich and Armey directed that the NRCC shift the focus of the ads toward issues of honesty and character. The decision apparently backfired, however, mobilizing angry Democratic voters and costing Republicans several closely contested House races. In the upheaval following the election, House Republicans held Linder accountable and replaced him with Representative Thomas M. Davis III (R-Va.). A month later, House Republicans chose Representative Dennis Hastert (R-Ill.) to be the new Speaker of the House, in part because he promised no grandiose programmatic schemes.[43]

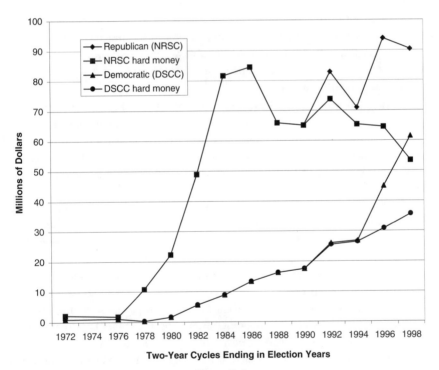

Figure 9.4
Senate Party Committee Receipts 1972-98
Source: Federal Election Commission reports.

The Senate Republicans

The National Republican Senatorial Committee entered post-1992 without any substantial paradigmatic reassessment, but the developments in campaign finance law in 1996 led to striking developments there as well. During the 1993–94 cycle NRSC Chair Phil Gramm of Texas capitalized on the committee's conventional strengths, and though the committee suffered from diminished receipts (see fig. 9.4, p. 195), it did remarkably well. Hostility toward President Clinton and frustration with a unified but ineffective Democratic Party government created an ideal opportunity. Several Democratic incumbents retired, and Gramm successfully recruited strong candidates.[44] Republican voters, mobilized by their party's high-profile House campaign, turned out in record numbers and swept Republicans back into majority control of the Senate as well.

In the aftermath of such sweeping success, NRSC chair Senator Alfonse D'Amato of New York found little reason to change anything as the 1995–96 election cycle began. Majority status revitalized the committee's fundraising and eased the task of candidate recruitment. Though several Republican senators had endorsed the Contract with America, there seemed to be little sentiment in favor of a broad Textbook Party initiative at the committee.

During the summer of 1996, however, the United States Supreme Court changed the rules of the game. In the *Colorado Republican Federal Campaign Committee* v. *FEC* decision described earlier, the Court ruled that party committees could make independent expenditures that expressly advocate the election or defeat of federal candidates, which the Federal Election Commission had previously held to be violations of the FECA. With their growing financial resources, D'Amato and the NRSC took advantage of the ruling immediately, and the committee intensified its efforts to raise soft money. Figure 9.4 (p. 195) shows that, although hard-money fundraising for the committee continued to stagnate (as it had for a decade), the infusion of soft money in 1996 produced a record NRSC budget.

Over the next four months the committee targeted more than $7 million of that money to about a dozen closely contested Senate races around the country. For example, the committee spent more than $1.2 million in Louisiana for advertising and other activities critical of Democratic Senate nominee Mary Landrieu (who ultimately won by fewer than 10,000 votes). They also spent nearly $1 million in New Hampshire against Democrat Dick Swett, who nearly unseated incumbent Senator Robert Smith. The *Colorado* ruling still held such spending to be illegal if coordinated with the candidate's campaign organization, and the DSCC immediately filed complaints with the FEC, but the NRSC insulated its activities enough to avoid legal violations.[45]

The committee spent another $7 million on "issue advocacy" advertising, but the independent expenditures clearly marked the most important innovation of the cycle, helping to salvage the Republican majority in the face of near defeat. At least one observer credited the injection of party money in the final weeks with saving several Republicans: "In the end, the NRSC was on the winning end of almost every contest that saw the committee spend heavily late in the game."[46] D'Amato and the committee drew scattered complaints for "micromanagement and consultant favoritism" in some campaigns, but those carried little weight in light of the election results.[47] The *Colorado* ruling and D'Amato's innovations had transformed the organization's work.

D'Amato's successor, Senator Mitch McConnell of Kentucky, quickly established himself as perhaps the most visible NRSC chair in recent memory. McConnell happily carried on the tasks of fundraising and candidate recruitment and worked even harder to establish himself as the leading national opponent to campaign finance reform. Even as he raised unprecedented amounts of soft money for the committee (see fig. 9.4, p. 195), McConnell led the Senate filibusters against the McCain-Feingold bill which would have sharply limited soft-money contributions.[48] McConnell and the NRSC also pursued court challenges to much of the remaining FEC regulations on the committee's campaign spending. The Federal Election Commission does not limit the amount of soft money spent in various ways by the NRSC and other national party committees, but it does require that such spending be matched with a certain proportion of hard money. With declining amounts of hard money to work with in a very competitive election, McConnell and the NRSC pressed for maximum flexibility, arguing that the FEC "ratios" interfered with the free expression they were entitled to under the Supreme Court doctrine expressed in the recent *Colorado* case.[49]

That case remains unresolved, but most Senate Republicans were satisfied with the work done in 1997 and 1998 by McConnell and the NRSC. Fighting Democrats to a standstill, the party retained its 55-45 majority in the Senate. Senator Chuck Hagel (R-Neb.) mounted a brief challenge to McConnell's reelection as NRSC chair in late November, arguing that McConnell's abrasive style and adamant opposition to campaign finance reform had hurt the party.[50] McConnell easily turned back the challenge.

The Democratic National Committee

As the conventional wisdom would predict, Bill Clinton's victory in 1992 initiated a difficult period for the Democratic National Committee. On one hand, Clinton and the rest of the new executive-branch party-in-government expected the DNC to transform itself into a political arm of the White House. On the other, party leaders and activists expected the organization to continue the successful professional work that had helped Clinton win in the first place. Though no one doubted that the organization should simultaneously pursue both missions, no one doubted that the two missions would conflict.[51]

Clinton set the process in motion by handpicking as chair David Wilhelm, manager of the 1992 Clinton-Gore campaign. With little prior exposure to the DNC's Accommodationist agenda, Wilhelm took office with a Textbook Party-influenced plan for supporting Clinton and the party-in-government. He shifted a large number of professionals from the Clinton-Gore organization onto the DNC payroll and collaborated closely with the White House in devising its initial political and legislative strategies. Their efforts were shaped in part by what Lawrence Jacobs and Robert Shapiro have called "a steady flow of survey data based on both private polls and compilations of published material."[52] Throughout Clinton's presidency, millions of DNC dollars have been set aside for nearly continuous polling and focus groups.

Clinton's and the DNC's fundraising success continued into the 1993–94 cycle (relative to 1989–90), and Wilhelm budgeted millions of dollars for polling and professional consultation for the White House. He also pledged to develop a large national issue advertising campaign and field operation in support of Clinton's economic stimulus package and health-care reform initiative. The field operation, he said, would identify and train volunteers across the country, who would in turn contact members of Congress and more than a million voters to lobby on behalf of the White House.[53]

Wilhelm's ambitious plans for the DNC quickly collapsed as Democratic members of Congress objected to the DNC's efforts to organize grassroots lobbying in their own districts and states. Twelve years of broad-based party building by Charles Manatt, Paul Kirk, and Ron Brown had created expectations that the DNC should support *all* Democrats, they argued, and the DNC should leave them to judge how they should vote on legislation. More importantly, they said, why should the DNC be spending millions of Democratic dollars on lobbying and consultants when members of Congress needed the campaign money to help in what was shaping up to be a difficult midterm election? Wilhelm backpedaled quickly, closed down the lobbying operation, and eventually laid off more than a quarter of his staff. He shifted several million dollars of committee funds toward a conventional Accommodationist program of supporting state parties and Democratic candidates in the midterm campaign, but his fortunes never recovered. In August of

1994, he announced that he would step down after the midterm election, and few mourned his passing.[54]

Once Wilhelm had departed, the DNC quickly reverted to more conventional form. Senator Christopher Dodd (Conn.) and longtime party activist Don Fowler of South Carolina were named co-chairs of the national committee early in 1995. Once it became clear that no Democrat would challenge President Bill Clinton's re-nomination, they focused the committee entirely on fundraising, party building, and laying the groundwork for Clinton's reelection, in close collaboration with the White House.[55] Financially, the committee achieved remarkable success, more than doubling its receipts from the already successful 1991–92 cycle (see fig. 9.2, p. 190). Even more than the Republican National Committee, however, the DNC remained heavily reliant on soft money, which was the source of 32.5 percent of the committee's money in 1992 and approximately half of the committee's money in the 1993–94 and 1995–96 election cycles.

This proved not to be a terrible operational problem, given that the FECA sharply restricted the amount of money the national committee could spend directly on the presidential elections anyway. To avoid those restrictions, the DNC simply transferred tens of millions of dollars to state and local Democratic parties throughout the 1995–96 cycle, much of that under the auspices of "agency agreements" and the "coordinated campaign" in support of Democratic candidates at all levels. The committee also purchased television time in late 1995, broadcasting issue ads criticizing Republican congressional proposals on Medicaid, education spending, environmental deregulation, and tax cuts for the wealthy. (The RNC emulated this strategy in early 1996.) Paul Herrnson and Diana Dwyre have noted that the ads killed two birds with one stone. "They were primarily intended to improve Clinton's reelection prospects, but the $42.4 million that the DNC spent on issue ads over the course of the election helped set the tone for many House and Senate campaigns." Though the ads later spurred an investigation of whether they violated FECA regulations, like Gingrich's GOPAC, they had their desired effect.[56]

Almost. Though Clinton came from behind and easily won reelection, DNC fundraising itself became an issue late in the 1996 campaign as Republicans increasingly criticized the committee's gathering and spending of unlimited soft money. Both Democrats and Republicans engaged in the practice, but in September and October the media increasingly focused on gifts to the DNC from individuals and corporations with foreign connections. Donors affiliated with one such organization, the Singapore-based Lippo Group, drew particular attention for their gifts totaling $452,000. Committee fundraiser John Huang, an Arkansas associate from Clinton's days as governor there, gained notoriety for the Lippo-related contributions, as well as an illegal $250,000 contribution (later returned) from a Korean corporation and a

$140,000 fundraising event at a Buddhist temple in southern California.[57] The controversy never harmed Clinton's reelection chances, but it discouraged enough Democratic voters to allow Republicans to retain control of the House and Senate.

In the aftermath of 1996, despite winning the White House, the DNC plunged into disarray. Two congressional committees and the Justice Department launched investigations into DNC fundraising, and the organization sank deeply into debt as it returned millions of dollars in questionable contributions and hired an army of lawyers.[58] President Clinton replaced DNC Chairs Dodd and Fowler with Roy Romer, the popular governor of Colorado, and party activist Steve Grossman, who set to work with the "demoralized" organization. They spent much of 1997 simply reducing the debt, and party activists around the country began to worry whether the committee would be of any assistance in the 1998 midterm election.[59]

Ironically, the Monica Lewinsky scandal may have rescued the committee. Shortly after press reports of the president's affair surfaced in mid-January 1998, contributions from party faithful to the DNC surged and remained strong for the rest of the year.[60] The press and the public virtually ignored the Senate Governmental Affairs Committee's report on 1996 DNC fundraising improprieties, and the parallel House committee abandoned its investigation.[61] President Clinton toured the country throughout the year, raising unprecedented amounts of hard and soft money for an off-year election. The DNC even took to using Independent Counsel Kenneth Starr's name in its own fundraising appeals.[62] Debates within the party then shifted to whether the DNC raised too much money, and House and Senate leaders called on the president to share the wealth.[63] By October the president was appearing with House and Senate candidates at successful fundraising events for their campaigns, and the DNC was able to provide a substantial amount of money for the party's get-out-the-vote program. Even as the president struggled through impeachment and trial after the 1998 election, the Democratic National Committee remained poised to become a forceful participant in the campaigns of 2000.

The House Democrats

The Democratic Congressional Campaign Committee entered the Clinton era of unified party government with some confidence. Representative Vic Fazio of California took over as chair in early 1993 and initially worked hard to collaborate with the Clinton White House and its legislative agenda.[64] This relationship, though it brought millions of dollars in DNC money into Democratic House campaigns, remained a two-edged sword. Collaboration on NAFTA (North American Free Trade

Agreement) in particular created problems for the DCCC when the AFL-CIO openly criticized the 102 House Democrats who had voted to ratify the trade agreement, threatening to withhold union campaign assistance from them in 1994.[65] Such threats diminished as the 1994 election drew near, however, as both party and union leaders responded to the Contract with America and the growing Republican challenge.

Democrats initially viewed the Contract with America as a blessing. It helped to spur record levels of campaign contributions to the DCCC (see fig. 9.3, p. 193), which outstripped Republican spending on candidates for the first time on record. Fazio challenged the Contract and the growing influence of the Christian Coalition as signs of extreme conservatism within the Republican Party and urged Democratic House candidates to do likewise. As the campaign unfolded, however, growing numbers of Democratic incumbents found themselves in close races, and the DCCC was forced to channel a large proportion of its money to defensive campaigns.[66] In the end, the Republican surge swept scores of Democratic incumbents from office and the DCCC's record-setting efforts were lost in the tide.

Those efforts nevertheless drew little criticism, and most Democrats looked elsewhere to explain their stunning defeat. As Representative Martin Frost of Texas took over as the new DCCC chair in the aftermath, he retained most of the committee's top staff and promised to expand both fundraising and services. DCCC Executive Director Matt Angle noted in a 1995 interview that although the dramatic change in House Democrats' fortunes required that the committee change its day-to-day business, the electoral role of the committee would remain unchanged. It would work to recruit candidates, contribute to their campaigns and help them raise money, and provide research and communication to them throughout the election cycle.[67] The committee would also work with pro-Democratic voter registration programs around the country and help to develop a growing effort to make the 1996 congressional election a referendum on the unpopular Newt Gingrich and the "radical" Republican agenda.[68] The DCCC and House Democratic leaders also collaborated with Senate Democrats to develop a "Families First Agenda" in response to the Contract with America, but there would be no broad Textbook Party initiative as at the NRCC. The Accommodationist paradigm remained intact for Capitol Hill Democrats.

The strategy nearly worked in 1996, as Democrats succeeded in recruiting an array of strong candidates in their targeted districts, then raised unprecedented amounts of money to support their campaigns. Ultimately, however, the national focus established in the 1990s for many of those House races carried the day. Voter turnout fell in 1996 relative to 1992 as many Democratic voters grew discouraged at their party's fundraising scandal. Republicans rebounded in the final weeks and retained control of the House.

Frost remained as DCCC chair for the 1998 midterm election cycle, but he shifted the focus of the committee somewhat. More than 80 House incumbents ran for reelection uncontested, leaving the committee free to target its efforts more narrowly on competitive races. In doing so, the Frost and the DCCC blended the use of issue ads and up-to-date technology with more old-fashioned efforts aimed at increasing the turnout of Democratic voters on election day. The committee spent about $6 million on television and radio ads emphasizing such Democratic issues as education and Social Security and taking Republicans to task for dwelling on scandal and personal politics.[69] Simultaneously, the DCCC collaborated with labor and other grassroots groups to develop a massive mobilization effort in September and October, capitalizing on voter anger with Kenneth Starr, the Lewinsky scandal, and the House Republicans' impeachment effort.[70]

In almost a mirror image of the 1996 congressional campaign, Republicans faded in the final weeks of the 1998 campaign and Democratic turnout surged. As a result, Democrats gained five House seats, marking the first time since 1824 that a president's party gained seats in a second-term midterm election. Republicans still controlled the House, but by such a narrow margin that Democratic control seemed within reach in 2000.

The Senate Democrats

Like their Republican counterparts, party leaders and staff at the Democratic Senatorial Campaign Committee entered the 1994 campaign cycle proposing tactical innovation but no fundamental rethinking of the organization's electoral role. Under the chairmanship of Senator Bob Graham of Florida, the committee drew on ideas from the successful 1992 Clinton-Gore campaign in stressing research and communication to enable Democratic candidates' "rapid response" to any attack.[71] The organization collaborated as closely as possible with the now-flush DNC, though Democrats' inexperience with unified party government created friction. Democratic senators bristled at the emergence of gays in the military as the administration's first high-profile policy initiative, then drifted close to mutiny as first NAFTA and then the President's budget proposals drew wide public criticism.[72] David Wilhelm and the DNC promising to stir up grassroots efforts to lobby senators did not help.

Still, the DSCC took in record amounts of money during the cycle (see fig. 9.4, p. 195) and its direct and coordinated contributions to Senate candidates outstripped the NRSC's for the first time. The committee continued to expand what Democratic senators viewed as a successful operation, and the organization responded to calls for help as the difficult election unfolded. Even after the Republicans swamped the Democrats in November, gaining eight seats and majority control of Senate for the first time since 1986, no one blamed the DSCC for the loss.

Proof of Democrats' confidence in the DSCC's approach came after the election. Incoming chair Senator Robert Kerrey of Nebraska retained Executive Director Don Foley and most of the committee's top staff when he took over in early 1995.[73] Foley himself, though troubled by the 1994 losses, promised to keep the organization on its Accommodationist track. He proposed tactical innovations in research, communications, fundraising, and candidate training, but viewed the organization's stability as strength during a difficult time for Democrats.[74] The committee supported efforts by the Senate Democratic caucus to create the "Families First Agenda" as a mild Democratic rejoinder to the Republicans' Contract with America, but it did not dominate Democrats' fall campaign the way the Contract had in 1994.[75] Thus, though the 1994 losses and minority status had created a genuine crisis, they did not fundamentally challenge the worldview and strategic analysis of anyone at the DSCC.

As at the National Republican Senatorial Committee, however, the Supreme Court's *Colorado Republican Federal Campaign Committee* decision impacted greatly on the DSCC. As Senator Alfonse D'Amato led the NRSC to take immediate advantage of the ruling, DSCC attorneys initially protested the increased injection of Republican soft money into Senate races. As their appeals fell on deaf ears, however, the committee quickly changed course and began raising its own funds for issue ads and "independent expenditures" on targeted races. The committee never matched its Republican counterpart, but the DSCC was able to raise and spend more than $1 million on those activities in the final months of the campaign. Its largest such expenditures came in three states: Oregon, where the committee spent $384,000 on ads attacking Republican Senate nominee Gordon Smith (who won); Georgia, where the DSCC spent $357,000 on ads attacking Republican Guy Milner (who lost to Democrat Max Cleland); and Kansas, where the committee spent $319,000 on ads attacking Republican Sam Brownback (who won). Despite these injections of cash—or perhaps because of them—the 1996 Senate elections proved to be a virtual standoff: the Republicans expanded their majority by two seats, to 55–45.

The 1998 Senate elections produced much the same result. Senate Democratic leader Tom Daschle (D-S.D.) convinced Kerrey to stay on as DSCC chair, and Kerrey reluctantly struggled through the national fundraising scandal that followed the 1996 election. He proved to be an effective chair, however, recruiting strong candidates and nearly restoring the committee's steady fundraising growth. Figure 9.4

(p. 195) shows that, like other national party committees, the DSCC grew increasingly dependent on soft money for its work, but Kerrey drew widespread praise for the committee's targeting of contributions and assistance.[76] Given that Republicans began the cycle predicting a filibuster-proof majority of sixty seats, Democrats were more than happy to come away from the election with a 55–45 split, no net change.

In fact, incoming 1999–2000 DSCC Chair Robert Torricelli (D-N.J.) had spent much of 1998 looking forward to 2000, when the large Republican "Class of 1994" would face the voters. "1998 is disproportionately a defensive effort and 2000 is clearly all-out offense," he had acknowledged in July.[77] Given the public backlash against Senate Republicans' handling of the Clinton impeachment trial, regaining a Democratic majority in the Senate in 2000 seemed like a reasonable goal as Torricelli stepped into the DSCC leadership.

NOTES

1. Thomas S. Kuhn, *The Structure of Scientific Revolutions,* 2d ed. (Chicago: University of Chicago Press, 1970).

2. See, for example, John Frendreis and Alan R. Gitelson, "Local Parties in the 1990s: Spokes in a Candidate-Centered Wheel," in *The State of the Parties: The Changing Role of Contemporary American Parties,* 3d ed., ed. John C. Green and Daniel M. Shea (Lanham, Md.: Rowman & Littlefield, 1999).

3. See Trevor Potter, "Where Are We Now? The Current State of Campaign Finance Law"; Anthony Corrado, "Money and Politics: A History of Federal Campaign Finance Law"; and Corrado, "Soft Money," in *Campaign Finance Reform: A Sourcebook,* ed. Anthony Corrado, Thomas E. Mann, Daniel R. Ortiz, Trevor Potter, and Frank J. Sorauf (Washington, D.C.: Brookings Institution, 1997). See also John F. Bibby, "Party Networks: National-State Integration, Allied Groups, and Issue Activists"; and Melanie Blumberg, William Binning, and John C. Green, "Do the Grassroots Matter? The Coordinated Campaign in a Battleground State," in Green and Shea, *State of the Parties.*

4. John F. Harris, "President Fills Top Positions," *Washington Post,* 14 December 1996, A1. See also Anthony Corrado, "The Politics of Cohesion: The Role of the National Party Committees in the 1992 Election," in *The State of the Parties: The Changing Role of Contemporary American Parties,* ed. Daniel M. Shea and John C. Green (Lanham, Md.: Rowman & Littlefield, 1994); Laura Berkowitz, Connie Krauss, and Daniel M. Shea, "The Evolving Role of the National Committees in the 1990s," conference paper, University of Akron, October 1997.

5. For an excellent illustration of such committees' constant efforts to recruit candidates, see Tim Curran, "Senate Democrats Have Y2K Theory: Some Are Looking Ahead to Take Back

Control in 2000," *Roll Call,* 9 July 1998, which documents party efforts to recruit Senate candidates for 2000 before the beginning of the fall 1998 campaign.

6. Walter Dean Burnham, "Realignment Lives: The 1994 Earthquake and Its Implications," in *The Clinton Presidency: First Appraisals,* ed. Colin Campbell and Bert A. Rockman (Chatham, N.J.: Chatham House, 1996). For an excellent broader analysis, see also Walter Dean Burnham, "Bill Clinton: Riding the Tiger," in *The Election of 1996: Reports and Inter- pretations,* ed. Gerald M. Pomper (Chatham, N.J.: Chatham House, 1997)

7. Rhodes Cook, "Democrats' Congressional Base Shredded by November Vote," *Congres- sional Quarterly Weekly Report,* 10 December 1994, 3517. See also Philip A. Klinkner, ed., *Midterm: Elections of 1994 in Context* (Boulder, Colo.: Westview, 1996).

8. Benjamin Ginsberg and Alan Stone, eds., *Do Elections Matter?* 2d ed. (Armonk, N.Y.: M.E. Sharpe, 1991).

9. Rhodes Cook and Deborah Kalb, "Though Vote Margin is Thin, GOP Outpolls Demo- crats," *Congressional Quarterly Weekly Report,* 23 November 1996, 3319–20.

10. For example, in the 1998 elections, party control was at stake in nearly a third of all state legislatures, a large number of which remain controlled by slim margins. Partisan control of eight chambers changed hands on election day. See Kevin Sack, "High Stakes and Antes in State Races," *New York Times,* 6 September 1998, A24; and "Election Results Still Give Edge to Democrats," press release, National Conference of State Legislatures, 11 November 1998.

11. Glen Bolger, " Lessons of Victory and Defeat '98: Republican Perspective," *Campaigns and Elections,* December/January 1999, 66. For a similar analysis by a nonpartisan observer, see Charles Cook, "Puzzling Through the Demographics of the Nov. 3 Vote," *National Jour- nal's Cloakroom,* 17 November 1998, http://www.cloakroom.com.

12. The following paragraphs draw on the definitive work of Corrado et al. in *Campaign Fi- nance Reform.*

13. *Buckley v. Valeo,* 424 U.S. 1 (1976).

14. See Bibby, "Party Networks."

15. *Colorado Republican Federal Campaign Committee v. Federal Election Commission,* 116 S.Ct. 2309 (1996). See Potter, "Where Are We Now?" 5.

16. Daniel R. Ortiz, "The First Amendment at Work: Constitutional Restrictions on Campaign Finance Regulation," in Corrado et al., *Campaign Finance Reform.*

17. Lyle Denniston, "Spending-Limits Case May Go to High Court; Cincinnati Campaign Law Designed as a Test," *Houston Chronicle,* 28 April 1998, A2; and Linda Greenhouse, "Justices Reject Appeals in Two Cases Involving Limits on Political Money," *New York Times,* 17 No- vember 1998, A11.

18. Carroll J. Doherty, "Senators' Votes Seem Set in Stone," *Congressional Quarterly Weekly Re- port,* 28 February 1998, 467.

19. Karen Foerstel, "'Soft Money' Restrictions Near Passage in House, But Senate Still Unreceptive," *Congressional Quarterly Weekly Report,* 1 August 1998, 2102; and Charles Pope, "McCain-Feingold Bill on Campaign Financing Proves Dead on Arrival," *Congressional Quarterly Weekly Report,* 12 September 1998, 2402.

20. David S. Broder and Thomas B. Edsall, "Lobbyist Takes Over GOP," *Washington Post,* 30 January 1993, A1.

21. Philip A. Klinkner, *The Losing Parties: Out-Party National Committees, 1956–1993* (New Haven, Conn.: Yale University Press, 1994), 193.

22. Ibid. 193–96; James A. Barnes, "Creating a Lean, Mean RNC?" *National Journal,* 27 November 1993, 2835.

23. Klinkner, *Losing Parties,* 194; Richard L. Berke, "Republican Gathering Raises Money, and Tensions," *New York Times,* 11 May 1994, A22.

24. Weston Kosova, "The Party's Over," *The New Republic,* 20 June 1994, 21–25. The Republican National Committee website is at http://www.rnc.org.

25. Paula Nowakowski, former RNC staff member, telephone interview by author, 15 March 1995; Kurt Anderson, RNC political director, telephone interview by author, 7 August 1995.

26. Paul Herrnson and Diana Dwyre, "Party Issue Advocacy in Congressional Election Campaigns," in Green and Shea, *State of the Parties,* 91.

27. *Campaigns and Elections,* August 1996; James A. Barnes, "Turnaround Time," *National Journal,* 10 August 1996, 1684–89.

28. Charles A. Babcock, "Anti-Tax Group Got Big Boost From RNC as Election Neared," *Washington Post,* 10 December 1996, A4.

29. Alan Greenblatt, "Barbour: A Tough Act to Follow," *Congressional Quarterly Weekly Report,* 25 January 1997, 250; Alan Greenblatt and Ronald D. Elving, "Nicholson, Romer Picked to Lead National Committees," *Congressional Quarterly Weekly Report,* 25 January 1997, 249–51.

30. Juliet Eilperin, "Veterans, Freshmen Shook Campaign Reform Loose for House Vote," *Washington Post,* 25 April 1998, A6; Ruth Marcus, "RNC Files Suit over Curbs on 'Soft Money' for Issue Advertising," *Washington Post,* 17 April 1998, A6; Thomas B. Edsall, "Abortion Proposal May Dominate RNC Meeting," *Washington Post,* 7 January 1998, A8.

31. William F. Connelly Jr. and John J. Pitney Jr., *Congress' Permanent Minority? Republicans in the U.S. House* (Lanham, Md.: Rowman & Littlefield, 1994); James G. Gimpel, *Fulfilling the Contract: The First 100 Days* (Boston: Allyn and Bacon, 1996). On the fundraising system and the subsequent legal problems it caused Gingrich, see Richard E. Cohen and Eliza Newlin Carney, "Gingrich's Trials," *National Journal,* 11 January 1997, 60–65; and Jackie Koszczuk, "All Eyes on the IRS as Agency Looks into Gingrich Case," *Congressional Quarterly Weekly Report,* 22 February 1997, 476–78.

32. Newt Gingrich, Richard K. Armey, and the House Republican Conference, *Contract with America* (New York: Times Books, 1994); Gimpel, *Fulfilling the Contract,* chaps. 1 and 2.

33. Maria Cino, NRCC executive director, telephone interview by author, 7 August 1995.

34. Nowakowski and Cino, interviews.

35. Lawrence R. Jacobs and Robert Y. Shapiro, "The Politicization of Public Opinion: The Fight for the Pulpit," in *The Social Divide: Political Parties and the Future of Activist Government,* ed. Margaret Weir (Washington, D.C.: Brookings Institution, 1998).

36. Cino, interview.

37. John Ferejohn, "A Tale of Two Congresses: Social Policy in the Clinton Years," in Weir, *Social Divide.*

38. Charles E. Cook, "Republicans Dodged a Real Electoral Bullet to Keep Their Majority," *Roll Call,* 7 November 1996, taken from the LEXIS-NEXIS electronic database; Juliana Gruenwald and Deborah Kalb, "Despite Push, Democrats Fail to Topple GOP," *Congressional Quarterly Weekly Report,* 9 November 1996, 3, 225–32.

39. Jackie Koszczczuk, "Embattled Speaker Scrambles to Save Eroding Power Base"; Rebecca Carr, "Subcommittee Lays Out Details of Gingrich Ethics Violations"; Donna Cassata and Elizabeth A. Palmer, "Chronology of Gingrich Ethics Case," *Congressional Quarterly Weekly Report,* 4 January 1997, 7–21; Rebecca Carr, "Using Weapons of Fax and Phone, War Team Never Gave Ground," *Congressional Quarterly Weekly Report,* 11 January 1997, 117–19.

40. Jackie Koszczczuk, "Gingrich Under Fire as Discord Simmers from Rank to Top," *Congressional Quarterly Weekly Report,* 21 June 1997, 1415–18; Jackie Koszczczuk, "Coup Attempt Throws GOP Off Legislative Track," *Congressional Quarterly Weekly Report,* 19 July 1997, 1671–74; Jeffrey Katz, "Shakeup in the House," *Congressional Quarterly Weekly Report,* 7 November 1998, 2989–92.

41. Amy Keller, "'Lean and Mean' Atwater Disciple Takes NRCC Helm As New Director," *Roll Call,* 18 November 1996; Thomas B. Edsall, "Parties' Core Backers Seen as Key to '98 Vote," *Washington Post,* 9 May 1998, A6.

42. Jim Vandetti, "Armey Wants Millions for Ads," *Roll Call,* 13 July 1998; and "First NRCC 'Issue Ad' Targets Dem Berkeley," *National Journal's CongressDaily,* 2 September 1998. Both citations were taken from the LEXIS-NEXIS electronic database. The campaign ultimately spent $25 million, including $5 million from the RNC.

43. Richard L. Berke, "G.O.P. Begins Ad Campaign Citing Scandal," *New York Times,* 28 October 1998, A1; Ruth Marcus, "Outside Money Wasn't Everything; 'Issue Ad' Strategy a Letdown for GOP," *Washington Post,* 5 November 1998, A39; Spencer Hsu, "Va's Davis Will Lead Key GOP Committee," *Washington Post,* 19 November 1998, A31; Chuck McCutcheon, "Hastert: Calm Resolve and Controversial Calls," *Congressional Quarterly Weekly Report,* 22 December 1998, 3319.

44. David S. Broder, "Republicans See Revival in President's Setbacks," *Washington Post,* 21 June 1993, A1.

45. Tim Curran, "'Independent' Money: Let the Hand-Wringing Begin Now That Both Parties Spent Big on Senate Contests," *Roll Call,* 21 November 1996; Federal Election Commission reports. Both citations taken from the LEXIS-NEXIS electronic database.

46. Curran, "'Independent' Money."

47. Charles E. Cook, "Campaign '96 is Finally Over," *Roll Call,* 12 December 1996, taken from the LEXIS-NEXIS electronic database.

48. Ellen Miller, "Message and Money: How the GOP Defeated Campaign Finance Reform," *The Hill,* 4 March 1998, 26.

49. Amy Keller, "With Request to FEC, NRSC Seeks to Free Up Hard Cash," *Roll Call,* 22 October 1998, taken from the LEXIS-NEXIS electronic database.

50. Carroll Doherty, "Showdown at the NRSC Corral," *Congressional Quarterly Weekly Report,* 21 November 1998, 3144.

51. James A. Barnes, "The Endless Campaign," *National Journal,* 20 January 1993, 460–63.

52. Jacobs and Shapiro, "Politicization of Public Opinion," 96.

53. Ruth Marcus, "The Windup and the Pitch," *Washington Post,* 7 March 1993, A1; Barnes, "Endless Campaign." Wilhelm's initiatives also included lingering Reform Party paradigm features as detailed in Task Force on DNC Structure and Participation, "Report to Chairman David Wilhelm," 13 June 1993.

54. Dan Balz, "House Democrats Tell Wilhelm DNC is 'Inept'; Lack of Confidence Said to Reach White House," *Washington Post* , 23 June 1993, A6; Ann Devroy and Donna Priest, "DNC Drops Health Plan Lobby Fund," *Washington Post,* 4 June 1993, A1; Thomas B. Edsall and Ann O'Hanlon, "Democrats Plan to Reduce National Committee Staff," *Washington Post,* 16 January 1994, A12; Lloyd Grove, "Man on a Tightrope," *Washington Post,* 20 April 1994, A1; Steve Daley, "Democratic Party Chief Wilhelm to Quit after November Elections," *Chicago Tribune,* 10 August 1994, A3.

55. Ann Devroy, "Clinton Reelection Machinery in Place Already," *Washington Post*, 3 August 1995, A9.

56. Herrnson and Dwyre, "Party Issue Advocacy," 91; Richard A. Serrano, "Reno Extends Investigation into Clinton-Gore Campaign Spending," *Los Angeles Times,* 9 September 1998, A5.

57. Anthony Corrado, "Financing the 1996 Elections," in Pomper, *Election of 1996,* 154–55.

58. Dan Balz, "Swimming in a Pool of Red Ink," *Washington Post National Weekly Edition,* 26 May 1997, 10.

59. Stuart Rothenberg, "Busted! Party Poverty Raises Some Questions for '98 Election Cycle," *Roll Call,* 2 October 1997, taken from the LEXIS-NEXIS electronic database; Ron Fournier, "DNC Fights Unrest with New Debt Figure, Promises More Help," *Associated Press,* 9 January 1998, http://wire.ap.org.

60. Ceci Connolly, "Party Hails Increase in Fund-Raising," *Washington Post* , 31 January 1998, A13.

61. The Senate committee's report is excerpted in "'White House, in Its Thirst For Money, Took Control'," *Washington Post,* 10 February 1998, A6.

62. Jonathan Salant, "Democrats See Ken Starr as Fund-raising Tool," *Associated Press,* 4 April 1998, http://wire.ap.org.

63. See, for example, Michael Kranish, "Focus, Spending of DNC Faulted," *Boston Globe,* 30 April 1998, A1; and Alexis Simendinger, "One Party, Different Agendas," *National Journal,* 9 May 1998, 1065.

64. Dana Priest, "House Democrats Get Battle Plan for Selling Health Care Reform Back Home," *Washington Post,* 11 August 1993, A4.

65. James A. Barnes, "Clinton's 1994 Political Machine," *National Journal,* 12 February 1994, 380; James A. Barnes, "Double Identity,"*National Journal,* 27 November 1993, 2834.

66. "Fazio Speech: Charges GOP Is Threatened by 'Radical Right,'" *American Political Network Hotline,* 22 June 1994, taken from the LEXIS-NEXIS electronic database; Gimpel, *Fulfilling the Contract,* 2–12.

67. Matt Angle, telephone interview by author, 31 July 1995.

68. Tim Curran and Benjamin Sheffner, "The Election Battleground: Dozen Senate Seats, Nearly 50 House Seats Are Toss-Ups," *Roll Call,* 20 May 1996, 1.

69. Janet Hook, "Wealth of Uncontested House Races Reflects Parties' Strategies," *Los Angeles Times,* 29 June 1998, A5; Peter Stone, "Issue Ads, The Weapons of Choice," *National Journal,* 31 October 1998, 2570.

70. See, for example, "Labor: Changing Election Strategy," *Hotline Weekly,* 27 August 1998, 2; and "Campaign Targets Come into Focus," *National Journal's Cloakroom,* 5 October 1998, http://www.cloakroom.com.

71. "DSCC Prepared: Response before Criticism," *Congressional Quarterly Weekly Report,* 2 April 1994, 815.

72. Barbara Sinclair, "Trying to Govern Positively in a Negative Era: Clinton and the 103rd Congress," in Campbell and Rockman, *Clinton Presidency.*

73. Tim Curran, "Kerrey Seeks Out 'New Style' Dems," *Roll Call,* 5 June 1995, 1.

74. Don Foley, DSCC, telephone interview by author, 2 August 1995.

75. "Democrats Offer a Families First Agenda," DPC Talking Points, Democratic Policy Committee press release, 25 June 1996.

76. Rachel Van Dongen, "Send Money: Parties Making Tough Calls On Senate Race Funds," *Roll Call,* 22 October 1998, taken from the LEXIS-NEXIS electronic database.

77. Quoted in Tim Curran, "Senate Democrats Have Y2K Theory: Some Are Looking to Take Back Control in 2000," *Roll Call,* 9 July 1998, taken from the LEXIS-NEXIS electronic database.

10

The Resilience of Campaign-Centered Politics

It's like deja vu all over again.

– Yogi Berra

Throughout the turmoil of the 1990s, the campaign-centered electoral order remained largely intact. The previous chapters show that the major parties' national organizations have come to play an important role in sustaining the new politics, and this chapter begins with a brief overview of their influence over politicians and other political professionals. Next the chapter explores recent changes in patterns of representation, deliberation, and choice, showing that new technologies and practices have not fundamentally challenged the central dimensions of campaign-centered politics. I close the book looking forward and asking a broader question: what are the implications of the new politics for representative democracy in America?

The Parties as Partners in the New Politics

The Accomodationist paradigm remains the dominant way Democratic and Republican leaders and activists think about and respond to the campaign-centered electoral order. Though the blending of Textbook Party strategies with Accomodationist analyses and strategies by House Republicans stands out as a striking anomaly, most leaders and activists within the national party organizations have embraced the inevitability of campaign-centered politics as conventional wisdom. In doing so, they have in turn exercised a surprisingly strong influence over many Americans' understanding of contemporary politics.

Party organizations' accommodation to the new politics has clearly influenced Democratic and Republican elected officials and candidates for national office. Through their analysis of the resources and skills thought necessary for a successful campaign, party leaders and activists influence the roster of candidates who run for president, Congress, and a host of lesser offices. More directly, professional campaign operatives at the party committees influence that roster by helping to recruit challengers and open-seat candidates they think can mount competitive campaigns for Congress. Once candidates gain their parties' nominations, the organizations continue to influence them by brokering their liaison with national interest groups and providing them with essential strategic information and advice as well as money. Further, the committees have played a role in helping congressional candidates shift their campaigns from local organization-intensive to media- and money-intensive operations. By implication, they have also increased the disjunction between congressional elections and the rest of state and local politics.

Party organizations during this period have encouraged the transformation of politics as a profession, though this transformation was well under way before the parties established their current role. New, more independent kinds of party professionals play a key role in campaign-centered politics, as Jeane Kirkpatrick and others noted more than twenty years ago.[1] Kirkpatrick argued in 1978 that these new professionals would be tied less to the party than their predecessors:

> Like the traditional 'pol,' professional campaign managers, political pollsters, and a host of media and direct mail specialists make their living out of politics by mobilizing and delivering support. . . . At the same time, [their emergence] weakened party organization because, although the professional of yesterday was dependent on, and identified with, the party organization, the contemporary professional is fundamentally independent of party. His [sic] income depends less on the party than on his skills.[2]

In many ways Kirkpatrick was right: campaign professionals now routinely work for a period as staff or contractors for the party organizations, then leave to join or establish independent, for-profit consulting firms.

Despite their apparent independence, however, the vast majority of such professionals remain within the party organization's orbit. From their consulting firms, they continue to work on contract with party committees, or they work with candidates who in turn coordinate aspects of their campaigns with party committees. Such mutual dependence is ultimately not very different from the old relations between the national party organizations and the local pols. As Robin Kolodny and Angela Logan have noted, parties and consultants now form interdependent networks of political engagement.[3]

This mutual dependence—and the creation of a new kind of political "establishment" in the United States—calls attention to voters as a third aspect of electoral politics influenced by Accommodationist ideas and practices. As noted in chapter 3, Americans have grown skeptical and hostile toward both candidates and campaign professionals. Although they consistently vote for candidates and initiatives advanced by campaign-centered politics, Americans have never become comfortable with its practitioners, its financial underpinnings, or its version of representative democracy.

Clear illustrations of that contrast emerged in surveys conducted in 1998 by the Pew Research Center for The People and The Press, which indicated that national politicians, officeholders, and political consultants view politics in ways that are strikingly different from the views of ordinary people. In its survey of members of Congress, appointees in the Clinton administration, and senior federal civil servants, Pew found that these officials badly misjudge the public's views about government in general. While the officials were right in perceiving that the public generally distrusts *politicians*, for example, the officials wrongly assumed that the public held a similar distrust for government activism in general.[4] Further, while, the survey indicated that public officials—particularly Republicans—tend to view government and policy in partisan and ideological terms, most Americans consider policy questions more pragmatically.

As long as most ordinary Americans continue to approach politics as "ideological conservatives and operational liberals," they will continue to be irritated by the constant battling, spinning, and polarization of campaign-centered politics, viewing it as noisy, manipulative, and an impediment to constructive public problem solving.[5] The Pew survey indicates that consultants, in contrast, view the permanent campaign as a vehicle for genuine democratic expression. They argue that campaigns are won most often because of content, whereas weak candidates with unpopular stands will usually lose.[6] Even so, *Campaigns and Elections* editor Ron Faucheux, the most visible spokesman for the consulting profession, acknowledges that races in a closely divided electorate are most often decided by turnout, and new politics practitioners have become adept at manipulating its outcomes by mobilizing supporters and discouraging opposition voters. "How do you win an unwinnable election?" he asks. "Make sure the people who turn out on election day are unrepresentative of the voting public."[7] While this is certainly good professional advice, well within the conventional wisdom of the new politics, it reveals a strategic mindset that discourages many Americans and helps to explain much of the political turmoil of the 1990s.

The campaign-centered electoral order is comprised of distinct values and practices of representation, citizen deliberation, and choice. Cumulatively, these values and practices constitute America's contemporary approximation of representative democracy. Though the order has generated skepticism and even hostility from a substantial number of Americans, it remains remarkably resilient. Though several developments of the 1990s—on all three dimensions of electoral politics—continued to bring marginal changes, the essential contours of the order remain in place.

Representation

Even as the "permanent campaign" remains conventional practice, in recent elections representation has come to be mediated and coordinated in rapidly changing ways. From one perspective, the wider use of communications and computer technology has enabled representation to become even more fragmented and impersonal. In 1992, for example, Democrat Jerry Brown took advantage of inexpensive 800-number services in raising funds from and communicating with his far-flung presidential campaign constituency, a practice immediately imitated by several professionalized campaigns across the country.[8] By 1996, the strategy became common.

More important, broad public access to on-line computer services has allowed millions of Americans to form and join new, electronically-mediated "virtual" groups focusing on almost every imaginable interest. Candidates, parties, and advocacy organizations have established their own World Wide Web services to enter this arena. As recently as early 1996, it seemed to many that the Internet would play only a marginal role in campaigns and elections. Too few Americans were on-line, the demographics were too skewed toward young, affluent, and well-educated men, and those who were on-line showed little interest in politics.[9] Yet, by the November 1996 election it became clear that the Web could be an important part of campaigns. According to consultant Mike Connell, "the Clinton and Dole campaigns reported that nearly one-third of their volunteers became involved in the campaign via the Internet (website or e-mail)."[10] By 1998 nearly every major candidate for the U.S. Senate, most candidates for statewide office, most sponsors of statewide ballot initiatives, and many U.S House candidates had established web pages. The number of Internet users had expanded dramatically as well, to nearly a third of the adult population. The demographics of those using the Web continues to approach those of the general population. Politics on the World Wide Web is coming of age very quickly, but because there are no clear patterns of political use yet, it is impossible to predict how it will ultimately affect representation in American campaigns and elections.[11]

On a more conventional subject, the 1994, 1996, and 1998 election campaigns witnessed the resurgence of more old-fashioned partisan groups, with immediate effects. After a long period of decline in the group focus of major party politics, both parties have clearly begun to adjust to new group conditions and form stronger partisan group alliances. The most important component of Republican adjustment has been among white evangelical Protestants, 16 percent of whom have shifted their partisan allegiance toward the Republicans since the late 1970s. In collaboration with grassroots organizing efforts by the Christian Coalition, the Family Research Council, and other groups, Republicans drew heavily on this constituency in winning control of Congress in 1994.[12] Democrats, in response, worked during the 1996 and 1998 campaigns to reestablish their historically effective electoral collaboration with the AFL-CIO and other labor unions, and the party's mobilization and turnout work with African Americans and Latinos proved especially important in congressional elections.[13] These developments suggest that the apparent decline in group politics during the 1970s and 1980s may have reflected not a decline in group life among Americans, but rather a reshuffling of the relationships between group life and partisan politics. If that is so, a resurgence of group politics may pose a challenge to representation mediated by professionalized campaigns and Accommodationist parties, two of the central features of the campaign-centered electoral order.

The transformation of campaign finance regulation described earlier has obvious and dramatic implications for representation. Supreme Court decisions and the failure of the Republican-controlled Congress to pass reform legislation in response means that the *financial* participation of groups in American national elections is now virtually unregulated.[14]

Deliberation

The quality and character of public political discourse continues to undergo similarly unpredictable changes. For example, 1992 marked the emergence of televised "town meetings" as an effective political forum for voters and candidates at all levels. Though they varied widely in format from nearly unscripted to quite rigidly controlled, such forums became so widely accepted that they served as the model for a high-stakes debate among President George Bush, Governor Bill Clinton, and Ross Perot. As public anger—toward government in general and incumbents in particular—grew in the mid-1990s, public participants in such events frequently pursued their own political or even personal agendas, raising the issues they wanted on the terms that they wanted regardless of the plans of campaign professionals who had organized the events. Thus, for example, during a 1996 MTV forum the President of the United States was asked what kind of underwear he wore.

"Talk radio" also emerged as a powerful and uncoordinated force in the early 1990s, revitalizing and updating a deliberative forum that local AM stations and national radio networks had used for decades. Liberated by the elimination of the Federal Communication Commission's "Fairness Doctrine" under President Reagan, hosts such as Rush Limbaugh and others established their shows as sounding boards for partisan politics and policy debates. By 1994 more than 20 million Americans tuned in to Limbaugh's show each week on more than 660 radio stations, and Republican leaders lauded him as the catalyst for their successful campaign to retake control of Congress.[15] Competitors of every political stripe continue their efforts to match Limbaugh's success.

The Internet emerged in 1996 as an important forum for political deliberation as well, and its importance continues to grow rapidly. Initially, campaigns mostly used the Internet for e-mail communication with supporters and donors, but the shift to the World Wide Web has brought increasing amounts of information and debate.[16] An entire industry has sprung up, offering a full array of campaign-related services, many of which are targeted at shaping public opinion and mobilizing voters. The Monica Lewinsky scandal of 1998 provided the final push: with the posting of Kenneth Starr's report on dozens of websites and hundreds of other websites devoted to debating the minutiae of the scandal, the World Wide Web became for a time a central forum for American political discussion and debate. Industry monitor RelevantKnowledge reported that traffic to news-oriented websites jumped 43 percent during the week Starr's report was published, and CNN reported that it transmitted 34.26 million "page impressions" (responses to requests for copies of a posted web page) on September 11 alone.[17] Exit polls from the November 1998 election found that 40 percent of voters reported using the Internet regularly.[18]

The World Wide Web, along with electronic bulletin board systems or BBSs, specialized cable networks and programs, and grassroots networks of fax "telephone trees," demonstrates that Americans have invented ways to use emerging technologies to carve out new "public spaces" for discussing and deliberating over the issues of American elections. Whether professionalized campaigns and Accommodationist parties can adapt and strongly influence these spaces remains to be seen.

Choice

Finally, recent years have brought striking changes in mechanisms of electoral choice. In 1993 President Clinton and a Democratic Congress passed the "Motor-Voter" bill, which enabled citizens to register to vote as they applied for driver's licenses, public assistance, and other public services. The legislation's implementation in 1995 and 1996 brought more than 9 million more Americans into the electoral process by November 1996, raising the number of registered voters to nearly 143 million, or 72.8 percent of those eligible.[19] Yet both the number and proportion of Americans voting declined in 1996, to about 105 million voters, 49 percent of eligible adults. Researcher Stephen Knack found that long-term turnout declines slowed in 1996, perhaps as a result of Motor Voter, but that is a small consolation.[20] The decline continued in 1998.

Initiatives and referenda grew increasingly popular during the 1990s as direct means for voters to enact legislation and state constitutional amendments. In one focused use of those direct means, more than 25 million Americans between 1990 and 1994 voted to limit the time politicians can remain in state and national office, passing term-limit referenda in sixteen states.[21] In early 1996, Oregon held the first mail-in election for a U.S. Congressional seat, as voters elected Senator Ron Wyden in a surprisingly high turnout.[22] Two years later, Oregon voters approved Ballot Measure 60, mandating that all future state elections be conducted by mail.

Looking Ahead

These developments have the potential to reorient electoral politics in the United States in fundamental ways and to displace a campaign-centered electoral order that has proven resilient for nearly forty years. Yet, as Thomas Kuhn wrote in his study of scientific revolutions and battles over competing paradigms, it would be difficult to recognize and understand such a transformation even if it were under way.[23] The news would not come from "the pros" because contemporary political professionals are caught up in the particulars of individual campaigns—candidates, issues, changing public opinion, new technologies, and tactical developments. Such professionals often look backward rather than forward, drawing their lessons from the past and "fighting the last war." Campaign observers and ordinary citizens suffer from the same limitations, repeating past inquiries and asking familiar questions, even if the changing world threatens to render those questions irrelevant.

Still, if a new electoral order is indeed emerging, the findings of this book enable us to make modest predictions. Displacement of the campaign-centered electoral order would bring a turbulent period of political confusion like that of the 1950s and 1960s, as Americans struggled to develop paradigmatic explanations for—and strategies to enable effective competition in—this new order. We could reasonably expect that political activists and analysts would again develop competing paradigmatic explanations and strategies for the new order, just as they did in the 1960s and 1970s. And, once again, competition among those paradigmatic visions would likely play itself out among factions within American political parties, just as described in earlier chapters of this book.

For now, however, we remain in a resilient campaign-centered electoral order, with the national party organizations firmly ensconced in their Accommodationist role. It is essential to note that the resilient order and the ensconced paradigm may leave us little to celebrate. We have increasing evidence that voters find the politics of this system alienating and demeaning, and they have a point. John Coleman rightly argues that we should not simply "accentuate the positive, ignore the negative."[24] As I noted earlier, representative democracy built around campaigns—rather than parties or even candidates—raises broad concerns about the health of our political system. Much of this system is mediated and coordinated by professionals who build ad hoc campaign organizations for each candidate and initiative on the ballot. When election day is over, these ad hoc aggregations of pollsters, strategists, fundraisers, field-operations specialists, and so on dissolve into thin air, only to recombine with different participants in the next campaign.

Representative democracy requires more than campaigns. A healthy representative democracy requires sustained channels of communication between citizens and the government representing them. Though skilled professionals may mediate a citizen's or a group's representation to a candidate during a campaign, once the candidate is in office or starts a new campaign, the mediating organization often vanishes entirely. In the case of ballot initiatives, the election does not even leave behind an officeholder as a point of citizen contact. How can such a system serve as a foundation of a healthy representative democracy? It cannot. Campaign-centered politics offers no means for establishing consistent representative or deliberative relationships between citizen and officeholder *even if* a candidate or officeholder wanted to do so. The analysis in this book helps explain this thinning of democratic communication, but it does not justify its existence.

The party organizations remain after election day, of course, as do the party caucuses in legislatures. But this book has shown that these organizations serve primarily as facilitators of campaign-centered politics, in service to candidates and their professionalized campaigns. The party organizations themselves have very little contact with voters, and voters in turn know little about them. Certainly few ordinary Americans would look to national party organizations as a means of communicating with their representatives or their government. So today's national party organizations and caucuses, by accommodating rather than mediating campaign-centered politics, offer representative democracy little help.

The plain fact is that advancement of representative democracy has always been what sociologist Robert Merton would have called a "latent" function of parties.[25] Political activists and leaders have organized and developed political parties in order to advance their own interests and values. Their goal was winning control of government, not the advancement of abstract principles. Perhaps under prior electoral orders, the most effective means of winning elections improved linkages between citizens and officeholders and simultaneously advanced the quality of representative democracy. Under those circumstances, political parties often were bulwarks of democracy, as one 1960 textbook proclaimed, and it is possible to imagine that they could play such a role again.[26] But political activists and leaders in contemporary America have decided that competition in the campaign-centered world requires a different kind of politics, one far less congenial to sustained democratic linkages.

Voters themselves must share some responsibility for these developments. Like political activists and leaders, voters have approached parties with an eye to their own interests and values. A substantial majority of them have remained partisan, but their partisanship cannot necessarily be interpreted as active support for the principles of democracy. Those who are loyal to parties see the parties as advancing their own interests and values. In any case, a decisive segment of American voters no longer even pretend to be loyal to parties or partisanship, and they make little effort to establish and sustain linkages to those who represent them.

This problem is particularly troubling in the context of an increasingly deregulated campaign finance system. One clear characteristic of campaign-centered politics is its financial expense: it takes a lot of money to build a professionalized campaign organization and contest an election using modern technology for polls and advertising. Theodore Lowi and Benjamin Ginsberg have even described the emergence of the new politics as principally a transition "from labor-intensive to capital intensive politics."[27] Campaigns once required marshaling partisan armies of campaign workers; now they require marshaling immense amounts of cash. In 1996 the average winning campaign for the Senate cost nearly $4.7 million, while the average winning House campaign cost two-thirds of a million dollars. Cumulatively, campaigns for national office in 1996 cost $2.2 billion. Preliminary estimates indicate that 1998 congressional campaign spending nearly matched 1996 levels even in an off-year election.[28]

The problem is not the money. American businesses spent far more than $2.2 billion in 1998 advertising beer, Barbie dolls, and bath soap, and none of us worries about that. The problem is that the financial side of campaign-centered politics is so undemocratic, involving only the smallest minority of Americans. Though millions of Americans contribute financially in some way to campaigns, the bulk of the money is raised from those giving $200 or more. Larry Makinson and his colleagues at the Center for Responsive Politics note that in all, some 630,000 donors answered the call in 1995-96, giving $200 or more and providing nearly $600 million in the 1996 elections (*not including* money they gave to PACs or to the parties' soft money accounts). Despite their financial importance, these donors make up less than $1/4^{th}$ of 1 percent of the nation's population.

Indeed, if you look solely at those who gave $1,000 or more, you find that the number of donors is something under 235,000—about $1/10^{th}$ of 1 percent of the American public.[29]

In short, the proportion of Americans who finance and most directly influence the conduct of campaign-centered politics is extremely small.

Party organizations may succeed in capturing and channeling a growing share of that money, but their success does not mitigate the effects of money on our democracy. Further, both parties and campaigns are increasingly funded by soft money, which is raised in even larger denominations from an even smaller share of the voting public. The Supreme Court may yet allow the regulation of such funds, but until it does, campaign-centered politics will increasingly be the province of those who can afford it. The spending goes up and the turnout goes down.

So challenges remain for the future. American democracy is a work in progress, and if history is any guide, political parties will be at the center of the next transformation.

NOTES

1. Jeane J. Kirkpatrick, *The New Presidential Elite: Men and Women in National Politics* (Beverly Hills, Calif.: Sage, 1976). See also B. Bruce-Briggs, ed., *The New Class? America's Educated Elite* (New York: McGraw Hill, 1979).

2. Jeane J. Kirkpatrick, *Dismantling the Parties: Reflections on Party Reform and Party Decomposition* (Washington, D.C.: American Enterprise Institute, 1978), 11–12.

3. Robin Kolodny and Angela Logan, "Political Consultants and the Extension of Party Goals," *PS: Political Science and Politics* 50 (June 1998): 155–59.

4. Pew Research Center for The People and The Press, "Public Appetite for Government Misjudged," 18 June 1998. Published at http://www.people-press.org/leadrpt.htm.

5. Lloyd A. Free and Hadley Cantril, *The Political Beliefs of Americans: A Study of Public Opinion* (New Brunswick, N.J.: Rutgers University Press, 1967); E.J. Dionne, *Why Americans Hate Politics* (New York: Simon and Schuster, 1991).

6. Pew Research Center for The People and The Press, "The Views of Political Consultants: Don't Blame Us," 18 June 1998. Published at http://www.people-press.org/con98rpt.htm.

7. Ron Faucheux, seminar, Los Angeles, 26 June 1998.

8. James Ceaser and Andrew Busch, *Upside Down and Inside Out: The 1992 Elections and American Politics* (Lanham, Md.: Rowman & Littlefield, 1993), chap. 3.

9. For a skeptical view of the political usefulness of the Internet, see Gary Chapman, "For Now at Least, the Net Is Not a Political Animal," *Los Angeles Times,* 16 September 1996, B7.

10. Mike Connell, "Avoid Cyberspace Rip-Offs," *Campaigns and Elections,* June 1998, 48.

11. David Birdsell, Douglas Muzzio, David Krane, and Amy Cottreau, "Web Users Are Looking More Like America," *Public Perspective,* April/May 1998, 33–35; one set of enthusiastic predictions can be found in Wayne Rash Jr., *Politics on the Nets: Wiring the Political Process* (New York: W.H. Freeman, 1997).

12. Pew Research Center for The People and The Press, *The Diminishing Divide: American Churches, American Politics* (Philadelphia, Pa.: Pew Center, June 1996); Dan Balz and Ronald Brownstein, *Storming the Gates: Protest Politics and the Republican Revival* (New York: Little, Brown, 1996). For background, see Robert Booth Fowler and Alan Hertzke, *Religion and Politics in America: Faith, Culture, and Strategic Choices* (Boulder, Colo.: Westview, 1995).

13. See, for example, Frank Swoboda and Thomas B. Edsall, "AFL-CIO Endorses Clinton, Approves $35 Million Political Program," *Washington Post,* 26 March 1996, A6; Steven Greenhouse, "Republicans Credit Labor for Success by Democrats," *New York Times,* 6 November 1988, A28; and Celinda Lake, "Lessons of Victory and Defeat '98: Democratic Perspective," *Campaigns and Elections,* December/January 1999, 67–68.

14. Note that the Republican-controlled House of Representatives passed campaign finance reform legislation in August 1998, but Senate supporters of the bill lacked the votes to end a filibuster against it. See Edwin Chen, "House Backs Bill to Reform Election Spending," *Los Angeles Times,* 4 August 1998, A1; and Edwin Chen, "Clinton Under Fire; Senate Blocks Reform of Campaign Financing," *Los Angeles Times,* 11 September 1998, A28.

15. Kathleen Knight and David Barker, "'Talk Radio Turns the Tide'? The Limbaugh Effect: 1993–1995," paper presented at the annual meeting of the American Political Science Association, San Francisco, August 1996; Howard Kurtz, *Hot Air: All Talk All the Time* (New York: Times Books, 1996); Diana Owen, "Who's Talking? Who's Listening? The New Politics of Radio Talk Shows," in *Broken Contract? Changing Relationships between Americans and Their Government,* ed. Stephen C. Craig (Boulder, Colo.: Westview, 1996).

16. Ron Faucheux, "How Campaigns are Using the Internet: An Exclusive Nationwide Survey," *Campaigns and Elections,* September 1998, 22–25.

17. Data reported in *NetPulse* 2, no. 18 (17 September 1998), http://politicsonline.com/news/.

18. Voter News Service, "1998 Exit Polls: Vertical Percentages For All Voters," 17 November 1998, http://www.cloakroom.com/members/polltrack/races/1998/exitpolls/vertical.html.

19. Chuck Alston, "Democrats Flex New Muscle with Trio of Election Bills: Some Republicans Say That 'Motor Voter,' Campaign Finance and Hatch Act Bills Add up to Permanent

Power Grab," *Congressional Quarterly Weekly Report,* 20 March 1993, 643–45; "Impact of National Voter Registration Act Contained in FEC Report to Congress," Federal Election Commission press release, 19 June 1997.

20. Stephen Knack, "Drivers Wanted: Motor Voter and the Election of 1996," paper presented at the annual meeting of the American Political Science Association, Boston, September 1998; "The Turnout File: Voting and Registration, 1992–1996," *Roll Call,* posted at http://www.rollcall.com/election/turnoutchart.html, downloaded 4 August 1998.

21. "The Term Limits Movement Goes to Court," *Party Developments* I, no. 2 (1 January 1995).

22. Robert Marshall Wells, "Wyden Narrowly Scores Win in Bid for Packwood Seat," *Congressional Quarterly Weekly Report,* 3 February 1996, 310–12.

23. Kuhn, *The Structure of Scientific Revolutions,* chaps. 6 and 7.

24. John J. Coleman, "Resurgent or Just Busy? Party Organizations in Contemporary America," in *The State of the Parties: The Changing Role of Contemporary American Parties,* 2d ed., ed. John C. Green and Daniel M. Shea (Lanham, Md.: Rowman & Littlefield, 1996), 373.

25. Robert Merton, "Manifest and Latent Functions," in *Social Theory and Social Structure,* 2d ed. (New York: Free Press, 1968).

26. Clinton Rossiter writes, "No America without democracy, no democracy without politics, no politics without polical parties," *Parties and Politics in America* (Ithaca, N.Y.: Cornell University Press, 1960), 1. For an excellent sampling of the current debate on the role of parties in American democracy, see John K. White and John C. Green, eds., *The Politics of Ideas: Intellectual Challenges to the Party after 1992* (Lanham, Md.: Rowman & Littlefield, 1995).

27. Theodore J. Lowi and Benjamin Ginsberg, *American Government: Freedom and Power,* 5th ed. (New York: Norton, 1998), 507.

28. Larry Makinson, ed., *The Big Picture: Where the Money Came from in the 1996 Elections* (Washington, D.C.: Center for Responsive Politics, 1997); "1998 Congressional Financial Activity Declines," Federal Election Commission press release, 29 December 1998.

29. Larry Makinson, "Who Paid for This Election?" in Makinson, *Big Picture,* 1.

Index

Project 500, 106, 144
public confidence, erosion of, 33, 34, 213

radio
    advertising campaigns and, 20, 97, 202
    category politics and, 44
    effect on representation of, 54
    emergence of nonpartisan, 16
    talk, 216
radio production assistance
    Democratic, 141, 157, 183
    Republican, 95, 183
Rayburn, Sam, 119, 122
Reagan, Ronald, 2, 103, 112, 137, 184
    and campaign finance, 93
    and "Fairness Doctrine," 216
    and use of marketing research tools, 42
    presidential nomination of, 162
    presidential victory of, 135
reapportionment, 18, 19
referendum campaigns, 4, 24, 27, 217
reform
    of campaign finance, 188
    of delegate selection procedures, 72–74
    mid–20th century, 18
    turn of the 20th century, 15
Reform paradigm, 8, 76, 77–83, 98
    decline in interest of, 84–86
    Democrats and, 98
    origin of, 70–75
    Republican support of, 94
reformed party-centered politics, 15–16, 118
representation, 3, 5, 8, 12–16, 24, 27, 61, 74, 96, 214–15
    coordinated by state and local parties, 22
    erosion of public confidence in, 33, 34
    fragmentation of, 33, 39, 214
    inequities in Democrat delegations, 73
    interest groups & organizations, 17, 18, 39, 54
    minority, 18
    for new liberals, 71
representative democracies
    campaign-centered compared with party-centered, 26–27
    components of, 218
    doubts about, 8
    electoral dimensions of, 3–4
    limited & lack of during colonial era, 12
Republican Congressional Leadership Council, 126
Republican National Committee (RNC), 5, 58–59, 96–97, 112, 123, 162, 163, 189–91, 192
    fundraising by, 190–91
    and hard money, 110
    headquarters of, 93–95
    revitalization of, 125
Republicans, 15
    congressional campaign committees of, 191–97
    and National Policy Forum, 189
    organizational development by, 93–97
    See also National Republican Congressional Committee (NRCC)

"responsible party government," 56
Reuther, Walter, 38
Robb, Chuck, 176
Roberts, Spencer, 54
Rollins, Ed, 146
Romer, Roy, 200
Roosevelt, Franklin D., 16
Roth, William, 127

Salmore, Barbara, 24, 25
Salmore, Stephen, 24, 25
Sanford, Terry, 173
scandals
    Clinton/Lewinsky. *See* Lewinsky, Monica
    House of Representatives, 147
    See also congressional investigations
Schattschneider, E.E., 42
Schlesinger, Arthur, 155
Schumpeter, Joseph, 40
Senate campaign committees, 58, 59, 154, 155
Senate Governmental Affairs Committee, report on DNC fundraising, 200
Shafer, Byron, 12
Shapiro, Robert, 198
Shays, Christopher, 188
Shays-Meehan bill, 191
Shefter, Martin, 34
Shelby, Richard, 173
Sheppard, Audrey, 172
Short, Robert, 76
Silbey, Joel H., 11, 13
Sisk, B.F., 136
Smith, Charles, 23
Smith, Gordon, 203
social equality, 19
social welfare policy, 55
soft money, 93, 107, 109, 163, 187, 188, 220
    DNC reliance on, 199
    Republican, 196–97
Sorauf, Frank, 33, 54
"Speaker's Club," 138
split-ticket voting, 15, 20, 125
"spot" commercials, 20
stagflation, 124
    Kemp-Roth remedy for, 127
Starr, Kenneth, 194, 200, 202
Starr report, posted on the Internet, 216
state apportionment, 73
state elections, decrease in, 15
state government
    nonpartisan, 15
    party loyalties and, 14
state parties
    displacement of, 50, 51–54, 75
    during party-centered era, 22
    lost control of elections by, 20
"State Party Works!" program, 101, 106
state politics
    Democratic mobilization programs and, 106, 109
    Democratic campaign plans, 110
"states' rights" presidential bid, 19
Stephanopoulos, George, 110
Stevenson, Adlai, 49
"straight-ticket" voting, decline in, 16

Strauss, Robert, 77, 84, 86, 98, 141, 158, 160
suffrage rights, 3, 5
　of African Americans, 18
　expanded, during party-centered era, 14
　of nonwhites, 18
　of white males, 6, 12, 14
　women's, 15, 16
survey research, 22, 60, 96, 183
　campaign committees and, 60, 62
　companies and categories, 40–44
　congressional, 184
　Democratic assistance programs and, 139
　displacement of state/local parties and, 54
　pre-computer, 120
　Republican campaigns and, 95
　statewide, 107, 158
　voter abstention and, 35
　voter individuality and, 22
　See also polling and pollsters
Sweeney, William, 129–35, 138, 145, 159, 166
Swett, Dick, 196

telethons, 84, 103
television, 20, 122
　campaigns using, 20, 21, 84, 97, 202
　category politics and, 44
　effect on representation of, 54
　and "town meetings," 215
television production assistance
　Democratic campaigns, 141, 157, 183
　Republican campaigns, 95, 183
Textbook Party paradigm, 8, 61–62, 67, 69, 75, 76, 77, 100, 110, 111, 156, 182, 183, 185, 198
　academic analysis of, 56–57
　Accommodationist paradigm blended with, 143, 192–94
　Accommodationist paradigm vs., 159–60, 166–67, 174–75, 143
　argument for, 134, 140
　Republicans and, 94, 146, 191
　resistance to abandoning, 98
　revival of, 188, 189
Thurmond, Strom, 38, 49, 59
Times Mirror media conglomerate, 41
Torricelli, Robert, 204
Truman, Harry, 49, 52
Tully, Paul, 109, 110
Twenty-Sixth Amendment, 18
two-party politics, 14, 56
U.S. Supreme Court
　ruling of, on FEC, 196
　ruling of, on Federal Election Campaign Act, 187, 188
urban development policy. *See* housing and urban development policy

Vander Jagt, Guy, 94, 123, 125, 127, 146, 147
Vietnam War, 19, 71
voter identification, 106, 135, 186
voter registration, 186

and DCCC, 201
Democratic Party's use of, 107, 109, 183
and DNC, 84
and "Motor-Voter" bill, 216
Republican Party's use of, 95, 97, 183
state regulated, 15, 16
voter turnout
　decline in, 15, 16, 18, 35, 54, 201, 217
　Democratic Party's use of, 107, 183
　importance of, 213
　Republican Party's use of, 95, 183
voters
　alignments and realignments of, 22
　coercion of, 13, 14, 15
　and deliberating modern elections, 24
　divided, 186
　and following local leaders, 13
　legal age of, 18
　misunderstanding of American politics by, 7
　perspective of campaign-centered politics on, 26, 176, 213
　Republican Party's targeting of, 95, 97
　responsibility of, 219
voting
　abstention from, 35, 125
　decline in "straight-ticket," 16
　private, during reformed party-centered era, 15
　public, 12, 13, 15
　restricted to white male property owners, 12
　split-ticket, 15, 20, 125
　See also elections; suffrage rights; voter identification; voter registration; voter turnout; voters
voting rights acts, 18

Wallace, George, 19
Wallace, Henry, 49, 59
Ware, Alan, 53
Washington, George, 23, 25, 27
WASPs, 33, 37
Watergate, 2, 125, 159
Wattenberg, Martin, 17, 35
Wertheimer, Fred, 39–40
Wester, William, 131, 166, 167
white conservative Christians, partisan groups of, 37
White Evangelical Protestants, 33, 215
white males, suffrage rights of, 12, 14
white southerners, 33, 37
Wilhelm, David, 198, 202
Wilson, Bob, 123
Wilson, James Q., 53
Wirthlin, Richard, 42
Wofford, Harris, 176
women
　lack of representation of, 13
　suffrage rights of, 15, 16
　and targeted advertising during Reagan-Bush campaign, 42
Wood, James, 23
Wright, Jim, 129, 145, 146
Wyden, Ron, 217